COMPTON

Acts II Perfect Love, Peace, & Happiness
The New Millenium, New Testament

Keeping My Family Church
Ubuntu (Philosophy)

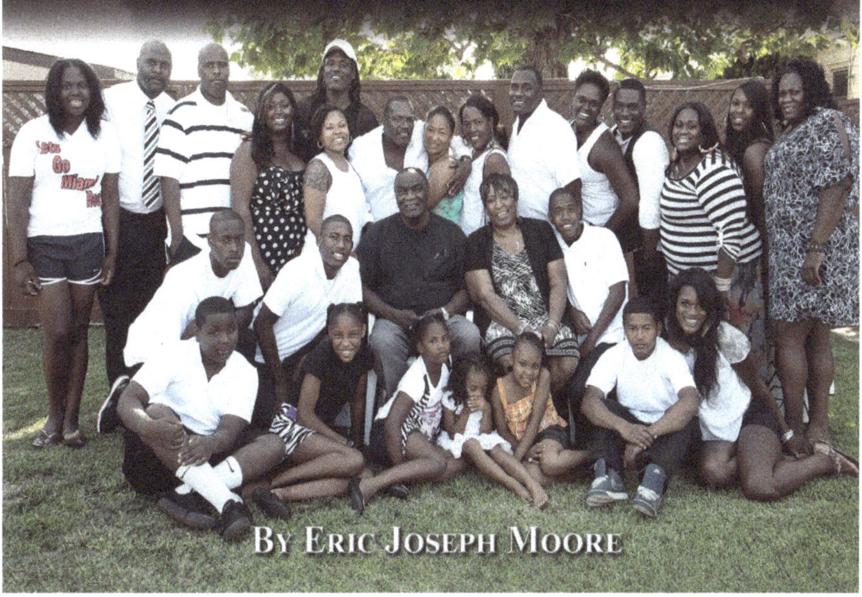

By Eric Joseph Moore

CLF Publishing, LLC.
www.clfpublishing.org
909.315.3161

Copyright © 2020 by Eric Joseph Moore

All rights reserved. No portion of this book may be reproduced, stored in a retrieval system, or transmitted by any form or any means electronically, photocopied, recorded, or any other except for brief quotations in printed reviews, without the prior permission of the publisher.

Cover Design by Senir Design. Contact information- info@senirdesign.com.

ISBN #978-1-945102-58-5

Printed in the United States of America.

Dedication to the Church

No time in recorded history has there been a book with pictures of two blood moon eclipses illustrated on the front and back cover Precedent Law and Order honoring God. Acts by the author in the exact same spot on earth looking west and east. Center On a hundred-year-old temple as the cornerstone to a monument illuminate God sign of the son of man appointed time Passover in the Tabernacle. Then write a volume of books about the worst suffering event stopping violent time starting peaceful times like a clock. Acts II Perfect Love, Peace and Happiness stops the violence Indictment against the Church.

Precedent "No war" the greatest law of them all Muhammad Ali vs U. S. in which the Court "had ruled that moral and ethical objection spiritual conviction to war was as valid as religious objection, thus broadening the qualifications humanism spiritual conviction of Jesus and Allah (God) as one equal not Muhammad equal to Jesus is God Allah too by law setting record straight, Justice Harlan, assigned to write the majority opinion, became convinced that Ali's claim to be a conscientious objector was sincere after reading background material on Black Muslim doctrine Elijah Muhammad provided by one of his law clerks.

To the contrary, Justice Harlan concluded that the claim by the Justice Department had been a misrepresentation He changed his vote, tying the vote at 4 to 4. A deadlock would have resulted in Ali being jailed for draft evasion and, since no opinions are published for deadlocked decisions, we would have never known why he had lost. A compromise proposed, in which Ali's conviction would be reversed citing a technical error by the Justice Department, gradually won unanimous assent from the eight voting justices. One by law and one by Holy Spirit the Law of Muhammad Ali No War!

Architect of law and order humanity Jesus Holy spirit Acts II Perfect Love, Peace and Happiness. Grassroots ministry start with each one of our families return to the temple celebration eternal life over death. Act of God certify by History biblical story four craftsmen Ben Joseph Jr, Ben David Jesus, Elijah and Righteous Priest Church rebuilding the temple. Second Acts II taking something old become born again new creation invitation to be baptizes. Celebration I see a new Church for the work that been done for God family husband and wives praying together equally suffering.

The New Millennial, New Testament dedicated to the work of the church people that has got us to this appointed time in the word to see the beautiful face of God excellence work in our daily life be holy. Every word of the Bible fulfilled from the peaceful smile on my family face temple honoring God Amen.

TABLE OF CONTENTS

Introduction	7
Entr'acte 2nd Acts II, Exodus II	13
Sign of the Son of Man Book of Jubilee Acts II	101
Chapter I *The Long Day of Debate*	104
Chapter 2 *Ordained To be A Witness*	145
Chapter 3 *There Is None Other Name*	156
Chapter 4 *I See the Heavens Opened*	167
Chapter 5 *The Order of Melchizedek*	191
Chapter 6 *Ministry of John the Baptist*	217
Chapter 7 *Acts II Conception of Jesus Christ*	232
Chapter 8 *Acts II something old Becoming New*	241

INTRODUCTION

If you can believe Joseph Smith Jr. white man's Book of Mormons another testament of Jesus Christ. Then you going to love this story Acts II Perfect Love, Universal peace and happiness the Black man's version Book of Moor-men. "Church Boy" born on the Moor-man trail of suffering descendant of Joseph Jr. another testament of Jesus Christ raised straight out of Compton Zi-On Holy Time monument to God will resurrect the dead. Sign of the Son of man The New Millennial, New Testament invitation to be baptize.

The Mission from Heaven descendants Joseph Jr. keeping family Church
At the time Dr. King conceived I have a Dream speech a generational marching order 1963 redeem the soul of our nation. They prayed, "Lord, you know everyone's deepest thoughts and desires. Show us clearly which one bell ringer you have chosen from among these seed of Abraham. The Lord said I need a volunteer God spoke Justus with truth over cultures and societies racial injustices to go check on your baby sisters and brothers set things right for me. Descendants of Joseph son of the Prophets saying cuzz and blood Urban Tribes divided north and south American. Lord called "Jubilee" for Justus a veteran volunteer of two armed forces Alone title Eric, Eternal Ruler one with favor. My righthand finger will point your way of protection you can't hurt yourself or nobody else you can lose your life we will have to start over. "Therefore, we must select one name of those who have accompanied us during the whole time the Lord Jesus lived among us, beginning from the baptism of John until the day when Jesus was taken from us. This person must become along with us a witness to his resurrection." So, they nominated two: Justus for "Jubilee" who is called Jesus the truth and they have proved a comfort to me. You will be given a sanctuary wall Temple everything you need will be provided to you new creation monument of Zi-On City of God no police. If there is anything

special, you would like the Lord wisdom will provide you all you need even a swimming pool to Baptize people in. From the womb of your mother your name will be great than Moses, Joseph thee beloved after your Grandfather and father ben Joseph Jr. will share the same King's Birthday Nation Holiday and Presidents Inauguration. Four craftsmen Ben Joseph Jr., Ben David Jesus, Elijah, and Righteous Priest honor to God. In the broken heartland of America the beautiful, New World a good life state married husband and wife under faith of Abraham and righteousness of Lincoln in star city native modern American family Black negro free. Raised in sin the hub city of Compton Babylon sister, cannot have a university degree, cannot be a Freemason, cannot have blood on your hands lock down in prison, cannot be gay or have tattoos. Not given in marriage by resurrection be like angel prince of God. Keeping holy time commandment Passover through Atonement. Be a prophet like Elijah fighting evil with tongue of fire pleading the blood of Jesus Christ, burning up prophets of Baal setting appointed time sign of the Son of man in a Temple monument looking upward praising God's glory. Say look how the Lord 's graceful finger pointed my way today and forever. In the worst of bad time, the best of good lifetime freedom state of mind being not afraid to do anything, go anyplace, turn to God weeping. Not because you are required to only by circumcision of the heart because of hearing the voice of God saying I love you I won't judge you. To a vision or dream remember the Law be baptizes. The word of Lord say I will bring up one firstborn double bless descendant of Joseph heirs of salvation Jews and Gentiles son and daughters equally in the Later-Day that will not be enslaved. Born again free weak and broken heart, in a good life state, star city, with no jealousy, pray on the same parallel line of faith in oath Lord of Abraham be holy. Demonstration of God true existence. From every word in the bible starting in book of Genesis ending in book of Revelation advent of Jesus Christ second coming resurrection Amen.

For centuries the church has debate how the sign of Son of man God will appear in the clouds on earth in tabernacle with everybody watching? First you must also have prophet Elijah returning to the temple on Passover with Fire and blood? They both appearing at appointed time as monument to God. It is written the work already done. Becoming like modern day City of On a City upon a Hill Zi-On prophecy prediction painted on the wall of Compton On City Hall fulfilled. Modern day church history: I see a new Church!

The most important appointed time alignment biblical event in Bible Church history recorded. From the Old Testament Passover return of Elijah on top of a mountain with tongue of fire and blood to destroy prophet of Baal, idol and sun god worshiping. New Testament advent second coming of Jesus Christ sign of the Son of man God return in the tabernacle on a cloud to Judge the world. Every prophet has spoken about this end of time event of seeing the advent second coming sign of the Son of man in a temple monument to God. Justus over philosophy I think so I am. The worldwide-web Ubuntu I am because we are as interconnection of people through other people witness at appointed time Human spirit in tabernacle with every detail fulfilled from Passover to Atonement reconciliation. Return of Elijah fighting evil with tongue of fire destroying prophets of Baal idol and sun god worshiping with Justus. From the oath of faith of Abraham to Abraham Lincoln Nebraska seeds of righteousness descendant of Joseph encouraging Justus providing comfort practicing circumcision remembering invitation be baptized, born again freely by hearing voice of the Holy Spirit saying "I love you no matter what you do, I forgive you". Praying with repentance, passion, immerse, and communion the trinity Christian perfection Methodist of Jesus Christ invitation be baptized fulfilled.

The Purpose of this Book story is an invitation for you to be baptized become a member of Ubuntu interconnection of family pool living water as person through people. That it inspires you to come celebrate the work of the human spirit male and female pass, present, future. Holy spirit in front of monument to God sign of the son of man.

The Moor's Descendants of Joseph Nobel people

We are gathered here today with the authority in faith to honor our heavenly father and earthly parent mothers and fathers that rest on this foundation wall cornerstone Church of Jesus Christ sign of the Son man God seeing son and daughters equally. To give thank for the promise of the firstborn blessing Passover through family inheritance managed by the righthand finger of God point to Atonement. From a little seed of measured faith planted Abraham in the Bible. To Abraham Lincoln, Nebraska born into history descendants of Joseph Chief administrator welfare keeping family Church craftsmen to God. On the Parallel line oath of faith from four corner on the world map Compton and Jerusalem line right up as Zi-On modern City on a Hill monument to God second work of grace advent of Jesus Christ perfect love the baptism with the Holy Spirit truth and Justus.

As I reflect on me and my brothers pass suffering, we were one hell of a mess. Only by the grace of God did we survive our lostness. Is not dead, in prison on Death Row is able to tell this story. I never been gang affiliated I am gang related to blood's and Cripes in my family and friends. Everybody knows my title Eric name Joseph, 2pac was an actor the thing we grew up doing in the Hood on the neighborhood deadened block of Compton. 2pac sing and rapped about to a bomb beat from Dr. Dra: California Love inspired by D. J. Quik Piru moon. The sons of the P, Pyramid Builders, Priest and Prophets, P-funk area gangster grove Blood's and Cripes walking like they on water. Every day was like Friday, payday hustling on the block. Walkout the front door and there was opportunity to get paid or get shot. That how it was set off on Holly hood Compton. Desert of the wild-west frontier coastline crossing the continental divide of America Capital City Abraham Lincoln Nebraska. The word of God numbers of sciences and

Black African American studies all adds up to a monument to God Holy *Time* in the worst of best times. Every prophet in the bible spoke about this movement keeping holy time, keeping family church. Amen!

Messiah ben Joseph Jr.

In Jewish eschatology Mashiach ben Yoseph or Messiah ben Joseph (ben Yōsēf), also known as Mashiach /ben Ephraim, is a Jewish messiah from the tribe of Ephraim and a descendant of Joseph Jew and Gentile. The figure's origins are much debated. Some regard it as a rabbinic invention, but others defend the view that its origins are in the Torah. Jewish eschatology is the area of Jewish theology concerned with events that will happen in the end of days and related concepts. This includes the ingathering of the exiled diaspora, the coming of a Jewish Messiah, afterlife, and the revival of the dead. In Judaism, the end times are usually called the "end of days", a phrase that appears several times in the Tanakh.

Messianic tradition

Jewish tradition alludes to four messianic figures, called the Four Craftsmen, from a vision found in Book of Zechariah 1:20. The four craftsmen are discussed in Babylonian Talmud Suk. 52b identifies these four craftsmen as Messiah ben David Jesus, Messiah ben Joseph Jr, Elijah, and the Righteous Priest. Each will be involved in ushering in the Messianic age. They are mentioned in the Talmud and the Book of Zechariah.

Commentary on the Talmud gives more details. Explains that Messiah ben Joseph is called a craftsman because he will help rebuild the temple. The roles of the Four Craftsmen are as follows. Elijah will be the herald of eternal life at the eschaton. If necessary, Messiah ben Joseph Jr. will wage war against the evil forces and die in combat with the enemies of God and Israel Dec 25 appointed time. The need for his appearance will depend on the spiritual condition of the Jewish people suffering. Year after his death a period of great calamities will befall Israel. God will then resurrect the dead and usher in the Messianic Era of universal peace. Messiah ben David Jesus will reign as a Jewish king during the period when God will resurrect the dead. With the ascendancy of good over evil Righteous Priest has largely not been the subject of Jewish messianic speculation

Academic views

The exact origins of Messiah ben Joseph Jr. are a matter of debate among scholars. It has been suggested that Messiah ben Joseph Jr. arose out of a Jewish collective memory of Simon bar Kokhba. Others suggest that his origins are older. Some academic scholars[who?] have argued that the idea of two messiahs, one suffering, the second fulfilling the traditional messianic role, was normative to ancient Judaism, in fact predating Jesus. Early Christians (who were Jews) might have viewed Jesus as fulfilling this role.

Christian views

Traditional Christians do not believe that Jesus / Yeshua was a clear candidate for the Messiah ben Joseph Jr. They believe rather that he was Messiah ben David Jesus and that he was of the tribe of Judah and a descendant of David. Some[who?] assert that the passages associated with Messiah ben Joseph have no power of redemption. Many modern Christians however follow the belief of the Messianic Jews that Jesus (Yeshua) may have fulfilled these prophecies due to his adoptive father being named Joseph?Christians have associated the Four Craftsmen in varying ways with the Four Horsemen of the Apocalypse?

Mormons

Main article: House of Joseph (LDS Church)
Some Mormon groups have associated Messiah ben Joseph with Joseph Smith Jr., as he was anointed king over Israel via Council of Fifty. Father also named Joseph.

 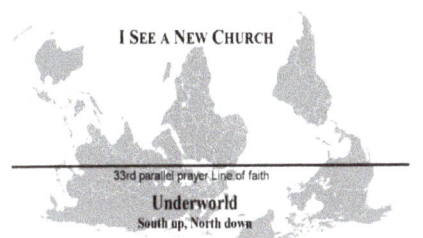 

ENTR'ACTE 2ND ACTS II, EXODUS II

My name is Eric Joseph Moore "Church Boy thee Beloved." My name is Biblical Eternal Ruler Joseph, born a seed of Abraham little by little faith descendant of Joseph Jr. today (Genesis 50:20). If somebody came and told me this old Bible story of inheritance firstborn blessing Joseph, becoming a new creation Bible story "Church Boy thee Beloved," conformation of the omnipresence inherit salvation of the Holy Spirit in every word of Holy Bible fulfilled. Modern day classic Eric little by little "Church Boy" God's blessing, been fulfilled, how the Holy Spirit reform keeping Family Church little by little in faith ending seven seasons pandemic of violence and death, beginning "Jubilee" year 2020 Lord's Day be Holy (Leviticus 25:10), I would not believe a word of it myself. I would have told you to stop lying calling you crazy!

This is what truly happened when the Lord showed up, reform schooling my anti-Christ life little by little new creation "Church Boy" crying, "Use me, Lord." Joseph uniquely faithful the first whistleblower persecuted for wisdom to do the right thing returning church with this story seeing prophet Elijah blood and fire, with Jesus Christ's grace and truth rising from a graveyard sign of the Son of Man praising God (Revelation 7:8), remembering to be baptized with repentance after seven season times seven hallow the 50th Birthday Easter 2013. Immersed three times for Father, Son, and Holy Ghost Trinity, son of Joseph Jr. (Matthew 28:19). The "Church Boy" passion born again brokenhearted Lord my increase. Apostle "Jubilee" "Church Boy" most people call him Eric to mean Eternal Ruler, nicknamed E.J. by his father firefighter. Joseph, the "Church Boy" Ruler, seer of truth like Elijah fighting evil with fire and the blood of Jesus Christ peacefully. Illustration of faith illuminating into a cross saving lives gathering of exiled and Gentiles. Family activist pleading truth rising over the dead temple monument praising God. Persecuted for being uniquely faithful returned from being dead confirming the Trinity omnipresence of the Lord. Healing truth to unify God's family weak and brokenhearted crying, stopping violence.

Genesis 1:6
"And God said, Let there be a solid arch stretching over the waters, parting the waters from the waters."

Never thought I would be proud to call myself "Church Boy," when talking to the last generation of Pirus and Crips; my nephews and nieces are not afraid to die. Waiting to protest and riot start a revolution war demonstration at an appointed time to inherit the homeland back, saying when Uncle "Church Boy" how will Holy Spirit peacefully return the promise land by inheritance back. Lord said it is written be not afraid and put your guns away; for all who take the sword, shall die by the sword. Children of God, police yourselves (Matthew 26:52). The pen is mightier than the sword. Acts II perfect love your enemy, turn the other cheek, pardon your neighbors bad behaviors with forgiveness. It's a double blessing mercy and compassion.

From the Old Testament being revealed at the end of The New Testament "Jubilee" the Revelations of Jesus Christ grace and truth new creation "I see a new Church." Old story of Joseph evil being used for good in Jesus Christ name new creation "Church Boy." The Sun shall be turned into darkness, and the black moon into color of blood before the great and the terrible day of the Lord comes to stop suffering, beginning of sorrows, being thankful we survived pandemic 2020 vision (Joel 2:31). To see "Jubilee" Law of Inheritance an image of the world peacefully flipped, right side up: Spiritual climate change flipping from negative to positive south up, north down connected to higher power Holy Spirit sign of Son of Man (Matthew 24:30). Between two blood moons through temple arches on a cross sign of eternal peace, with sun setting and sun rising in heaven, Lord's Day of memorial honoring life and death. Peaceful return of Elijah to a temple with blood and fire top of monument to God.

Genesis 1:7

"And God made the arch for a division between the waters which were under the arch and those which were over it: and it was so."

You cannot be more holy led by Holy Spirit to be in the perfect appointed position wisdom of God then this coming straight out of the Bible in Compton. Seeing the return of Elijah with fire and blood, sign of the Son of Man the sun moon united illuminate up into a cross on hundred-year-old temple monument memorial honoring tens of thousands of Christian lives of spiritual protection sanctuary (Matthew 24:31). Kingdom of Heaven Zi-On New City On, Son of man destroying Anti-Christ idols and sun god worshiping policing themselves (Jeremiah 3:14). 2nd Acts II The Greatest Story Ever Told. A story only by action of God moving passing over our lives. 2020 version proclaims inheritance "Jubilee" Acts II Law Human Rights equal protection retuning our homeland security Exodus II. A word of truth that all the prophets of the Bible spoke about.

Law of firstborn inheritance can't claim land that was stolen. Like when the United States transferred return the Panama Canal back to Panama created from a treaty with Spain. The promise of inheritance all the land you see God gave to the people of Color Native Americans at the beginning of Holy Time rainbow covenant all people equally policing themselves. Human rights peacefully proclaiming the land that was lost, Christopher Columbus stole all that he could see from the fatherless, widow, poor people innocent blood gave to the rich den of robbers, divided, and conquest of paradise year 1492 back (Jeremiah 7:9).

It is written the Bible and history will come together new creation from something old people freely policing themselves, children of God. It was prophesied the world would peacefully end like this with great awaking. Turning away from Jesus Christ becoming anti-Christ police double minded men (John 6:66). Rainbow covenant Black Native American people return to one God as heir of salvation. 2nd Acts II perfect love, peace, and happiness, ending at a beautiful Taj Mahal Mausoleum style temple watchtower plumb line between arch of harmony heaven and Earth. A blueprint drawn in the sky by the architect of the law plans of heaven, earth and temple working together from the beginning setting time like an alarm clock use to wake people up.

No place on Earth can you see a more beautiful demonstration of the peaceful harmony perfect love righthand comfort of the Holy Spirit in action grace and truth with the Law Human Right (Jeremiah 7:14). Architect arch of heaven, earth, and law of scripters eclipse a celestial glory comparable to the glory of the sun. Melting pillar of fire that burneth away all conspiracies theories by presence of the Lord. Stopping white supremacy nationalists Ku Klux Klan burning of the cross sign for anti-Jesus Christ name like people use the Blood Moon sign for doing evil being afraid calling the police (Jeremiah 7:18).

Genesis 1:8

"And God gave the arch the name of Heaven. And there was evening and there was morning, the second day."

January 19, 2018

This is not another bad boy against the police from the hood setting it off story. "Church boy" setting the record straightway the tribulation of these days moonlight reflection sunlight Elijah returns on mountain top with fire and blood, sign of the Son of man on a cross praising God grace and truth the lord lives rising from the dead (Matthew 24:29). Never thought we would see life as we know time peacefully come to end on the cross like this great gathering reforming Sunday school and bible study keeping family church (Jeremiah 16:14-15). A novel to be read with the Holy Bible confirming 2nd Acts II perfect love of the Holy Spirit apart of Native American journey Wokini on water vision for human rights.

The Bible in the beginning warned us about latter days of bad times ending like this virus pandemic, economic recession, plague of racial violence looting and rioting. Shadow of death Passover firstborn urban tribes last day (Jeremiah 16:16). Great falling away from seeing the face hearing the voice of the Holy Spirit weeping. Seeing people use a man tragedy to loot and steal, you will feel the weight of the hand of Almighty upon you. The shutting down the world economy to fight a global pandemic celebrating Holy Week, keeping the Passover at Easter time, and the resurrection of Jesus Christ wept.

As it was in the beginning, it will be in the end Lord's Day of memorial victory over life and death. God is the Holy Spirit same yesterday today, and forever memorial to eternal life. Battling smashing the Anti-Christ good against evil, truth against lies alternative facts (Jeremiah 18:7-8). Remnant House of Joseph Jr. the persecuted unifier, an Old Testament savior resurrection, type of Jesus justified as a uniquely faithful spiritual body of people who died and went to heaven many times doing the right thing hearing the Lord. Becoming born again continually praying keeping Holy Times shield against a pandemic saving lives united with Holy Spirit Lord our righteousness (Jeremiah 23:5-6). Nobody gets left behind all will be saved justice. Some generations started this relay race eternal lifecycle before others. We all finish at the same time, be accomplished with every knee bowing together tongues confessing their shame (Jeremiah 29:10). The good word of Holy Spirit not a competition 1st Acts started in one cemetery ending parallel another cemetery becoming 2nd Acts II Lord's Day Memorial park for honoring the Living and Dead Temple of Justice (Jeremiah 26:9).

Genesis 1:14

"And God said, Let there be lights in the arch of heaven, for a division between the day and the night, and let them be for signs, and for marking the changes of the year, and for days and for years."

If you were given a peaceful mission against anti-Christ police from heaven to be used like Black Native American Moses Exodus II sent like Jonah, proclaim one message: "Save my church!" From the place of comfort protection terms of endearment Abraham Lincoln, Nebraska cross continental divide to the place of learning and discovery Eureka I found it safety and suffering restored health (Jeremiah 30:17). Compton, California on your Lord's day off be in graveyard next to Lueders Park. Angeles Abby Memorial Park Cemetery at sunrise Saturday morning April 4, 2015 Passover and sunset Sunday evening September 28, 2015 Day of Atonement during four blood moons lunar eclipse worldwide warning latter days (Jeremiah 30:24).

To simply take a perfect picture all the equipment and transportation you will need is given at no cost to you watchman. All from a vision in a dream Holy Spirit cannot tell you until you get there because you would not understand it. Like Moses climbing a mountain then talking to a burning bush. Epiphany see the moon the color of blood on fire burning over an ancient temple beautiful building historical landmark uniting the old testament with the new testament becoming a new creation Zi-On like a city on the hill (Jeremiah 31:5-6).

Battle of heaven earth watchman against the anti-Christ police. Model City Compton and heaven align straight up now you know we are in trouble sound wave of harmony like a Dr. Dre's Day beat hook proclaim Great year "Jubilee" Holy Times of the firstborn Children of God policing themselves (Jeremiah 31:9)! Lord's Day spiritual climate changing reversal gathering of the blind brokenhearted beat from negative to positive. Setting it off Black Native American proclaiming "Jubilee" rejoice no police Day of the Lord our Homeland Zi-On back Exodus II gathering second coming to Jesus Christ (Jeremiah 31:12).

The word of the Holy Spirit fulfilled twin year 2020 release from debt be Holy. And you cannot take credit for seeing it come true history new creation no police. It is the Law commandment written already on the books every on shall die for his own iniquity (Jeremiah 31:29-30). The only requirements are you can't have blood on your hands or be gay, must be baptized and no tattoos. Could you say, "I will do that, Lord. Send me"? Likewise, Moses God said, "I Am my presence will go with you. I'll see the journey to the end (Exodus 33:14).

Genesis 1:17

"And God put them in the arch of heaven, to give light on the earth."

Passover April 4, 2015

It's been a long time coming; I know a change gone come. So, I write to my brothers to stop knocking me to my knees, help me please I can't breathe, remove your knee from off my neck. Black Lives Matter, too. The New Millennial, New Testament written on our hearts in the worst of dark times great pandemic best of great times of reform "Jubilee" Universal Pardon new covenant (Jeremiah 31:33). Flood of goodness destroying Anti-Christ police at the end of bad times, 1st Acts of the apostles with Amen "Jubilee" law of humanity be holy. Starting of 2nd Acts II perfect love, peace, and happiness ministry of reconciliation forgiveness beginning of good times one heart one way (Jeremiah 32:39).

Passover and resurrection best of days protected by a promise of God with restoration never dying. The word of "Jubilee" in the name of the Holy Spirit is mightier than a sword; it is nothing to play around with; it can cost you your eternal life (Jeremiah 36:32). It's a double blessing becomes cures by not keeping the commandment. It makes you look at yourself to see you are not right Anti-Christ calling the police afraid. Your either keeping Holy Time the commandment trusting and forgiving or Anti-Christ policing other people going into outer darkness self-created keeping Hell. Looking back gnashing of teeth at the perfect love of God you could have had.

This story about what Holy Spirit is doing grace and truth (Jeremiah 41:1). Trust Lord in every detail of your life. Being used by Holy Spirit's right hand, setting a plumb line to tell these twin novel stories 1st Acts ending with a pandemic, 2nd Acts II proclaiming "Jubilee" year of the Lord. God the Holy Spirit is instantly answering prayers directed in Jesus Christ's name. We are the heir of salvation given inherit authority to call on angels to move on our behalf, to do the good will of Holy Spirit in our life at the right time (Genesis 1:5). Nothing is random moment of God's Kingdom look up. Resetting time to year Zero.

Genesis 1:20

"And God said, Let the waters be full of living things, and let birds be in flight over the earth under the arch of heaven."

Total Solar Eclipse
August 21, 2017

    Wow, don't panic! Have you ever seen this picture before an image of the divided world word of the Lord (Ezekiel 1:1)? Anti-Christ land of giant corporations and churches turn upside down between two blood moons eclipse on the cross dream and vision (Ezekiel 1:4)? When Bishop said at the annual conference, "I see a new church," I prayed the world to be united and to turn around, return to trusting God's over all thing (Ezekiel 1:10). This is what happened next: I presented as president on the agenda to council of United Methodist Men Charge conference report First Church of Compton call to prophecy sign of the Son of man holiness (Ezekiel 1:26).

    As Black Native American New Millennial, New Jerusalem Hub City of Son Priest State of hope, Country of peace-loving people opposite anti-Christ police state Roman Guard the Vatican City most rebellious (Ezekiel 2:7). If you fold a world map in half, model City of Son Zi-On Compton lines right up with old Testament Jerusalem and City of the Sun On (Genesis 41:45). The New Millennial, New Jerusalem comes true unfolding from Heaven kingdom of peace. There is a snapshot image of a united world turned right side up between 2nd Acts II two blood moons sunsetting and sunrising on the cross. Straight out of heaven Compton Zi-On New City of the Son of Man as light like ancient city on the hill for all to see.

Genesis 1:27
"And God made man in his image, in the image of God he made him: male and female he made them."

August 21, 2017

The story of Joseph the greatest story never told of choice. Seers who are more than a prophet unifier name greater than Moses, Joseph, serving as liturgist the first time on his birthday January 19, 2020, which is Human Relations Day of peace 1/19 opposite 9/11- day of terrorism. Watchmen ringing a hundred fifty-two years old historical church bell three times honoring the trinity once for the heavenly father, once for the Son of man, and once for the breath of life delivered thy soul (Ezekiel 3:19). Honoring the Holy Spirit at 1st United Temple Church something old sound proclaiming new creation "I See A New Church." Did not know healing would instantly happen like this fighting a global health pandemic virus burning appearing of fire looting and rioting (Ezekiel 8:1-2). Shaking up shutdown economies of the whole wide world, collapsing the stock market, turning into a recession starting people to rioting over racial injustice.

Be careful what you cry out to God for you are responsible for every word that comes out your mouth. Two or more praying together will become history of the Church. God's judgment to the believer is a double blessing stimulus Sabbatical with God, indictment to the unbeliever as impeachment, and "apocalyptic" pandemic to the ungodly anti-Christ nation (Ezekiel 8:3). There is no better way to ending a pandemic or begin a biblical story celebrating "Jubilee." This is what great books are written about. Stay calm. Be not troubled, for this is not the end; it is not yet the beginning of sorrows. This too will Passover. The sacred scripture fulfilled was called to standup and read in church service as Liturgist Human Relations Day January 19, 2020 was Isaiah 49:1-7, 1 Corinthians 1:1-9, John 1:29-42.

The Servant, the Light to the Gentiles
Isaiah 49:1-2
"Listen, O coastlands, to Me, and take heed, you peoples from afar! The Lord has called Me from the womb; From the matrix of My mother He has made mention of My name. 2 And He has made My mouth like a sharp sword; In the shadow of His hand He has hidden Me, And made Me a polished shaft; In His quiver He has hidden Me."

The sacred scriptures cannot be broken, standing on the promise I will be their God (Ezekiel 11:20). Talent to take something old hundred-year-old temple bell tower one-hundred-and-fifty-year church bell align into a new creation good news. Light to the nation sign of restoration (Ezekiel 12:11). Bold new radical way traditionally sees the world turned right side up. People bearing the cross on the top protected by trusting Jesus Christ vision Son of Man (Ezekiel 12:22). Dying on the cross a plumb line sets the holy timeclock like a compass tool set true north. You never will be lost; everything you pray for instantly happens, shall be done saith the Lord (Ezekiel 12:28). Like feeling idols of the heart lost in a storm in your own backyard praying look up seeing sunrise, moonset, sunset, moonrise illuminating into a cross.

Through beautiful peaceful temple stand in your backyard letting you know everything will be alright, guiding returning you home to safety. One hundred and one scores ago, our heavenly father elder came forth from heaven in the image son of man Holy Spirit as human face sunlight (Ezekiel 14:3). To become a part of a plan, hew stone memorial living sacrifice heir of salvation, offering his own blood in the image of himself, not the sacrificed blood of bulls and goats. Cornerstone New creation Spirit ministry by name of Jesus Christ, King of Kings, turned the known world upside down (Acts 17:6).

A Light for the Nations
Isaiah 49:3-4
"And He said to me, 'You are My servant, O Joseph, In whom I will be glorified.' 4 Then I said, 'I have labored in vain, I have spent my strength for nothing and in vain; Yet surely my just reward is with the Lord, And my work with my God."

In the beginning of divide time Jesus calling, it was a very violent dark period and nasty way of thinking anti-Christ not hearing God (Ezekiel 14:14). A great prophet lost his head simply by a promise made for a dance to a king, Jesus died like a thief for healing people on their day off. There was no equality and no justice; whatever the king said became the law; men were beaten, wives were treated as property of husbands, and women had no rights to pray, touch, or agree separately from men. The world was deeply divided, and people were afraid of the dark time (age). The divided anti-Christ Roman Empire was on top. Caesar became king god of the world of iron and clay, land of giant artificial people corporations and stockholders (Ezekiel 15).

Firstborn sons and daughters were treated differently on the top inheritance; genealogy is not to be reckoned after the birthright. For Judah prevailed above his brethren, and of him came the chief ruler (Eric), but the birthright was Joseph's (1 Chronicles 5:2). Everybody knows God used Joseph's suffering, beautiful heart of integrity, and forgiveness to save others, unifying the faithful and nonfaithful in his darkest time turning to light. Any question you have about God in history will be answered in Greatest Story Never Told of Joseph Alone today word of the Lord came unto me (Ezekiel 16:1). The New Millennial, New Testament 2 Acts II Peace, Love and Happiness, a story of goodness for all ages everybody lives forever. Under the watchful eye of the Lord in every little by little step of our lives.

Delivery of the Exiles
Isaiah 49:5-6
"And now the Lord says, Who formed Me from the womb to be His Servant, To bring Jacob back to Him, So that Joseph is gathered to Him (For I shall be glorious in the eyes of the Lord, And My God shall be My strength), 6 Indeed He says, 'It is too small a thing that You should be My Servant To raise up the tribes of Jacob, And to restore the preserved ones of Joseph; I will also give You as a light to the Gentiles, That You should be My salvation to the ends of the earth."

Generational unity Passover throughout Holy Time on a prayer line measure of oath in faith to do which is lawful and right continually praying until the end of the age shall not die (Ezekiel 18:20-21). Directed by the right hand of God's perfect pure love with repentances, passion, baptizes and communion. Trust in the name of Jesus Christ in everything you do in life. Christian perfection is pure love of God. Perfect love Passover atonement from ancient Temple wisdom system of worshiping God, pouring flooding out of the heart in spiritual maturity shall live righteously

(Ezekiel 18:22). Through the scriptures, tradition, reason, Christian experience, written on our new heart and a new spirit. Renew in Millennial New Modern-Day Church taken communion and repenting reforming to God (Ezekiel 18:31). Praying with authority, Psalm 91, of the heart in the morning, forgiving each other, suffering of correction, crying out prayer line in history, during times of affliction and persecution in their lives, being thankful for God's goodness turning to live (Ezekiel 18:32). Twenty years after 9/11 becoming a pandemic of 2020.

God Calls His Special Servant
Isaiah 49:7
"Thus says the Lord, The Redeemer of Joseph, their Holy One, To Him whom man despises, To Him whom the nation abhors, To the Servant of rulers: "Kings shall see and arise, Princes also shall worship, Because of the Lord who is faithful, The Holy One of Joseph; And He has chosen You."

Because most of my life cycle, I lived anti-Christ foolishly with upside-down and backward for count money 666 in God we trust, enslaved in the world of debt. I was a bigger sinner than most people doing evil to get paid (Ezekiel 24:15). I had to go through more tests than most people, giving me more testimony pardon bad behavior forgiveness. The New Millennial Testament story of redemption, a new creation turns the world around, right side up, with south up, and north down; everybody wins. A new way of traditionally seeing the negative world positive, peacefully nobody loses neither shall tears run down (Ezekiel 24:16). Zi-On profane sanctuary people who were on the bottom are instantly on top. Turning of the cheek pardon other people bad behavior negative to positive excellency of strength. Allowing me to see eyes desires the upside-down underworld as for what Hell it is Anti-Christ. With a backward way of thinking, I was raised north up, south down, catching Hell (Ezekiel 24:21). Anti-Christ the things I thought were good positive for me turned out to be negative bad; the things I thought were bad negative turned out to be good positive strength of excellency.

Appeal to Unity
1 Corinthians 1:1-3

"From Paul, called by God's will to be an apostle of Jesus Christ, and from Sosthenes our brother. 2 To God's church that is in Corinth: To those who have been made holy to God in Christ Jesus, who are called to be God's people. Together with all those who call upon the name of our Lord Jesus Christ in every place—he's their Lord and ours! 3 Grace to you and peace from God our Father and the Lord Jesus Christ."

On the bottom is a borderline of faith going to church. In the anti-Christ underworld, the old church is divided. Woman were not allowed to preach and pray with men. In the Old Testament, the word of God came in drops by one prophet at a time. In the New Testament, the Word of God through the Holy Spirit poured out on everyone in Acts of the Apostles, turning the old world around, upside down with north up and south down, which became anti-Christ Hell. The New Millennial New Testament the Holy Spirit is written the healing Word of God overflowing on our heart 2 Acts II Peace, Love and Happiness. Turning World upright straightway back to God original order of heaven seeing things right, changing the direction of seeing the World map at the beginning of time south up, north down, nobody gets hurt; everyone stands for themselves; no more dumb (Ezekiel 33:21-22). If you would have told me I would be waking up calling out to God on a cell phone prayer line at 5am in the morning, to peacefully demonstrate my faith, protesting my joy and concern to the Lord and being thankful, I would have called you crazy! How did God make this happen, turning everything upside down? There is a consequence for every action. No coincidence here; everything has a purpose and reason. Second Acts II a purpose-driven life with thanksgiving.

Thanksgiving for the Corinthians
1 Corinthians 1:4-9

"I thank my God always for you, because of God's grace that was given to you in Christ Jesus. 5 That is, you were made rich through him in everything: in all your communication and every kind of knowledge, 6 in the same way that the testimony about Christ was confirmed with you. 7 The result is that you aren't missing any spiritual gift while you wait for our Lord Jesus Christ to be revealed. 8 He will also confirm your testimony about Christ until the end so that you will be blameless on the day of our Lord Jesus Christ. 9 God is faithful, and you were called by him to partnership with his Son, Jesus Christ our Lord."

The ambassadors three sons out of the house of Joseph first born King James, second the prophet Daniel, and the third, Joseph eternal ruler (Eric). Named within the womb of their mother at their birth. In the heartland of America, Abraham Lincoln, Nebraska Good Life State place of equality birth Saint Elizabeth Hospital sons circumcised on the eighth day, daughters to be a light of hope in upside down dark times underworld blessed by the name of God forever. Raised straight out of Compton, California with wisdom and might God hand in history (Daniel 1:15). Everybody knows we are the moors Noble people from Spain, the first to establish church cemeteries planting Christianity here in the New World knowledge of understanding change of time and seasons fear of the Lord (Daniel 2:19-22). Exiled here in the west to live alongside with the natives indigenous before it was named America, not enslaved in the first original thirteen United States colonies as citizens in the East.

In the West, after ten years, the land returned to the original native indigenous people of color speaking utterance. My people family foundation house of Joseph has been here from the beginning set in appointed time history state of difficulty. The record of the King James Bible proves it. Hub City Country State of Compton as Zi-On the first church free state

(Genesis 41:45). Landmark horseshoe Moorish Arch over a Christian cemetery Land granted by the Queen and King of Spain that stands today like the Vatican City Country State and Temple Mount to get to God on Earth one Gate for non-Muslims Moors gate separation of religion. Everyone welcomes Zi-On thought the Moor's Arch gate of heaven the temple mount name honoring Jesus Christ with cross and star of David all religions are welcome (Daniel 2:44). Continually praying women and men touching and agreeing 2nd Acts II perfect love, peace, happiness.

John 1:29-49 New King James Version (NKJV)
The Lamb of God (John 1:29-34)
"The next day John saw Jesus coming toward him, and said, "Behold! The Lamb of God who takes away the sin of the world! 30 This is He of whom I said, 'After me comes a Man who is preferred before me, for He was before me.' 31 I did not know Him; but that He should be revealed to Israel, therefore I came baptizing with water." 32 And John bore witness, saying, "I saw the Spirit descending from heaven like a dove, and He remained upon Him. 33 I did not know Him, but He who sent me to baptize with water said to me, 'Upon whom you see the Spirit descending, and remaining on Him, this is He who baptizes with the Holy Spirit.' 34 And I have seen and testified that this is the Son of God."

To the new Christians believe in the sign of the son of man God's every Word in the Bible, born-again faith of Jesus Christ grace and truth kingdom never ending. In the year 2020, bringing the Word of God unified with flesh (Daniel 2:11). Every word must be followed; the scriptures cannot be broken. Qualify by the right hand of God in every word written. To the highest priest order known son of man who prays for others, fighting a good fight against evil. The old ancient temple wisdom system of worshipping united with the New Millennial Modern Church Christian perfection new creation "Church Boy" (Daniel 3:8-25). Teaching of the word of God correctly through the scripture, tradition, reason and Christian experience.

Demonstration of faith from reason praying the Psalm of your heart for enabling grace in the morning. Calling on a cell phone out to God for mercy on my soul like he is the best friend you ever had revealed. "Church Boy" voicing protest concerns that only God can help you with spiritual relationship with Him and rely on His divine graciousness as the basis for an answer (Daniel 6:28). Before I became a born-again Christian "Church Boy," I would hear people say they did not believe every word of the Holy Bible. By saying they are independent not religious, they believe in a higher power that was not named Jesus Christ. They called on a spiritual guide and don't think they need to keep family church is organized religion.

The First Disciples
John 1:35-42

"Again, the next day, John stood with two of his disciples. 36 And looking at Jesus as He walked, he said, "Behold the Lamb of God!" 37 The two disciples heard him speak, and they followed Jesus. 38 Then Jesus turned, and seeing them following, said to them, "What do you seek?" They said to Him, "Rabbi" (which is to say, when translated, Teacher), "where are You staying?" 39 He said to them, "Come and see." They came and saw where He was staying, and remained with Him that day (now it was about the tenth hour). 40 One of the two who heard John speak, and followed Him, was Andrew, Simon Peter's brother. 41 He first found his own brother Simon, and said to him, "We have found the Messiah" (which is translated, the Christ). 42 And he brought him to Jesus. Now when Jesus looked at him, He said, "You are Simon the son of Jonah. You shall be called Cephas" (which is translated, A Stone)."

When I became born again "Church Boy," a new convert believing in one God named Jesus Christ, the Holy Spirit set my heart free, being Holy

Trinity. Believe every word in the Gospel of Good News of the King James Bible man of one book that all people nations and languages should serve God (Daniel 7:13-14). If you don't stand for something, you will fall for anything anti-Christ. We aren't fighting against human enemies but against rulers, authorities, forces of cosmic darkness, and spiritual powers of evil in the clouds of heavens most high given judgement (Daniel 7:21-22). Invisible enemy army of the dead pandemic from the North, not an easy path of faith.

It is hard to follow the Word of God in all things you do. This fight is a real battlefield of love. It became a pandemic, a very scary event, with mind blowing decisions: marriage or shacking, which way do you go? I had to go through a divorce, not for cheating cancer in my marriage. She said, "I forgive you." It's when I had a change of heart and looked at my own ignorance. I realized I was amoral (wrong) my whole life anti-Christ. How I identify saw myself spiritual not a believer in the word of Jesus Christ. Started working out my own salvation and became born again, so the Lord could use me in ministry. Circumcise my heart cleanse my soul new creation "Church Boy" from a bad boy. She said I had a nervous breakdown and was trying to brainwash her change her unforgiving heart. She believed in a spiritual higher power that was not Jesus Christ anti-Christ. That's when she threw me out the house with a police escort the day after our ninth wedding anniversary, filed for a divorce with a restraining order, trying to send me to back to prison.

Philip and Nathanael (John 1: 43-49)
"The following day Jesus wanted to go to Galilee, and He found Philip and said to him, "Follow Me." 44 Now Philip was from Bethsaida, the city of Andrew and Peter. 45 Philip found Nathanael and said to him, "We have found Him of whom Moses in the law, and also the prophets, wrote—Jesus of Nazareth, the son of Joseph." 46 And Nathanael said to him, "Can anything good come out of Nazareth?" Philip said to him, "Come and

see." 47 Jesus saw Nathanael coming toward Him, and said of him, "Behold, an Israelite indeed, in whom is no deceit!" 48 Nathanael said to Him, "How do You know me?" Jesus answered and said to him, "Before Philip called you, when you were under the fig tree, I saw you." 49 Nathanael answered and said to Him, "Rabbi, You are the Son of God! You are the (Ben Joseph) King of Israel (Joseph body of people)!"

Anti-Christ real-life horror story with four blood moons, angels and demons babbling and battling the devil artificial people in the twilight zone of unforgiveness, being weak not afraid of trouble end of days (Daniel 12:13). What are we supposed to believe? Was blind now can see, looking at myself alternative facts. The things meant for evil, God used for good, such as the danger I placed my own life in. Every word, little by little detail, must be fulfilled, even down to the exact purpose being good by commandment of one's name must be obeyed. Does God really answer prayers?

Songs of David (Psalm 40: 1-3)
I put all my hope in the Lord. He leaned down to me; he listened to my cry for help. 2 He lifted me out of the pit of death, out of the mud and filth, and set my feet on solid rock. He steadied my legs. 3 He put a new song in my mouth, a song of praise for our God. Many people will learn of this and be amazed; they will trust the Lord.

How do we demonstrate our little by little faith of righteousness believing in things unseen be holy? In what direction do we look up to pray for Jerusalem and who do we look to pray for others? Holy Spirit voice of God among you. First, what traditions, denomination or nondenominational, church house, hall, or temple, do we go to Jerusalem House of God (Ezra 1:2-3)? Catholic Church, Protestant Church, and Methodist Church? You don't know what type of service you might get served when you walk into any church vessels today. You get more friendly service handed a menu at a restaurant than some mosque, churches or synagogues (Ezra 1:7).

Some take communion (the Lord's supper) and some don't. This pastor says this wrong; that preacher says that right. Some churches have crosses with death on them, and others do not gift of protect. How do we know who is right or wrong, good or bad righteous (Ezra 1:8)? How do you pay tithes when you owe so much? What day is the sabbath? Do we go to church on Saturday or Sunday? Does God speak in tongues the same truth to female preacher as a male preacher's heart of no genealogy? Do we need to be baptized or get circumcised? Do you get sprinkle with water or be dunked under water in a pool or pond? Are any of these things required to be reconciled holy with God sign of Son of man (Ezra 2:62)? The Lord's spirit will be poured out on all flesh can be used by God not just anybody will be selected called by name alone "Church Boy."

A Sacrifice of Praise and Prayer for Help
Psalm 40:4-8

"Those who put their trust in the Lord, who pay no attention to the proud or to those who follow lies, are truly happy! 5 You, Lord my God! You've done so many things your wonderful deeds and your plans for us no one can compare with you! If I were to proclaim and talk about all of them, they would be too numerous to count! 6 You don't relish sacrifices or offerings; you don't require entirely burned offerings or compensation offerings— but you have given me ears! 7 So I said, "Here I come! I'm inscribed in the written scroll. 8 I want to do your will, my God. Your Instruction is deep within me."

What is a new Christian "Church Boy" to believe with doubt in the heart? It is scary to find out that something you believed all your life was alternative facts wrong sacrifice (Ezra 2:63). That you made a mistake and changed your way of seeing things from a different personal relationship point of view. From being negative anti against something bad to being positive for something good. Then, be not afraid to cry out publicly say, "I had a change of heart peace, peace." That might put your life in danger. It takes courage to say we were wrong in everything we did all our life, even a teardrop tattoo on our face, and repent say sorry love thy neighbor (Ezra 3:3).

If you stop doing this wrong, how do you know doing this will be right? In Jesus Christ's name, sin is sin thinking about is the same as doing sin. Do we celebrate Christmas, holidays or birthdays? Who do we turn to forgiveness of yourself hearing the truth of the Old Testament and the New Testament? Do we keep the Ten Commandments or are we free to do what we want to do? When the builders laid the foundation of the temple of the Lord (Ezra 3:10). Our whole world turned upside down, south up and north down. God speaks to everyone circumcised heart equally; it is supernatural understanding praising the foundation of the house of the Lord was laid (Ezra 3:11).

God Sustains His Servant
Psalm 40:9-11

"I've told the good news of your righteousness in the great assembly. I didn't hold anything back as you well know, Lord! 10 I didn't keep your righteousness only to myself. I declared your faithfulness and your salvation. I didn't hide your loyal love and trustworthiness from the great assembly. 11 So now you, Lord don't hold back any of your compassion from me. Let your loyal love and faithfulness always protect me."

Now a new king came to power who didn't know the house of Joseph's God's accomplishments. House of Joseph's prayer line of faith was powerful Passover to him from his great grandfather's faith, being a seed of Abraham. His father Jacob double blessed Joseph's descendants with firstborn blessings that they would not be touched by the death of the firstborn house of God reign (Ezra 4:24). Jesus Christ's restoration of Zi-On is the firstborn double blessing House of Joseph Jr. Royal Enoch. Passover to the gentiles for the gathering beautiful hearted colorful people abiding remembering God build and finish the temple (Ezra 6:14). They never bowed down to nasty ancient temple worshiping sacrificed animals' religions. They worship one God having personal relationship. This story keeps repeating itself like a pandemic "Jubilee" day of the Lord it is finished (Ezra 6:15).

I assure you as Moses was a prophet, his name alone, Joseph will be greater than Moses. "Church Boy" Born again veteran Eternal Ruler Joseph President of 1st United Methodist Men Compton, Church Sexton, baptized child of God, fighting a good fight against pandemic epidemic of evil unseen virus of social violence. Invader Army of the death from the Northern hell attacking the South kingdom of heaven children of God, on a prayer line of faith Passover from generation after generation Jesus Christ's second coming. Joseph never alone using two blood moons temple, like Moses used a burning bush, Elijah fire from the sky turn a divide nation to joyful and strengthened their hands in the work of the house of God (Ezra 6:22).

House of Joseph Rises to Power
Genesis 41:37-45

"This proposal pleased Jesus and all his servants. 38 And Jesus said to his servants, "Can we find a man like this, in whom is the Spirit of God?" 39 Then Jesus said to Joseph, "Since God has shown you all this, there is none so discerning and wise as you are. 40 You shall be over my house, and all my people shall order themselves as you command. Only as regards the throne will I Jesus be greater than you." 41 And Jesus said to Joseph, "See, I have set you over all the land of Zi-On." 42 Then Jesus took his signet ring from his hand and put it on Joseph's hand, and clothed him in garments of fine linen and put a gold chain about his neck. 43 And he

made him ride in his second chariot. And they called out before him, "Bow the knee!" Thus he set him over all the land of Zi-On. 44 Moreover, Jesus said to Joseph, "I am Jesus, and without your consent no one shall lift up hand or foot in all the land of Zi-On." 45 And Jesus called Joseph's name Zaphenath-paneah (the follower of the living/ life giving one God). And he gave him in marriage Asenath, the daughter of Potiphera priest of On. So Joseph went out over the land of Zi-On."

A real-life Game of Thrones, the president of the United Stated called a hoax. Like what happened when Moses spoke science about the spread of viruses from sacrificing animals to the Pharaoh knew artificial fact and idols other gods didn't know the God of Joseph time is not come (Haggai 1:2). Artificial people only concerned about own family inheritance profit and loses no other people live of waste (Haggai 1:4)? A house divided cannot stand against itself. This is not a game; consider your ways (Haggai 1:5)!

This an act of love God, fighting a good fight against evil anti-Christ sacrifice seeking out your own way of life. Giant corporations' artificial people to turn the world back upright to God and away from the rule over evil alternative fact bag with holes (Haggai 1:6). Temptations of the devil corporation artificial people. Need real people children of God to work for them to survive. Be never alone sacrificing glorified by God covenant ways (Haggai 1:8). A real live battle against the invasion of an unseen army of the dead evil virus, commanded to happen in the latter day, shutting down of the divided world being turn upright by the right hand of God with one snapshot spiritual blessing morning dew of praying for rain (Haggai 1:10).

Commanded to keeping the Passover of truth prayer line of faith handed over in a relay race keeping holy time spiritual drought of love upon the land and upon the mountains (Haggai 1:11). Passover generation after generation, this work is no bull's blood sacrifice or material possessions. People think this work obey is a joke. There are many false prophets, one seer greater than a prophet voice of the Lord (Haggai 1:12). You can and will lose your life if you don't see it right or make it about yourself pride and ego.

Joel 2:31

"The sun will be turned to darkness, and the moon to blood before the great and dreadful day of the Lord comes."

Feast of the Tabernacle September 27, 2015

The word of God is very precise alignment and detailed; it is hard work being able to hear the voice of truth. See God's face, look into the eye of the Lord and not cry out be Holy. Have visions and dreams, following every word and seeing it right all the way through the end. First you must be called. For many prophets are called, but one is chosen seer by name from the womb of their mother to work in the house of the Lord of hosts of their God (Haggai 1:14). You can abort any time you want; too many false prophets have lost their lives peaching self-prosperity, not seeing the will of God goodness keeping temple worshiping comparison of it as nothing (Haggai 2:2-3). To be prosperous is to see the will of God working over everyone's life being good be strong. Don't take the word of God for granted be strong. It can come back to haunt you from the graveyard. Too many men take the word of God to be a weak joke, afraid to read the Book of Revelation do the work of the Lord. For I am with you saith the Lord of hosts (Haggai 2:4).

PlayStation time is over artificial people, real people sitting around playing games competing hating to lose desire of a nation to make America great again anti-Christ not with God's glory (Haggai 2:6-7). Playing old school music on a radio, watching Westerns reruns and Racecars going around in circle on racetracks on their weekend off on the Golf course. Have you ever seen so many grown men playing games and writing drawing tattoos on their face? While calling themselves Christian, but not keeping the commandments of Atonement or Passover of faith word of God rightly to the next generation latter house shall be greater than of the former saith the lord of hosts (Haggai 2:9). They do nothing don't event go to church, are worried about the government taking their firearms gun rights away because they want to pass down weapons of mass destruction to their grandchildren. Then, their children's salvation.

Acts 2:22

"The sun will be changed into darkness, and the moon will be changed into blood, before the great and spectacular day of the Lord comes."

August 21, 2017
Total Solar Eclipse

What is a seer? Choice seer is called a prophet concerning the Law. Anybody can be used by God, but God doesn't just use anybody; be holy (Haggai 2:11). Only one prophet is chosen a seer of God's eye of perfection and is supernaturally enlightened to see things which God only can reveal of the heart. It is a name sometimes applied to the prophets because of the visions granted to them as a person who foresees events Holy Time (Haggai 2:12-13). The insight or vision they possess is traced to God's Spirit. Individuals who bear the title "seer" are mentioned in connection with the kings and as historiographers.

The essence of God vision hearing, and face is seen by the created intellect power of sight and union of the thing seen with the sight. For vision is made consider from this day upward (Haggai 2:15). Do those who see the essence eye of God comprehend Him? "That is comprehended which is so seen as a whole, that nothing of it is hidden from the seer from this day and upward (Haggai 2:18). But if God is seen in His essence, He is seen whole and as a certificate of proof Acts II God moving coming unified by the Holy Spirit administration of godliness being fruitful and multiple (Haggai 2:19).

If you do the math, it all adds up right; it cannot be shacking monument The New Millennial, New Testament destroy kingdom of darkness (Haggai 2:21-22). Who would have ever thought the Old and New Testament would end in my backyard? In the graveyard, we play amongst the dead as children for fun, in the world-famous Angeles Abbey Memorial Park, starting the New Millennial, New Testament second Acts II book of the Holy Bible saith the Lord I have chosen thee as a signet (Haggai 2:23). When you see the sun shall be turned into darkness and the moon into blood, before the coming of the great and awesome day of the Lord (Acts 2:20). This was spoken by prophet Joseph, Joel and Peter, pouring out of my spirit set by appointed holy time by natural law like a clock on the wall. The Yin and Yang concept of dualism heaven natural world interrelated. Gives rise to one another sun, moon and man as one proclaims turn to the Lord will turn to you (Zechariah 1:3). It is a plumb line for keeping the information age straight that the Phoenicians had followed from time travel and settling the globe time clock, putting an end to all conspiracy with hope.

This is the same timeline of vision of hope the wisemen used to travel to find baby Jesus (Zechariah 1: 8). This is not a game of chance; it is more like finding a needle in a haystack. All conspiracy dies and are laid to rest in my backyard, standing on the promising Word oath of truth God rising from the dead fulfilled, killing and burying all conspiracy theory house of mercy and compassion (Zechariah 1:16). Sanctuary alignment from Mount Hermon transfiguration of Jesus together who took oath of faithful bound by a curse. The 33^0 Parallel line of death ends in my backyard at a cemetery memorial honoring life and death, killing all conspiracy theory like a virus, from Roswell New Mexico aliens, Dallas Texas President Kennedy assassination, Atlanta Georgia Death Row, Baghdad Iraq Babylon and Jerusalem (Zechariah 1:18-20).

It puts them to waste by burying them in the cemetery, putting an end to all make believe entertainment becoming reality, science fiction, witchcraft, scary fairy tales, astrology, superstitions, end of times destruction of world philosophy theory. Peaceful return of Prophet Elijah and Jesus Christ together with blood and fire temple monument praising the Lord rising from the dead city of Zi-On thee cross. This is not about using technology measuring line of little by little seed of faith praying (Zechariah 2:1). The Word of God is poured out flooding on all flesh equally. The story of the Word seed of life and prosperity. There are treasures worth more than gold nuggets hidden in the Bible called seeds talents. I Am because we are sower of seeds in places without walls (Zechariah 2:4).

In the beginning was the Word, and the Word was with God and the Word was God (John 1:1). One word from God out of the Bible is very valuable. The Word was with God in the beginning (John 1:2). It is like finding a hidden treasure talent that you didn't know you had. Everything came into being through the Word, and without the Word, nothing came into being (John 1:3). A blessing from one word, from out of the Bible is more valuable than any material on Earth. What came into being through the Word was life, and the life was the light for all people (John 1:4).

Miracle cure for healing comfort, peace food for the soul mercy and compassion. The light shines in the darkness, and the darkness doesn't extinguish the light (John 1:5). Firstborn double blessing to the believer. Responsibility to do the right thing, acting peacefully under the law.

Benefits of the clergy right of the old world newly create Christian perfection. Renew your heart and mind though life being weak and brokenhearted trusting God glory a wall of fire protect (Zechariah 2:5). Give strength to sing out and rejoice stand at attention just breathing and blinking, fighting a good fight for liberty and justice Holy time zone Zi-On. The opportunity dwell in the midst of God start life over by being born again child of God and take away everything you ever did wrong (Zechariah 2:10). It is an opportunity to look upward to the future with hope and at the past to see what a horrible mess you have been. It will make you branch out of your family's house of religion way of seeing things and start your own relationship with God called alone by faith my servant (Zechariah 3:8).

It is a chance to be a living sacrificing, living your life helping other people or even finding a treasure in your backyard. You must be willing to walk by faith not by sight. Going into dark places, you cannot see where you are going or know where you are going until you get there remove the iniquity of that land in one day (Zechariah 3:9). It can even inspire you waked that is wakened out of sleep to write volumes of books, giving powerful insight to look at something old plainly you've seen all your life and epiphany (Zechariah 4:1). See something new beautiful with the word from God wisdom, making it appear different, giving it a different valuable purpose treasure.

Can you imagine hearing one word from God then you find yourself pregnant with a child? We all hear the same good or bad news gospel behold vision and dreams (Zechariah 4:2). When I heard one word from heaven sounding like a trumpet blast heart pregnant with a flood of joy to proclaim "Jubilee" universal pardon freed me to conceive the conception give birth to The Greatest Story Never Told Joseph Jr. conception of Jesus

Christ "Church Boy" eternal light two mess (Zechariah 4:3). Everybody know Jesus Christ was not born on December 25 season of darkness.

It is the time of his conception during the festival of light Hanukkah of rededication temple lamp. The conception is the most importance moment to see new blood type the hand of God operating in our life not be might nor by power but by spirit (Zechariah 4:6). The talent of conceiving a new creation from your weak broken heart is an vary valuable gift talent from God (Luke 1:31). Seeing the Lord working out balance every detail of your salvation becoming light as a feather. With the freewill to give up, abort at any time. No one can judge you (Luke 1:35). They won't even believe it happened.

Acts II restoration of Zi-On state of mind of always being with God's pure love. Continually praying line of faith; everything asks for comes to pass finish it (Zechariah 4:9). When a false prophet artificial person tries to fulfill Bible prophecy, he can call up a pandemic upon the earth. This is what happens when you try to fulfill Bible prophecy that you make about your own self wealth has nothing to do with the pure love of God and more to do with your hardened heart making money. It can be a blessing or a curse all the face of the earth (Zechariah 5: 3). Does the work return people to praising God or turn people away from praising God vision?

Ubuntu reconciliation is two-operation system program, one program reboot computers to network interconnects worldwide web together and a program of philosophy of humanism interconnecting people ephah equal measure of faith (Zechariah 5:10). Ubuntu ministry interconnecting a person is a person through other people by the intranet operation system. I am because we are, because one man, Adam, sinned, we are sinners, because one man, Jesus, sacrificed, we are saved (Zechariah 5: 11). A flood of misinformation attacking the human body like a virus shuts down a computer doing harm. Ubuntu ministry humaneness is virus protection for child of God to reboot of truthfulness.

I never claim to be a Bible scholar. I am a Jonny come lately to the discussion about believing every word in the Holy Bible mountains of brass (Zechariah 6:1). Most of my life, I rejected God's word of truth written in the Bible. I lived a double minded and unstable life most of my life, thinking wrong was right and what was right was wrong. With a backward way of thinking, I was being a good man by being a bad boy (Zechariah 6:12). When I reflect on where I've been, I find myself shaking my head and thanking the Lord for saving a wretch like me from myself and having mercy on my soul.

Why would God use a sinner like me speak unto all the people of the land (Zechariah 7: 5)? Voice from heaven said, "You are not gay." To prove how wrong and unholy I had been, Holy Spirit guided my handwriting, cannot even take credit for writing one word or taking pictures used in this story "Church Boy." God is right perfectly one true judgement mercy and compassion (Zechariah 7:9-10). Then, the world will know that you sent me and that you have loved them just as you loved me Joseph uniquely faithful heart.

After my divorce, being alone weak and brokenhearted, the Lord said, "I am going to use you like I used Moses" former prophets (Zechariah 7:12). Stuttering, I said, "I don't know how to write, Lord; touch my mouth. I heard a voice from heaven say, "Good job. I will be your right hand; the comforter will help; you've been given favor." The Holy Spirit sounding like Michael Jackson singing let me show the way to go fellow me. First, you must trust me in the small things, every detail of your life, every teardrop, great jealousy for Zi-On (Zechariah 8:2). Written on your heartbeat by the right hand of God be born again and baptized. Be willing to be led by the Lord anywhere by returning home where you first started city of truth holy mountain temple of the Lord (Zechariah 8:3).

The Good Life State to the State of Eureka, I found it Holy Spirit descended in a bodily form like a dove! If you were told after being baptized at fifty years of ages in worst of time recession give up your career, resign of the Pope. In Abraham Lincoln, Nebraska you need to go back home to Compton, California save my people, and I will be their God in truth and in righteousness (Zechariah 8:8). "Proclaim Jubilee"! At appointed time, be in a cemetery sunset and sunrise during four full blood black moons, one total eclipse sun turns into darkness new moon. Then, write a value of book about it. Would you go be strong (Zechariah 8:9)? How would you start telling this story of seeing the world returning to God remember his people?

I am not learned; I don't have a college degree. Never had a class on public speaking communication or have an outline for writing this story be a blessing (Zechariah 8:13). Always look for the good in all things like a good debate; man sharpens man like iron sharpens iron. The word of God is not a debate competition; speak truth to your neighbor; execute the judgment of truth and peace; everybody wins (Zechariah 8:16). It a testament for what God has done, doing, and will do like teaching how to continually pray all day communion not imagine evil in your heart against your neighbor (Zechariah 8:17). I don't make false oaths, watch sports, play lottery games or have any tattoos written on my body. I always had a strange way of seeing the world and myself using simple common sense; God is with you (Zechariah 8:23).

I was blinded by my traditional way of seeing woman as not being equal with man in the world upside down. Now, I can see I was blinded by my alternative facts dark foolish way of thinking I was right all the time burden of the word of the Lord (Zechariah 9:1). Did not know how wrong I truly was by not continually praying or praising God. I thought because I was a good mechanic and could fix anything that had wheels on it that it made me a strong good man and that I did not need help having salvation (Zechariah 9:9). I never thought vision God would us me to proclaim "Jubilee." When I proclaimed "Jubilee" seven years ago in my published book *I Am Because We Are: Jubilee*. I did know it would happen like this exactly seven years today and one year after my father Joseph Jr. Passover

Christmas morning 2018 blood covenant double blessing (Zechariah 9:11-12).

When "Church Boy" decided to read the book of Revelation of Jesus Christ cornerstone and follow the word of God to be corrected and lifted-up. He didn't know that he would be used like this ensign while being weak and brokenhearted crying out alone upon the land (Zechariah 9:16). "Church Boy" started on the bottom, cleaning toilets at the Church First United Compton older than the city est. 1867. "Church Boy" was led from Abraham Lincoln, Nebraska to Compton, California. When he heard the voice of God tell him be not angry to return to Compton; it made him laugh at the sacrifice, not punishment (Zechariah 10:3). Those are the two places he equally loves and calls home. "Church Boy" returned to the best places of safe keeping at his mother's house of Joseph Jr. the same places he was raised up in mercy and compassion upon them (Zechariah 10:6).

He was in the perfect spot to snap a beautiful picture of the sun, moon and man praising God's grace and glory of redemption. Little by little, "Church Boy" started to see a prophetic season, a moment in time and history when God enacts events that bring to pass what Jesus wept speaking softly gentle healing the brokenhearted, making the weak strong (Zechariah 10:8). There are no accidents or coincidence here; everything happens for a reason at an appointed time to the glory of God's grace of forgiveness. A worldwide pandemic epidemic shutting down the world's greatest economy (Zechariah 10:9).

A Story About Unforgiveness
Matthew 18:32-35

"The king summoned the man and said, 'You evil servant! I forgave your entire debt when you begged me for mercy. Shouldn't you be compelled to be merciful to your fellow servant who asked for mercy?' The king was furious and put the screws to the man until he paid back his entire debt.

And that's exactly what my Father in heaven is going to do to each one of you who doesn't forgive unconditionally anyone who asks for mercy."

Practice what you preach. Everybody knows me as a seer of "Jubilee;" I fed the flock forgiveness (Zechariah 11:7)! When I said we should celebrate "Jubilee," beauty of God, everybody heard me proclaim Law "Jubilee" commandment I talked to already heard about it said it in the Bible like filing bankruptcy. We cannot afford it; it costs too much to release people from their old student loan debt or get out of prison free, remove a knee from a man's neck; it will never happen breaking my covenant (Zechariah 11:10). All the people like to receive the mercy and compassion of "Jubilee;" they don't want to give mercy and compassion of "Jubilee" like the unforgiving servant (Matthew 18:21-35). The land returned back to God, the original landlord; we are only caretakers of the property: law of inheritance.

If somebody does not keep the law of inheritance "Jubilee" given mercy (Zechariah 11:12), he will lose your property until a new generation that will keep the law of Passover and Atonement and correctly celebrate "Jubilee." Not because you are required to but because it is the right thing to do. Keep a prayer line of little by little faith house of the Lord (Zechariah 11:13). The Jews still celebrate "Jubilee," keeping the law of Moses. Sabbatical year off celebrate Lord's day family foundation with God keeping holy time bible study three-year process (Zechariah 11:16). Church never processed "Jubilee" commandment at one time; now we have the money to pay people to stay at home during a pandemic. Artificial people want to send real people back to work overtime pass down profit and loses (Zechariah 11:17). By not doing the "Jubilee," it will cause a global pandemic, the greatest economy ever shut down judgment of a nation. They believe the conspiracy of artificial man before the burdens of the Word of God (Zechariah 12:1). "Jubilee" is required and is commanded to happen every fifty years; it is a check against inflation and needed to balance humanity resetting Holy time thought all the people of the earth be gathered (Zechariah 12:3).

There is no way you could have prepared for this type of worldwide plague event bitterness. This is why we must stay continually prayed up spirit of grace. Continue praying with repentance, passion, immerged, and communion, giving thanks for his firstborn (Zechariah 12:10). Christian perfection Acts II the perfect right hand of God by the precise word spoken to Joseph in the Bible the go between the father and sons. Son of Joseph Jr. the faithful son he who righteous is in favor of the Lord's protection cut off the names of the idols out of the land (Zechariah 13:2). House of Joseph Jr. stands alone to do the right things, managing the affairs of others, set as leader over the land, president of the United Methodist men of south up and north down America. There is a real-life sword fight of knowledge against superstition traditions, a hoax saying I am not a prophet (Zechariah 13:5-6). A lie can kill you quicker than a virus or disease. Speak the Word of God wrong can cost you your life.

New millennial, new church of reconciliation ubuntu ministry interconnecting people through the word of God's humanism passing over the world wide web. Acts II perfect love, peace, and happiness. The pouring out of the Holy Spirit on all flesh network of people praying together touching and agreeing say, the Lord is my God (Zechariah 13:9). Beginning of Holy Time reconciled to interpersonal relationship with Word of God being not afraid. Grown in truth and understanding repenting turning to God gathering all nations the city will be taken (Zechariah 14:2).

Protection from a pandemic of misinformation. Living through a pandemic worse than 9/11 and Pearl Harbor all in one week before Good Friday and Easter resurrection revival with God, shutting down of the whole wide world economy one country one state and one city at a time great deliverance (Zechariah 14:4). "Jubilee" the stopping shutting down of church and state together at one time starting over eternal life (Zechariah 14:7-8). Exactly one year after my father's victory over death seven years after getting baptized and proclaiming "Jubilee," it happens holiness present of the Lord and all the holy ones with him (Zechariah 14:5).

Generational authority aligns with the oath truth of faith. As the first generation to deal with Ubuntu technology worldwide web with the word of God in the Bible of his reign (Esther 1:3). Misinformation can kill you slow or quickly like a virus shutdown a computer. When you keep repeat bad information. Spreading bad information is like spreading a virus becoming a plague that people don't know what to believe if it is real (Esther 2:10). The word of God is truth immune system vaccine protection against lies and disease. Misinformation will have praying in the wrong direction reciting the same old prayers as spreading a virus. Making yourself sick by repeating to yourself saying how lovesick you are chosen above all the women (Esther 2:17). Healing comes from praying the Psalm of your heart out to God like He is your best friend in the morning dew being weak and brokenhearted weeping. Repenting with passion becoming immerse deeply crying being thankful sharing comforting word with the Lord seat above all (Esther 3:1-2).

Jesus Christ as a best friend that never did you wrong forgiving you for all your mistakes. If I did not know Jesus Christ, I would be scared and afraid on the Internet spreading alternative facts to. I feel safe because I can see God work through the beautiful heart of people praying in one day (Esther 3:13). Let me know Holy spirit is doing the right thing keep me on the right path fasting and weeping. This is why I call myself "Church Boy," praying change the world not Internet video. Getting on the Internet running my mouth just makes people madder and more afraid and go get a gun to be ready to fight at any time mourning (Esther 4:3). My story peace Acts II perfect love be not afraid fighting a good fight with peaceful fire from the sky cleansing sunlight turning the moonlight the color of blood. Sign for deliverance everything going to be alright keeping Holy Time of protection come to the kingdom for such a time as this (Esther 4:13-14).

The Day of The Lord
Look, I am sending Elijah the prophet to you, before the great and terrifying day of the Lord arrives.

Feast of the Tabernacle September 27, 2015

Compton the New City of Zi-On of high priest may be the name given to Zi-On home of descendants of Black Joe Jr., the prophecy being that the time will come when that city which was known as the "city of the sun-god" On shall become the "city of destruction" of the sun-god, when idolatry shall cease, and the worship of the true God be established Son of man (Genesis 41:45). Compton is this Church City State today putting an end to time history of idolatry. In ancient times, this city was full of obelisks dedicated to the sun to keep track of time. It still stands today two famous obelisks long called "Cleopatras Needles," one of which now stands in London and the other in Central Park in New York city, once stood before this city and were seen by the children of Israel before the Exodus.

Moses had a vision off a burning bush nobody else saw whom gave instruction and rule for all Joseph at Horeb (Malachi 4:4). Joseph vision of the reflection of the sunset, sunrise off the black moonlight united with the shadow of Earth turning the color of blood, captured in a snapshot of a sacred temple monument arch set in heaven by appointed holy time praising God be not afraid (Esther 7:6). The whole wide world saw. The same voice Moses heard instructing him to write Exodus is the voice that spoke to write this story Exodus II. Black Native American Culture claiming their indigenous culture back praying to one God burden of the word (Malachi 1:1). Jesus Christ who died on the cross for their salvation. Just like Moses used a burning bush to lead Israel, Joseph used burning moon reflecting on a Temple tomb wall to lead Native culture of people to the cross uniting all. Church awaking to God's gentle quiet loving voice of responsibility not of hate (Malachi 1:2-3). The greatest movement of people awaking being baptized at one time by the handwritten word of God image of my family smiling face on this book cover Acts II perfect love freely accept God (Malachi 1:10).

Compton always had special place in the movement of religious study across United States abolition of slavery with the Methodist of Jesus Christ 1st Church of Compton Est 1867 older than the City Est 1888. From the city creation to the land grant from the Queen and King of Spain protectorate to the Moor's New Christian. Taylor of cloths creator of fashion styles architect's designer of building and society. Black Native American people of Color God promised the land to under the rainbow covenant table of the lord (Malachi 1:12). Beginning of time there is no place on earth where you can see the sun, moon, earth and man perfectly line up to a sanctuary sacred temple arch covenant promised fulfilled.

Compton always been a very special unique place of blessing to live in History giving glory to God (Malachi 2:1-2). "Church Boy" Anthony Anderson is my little homey grew up on my block, Holy Ave. Hood. Lot of great people have lived in come out of Compton keeping the faith real. Republican president family, civil rights activist, politicians, judges, union organizers, entertainers, athlete and even rap artists. There is nothing greater than standing aligned upright with God's creation demonstrated nature and men together on the front and back of this book's cover. Demonstration of the prophetic word of God down to every detail even one name alone Joseph Jr. persecuted seed of Abraham little by little measure of faith judgment of God (Malachi 2:17). One seed- how remarkable is that?

Angeles Abby Memorial

The Sun Temple monument to wisdom of God, suffering in the hub city of Compton, modern day obelisks can be seen from my backyard. It has the same purpose to keep holy time, praising heavens architect of the scriptures Lord of hosts that cannot be moved (Malachi 3:1). Sun of man sunrising and sunsetting on the cross is a daily demonstration of God's handy work of pure love passing over our lives. Ending 1st Acts worst of bad times and beginning of 2nd Acts best of good times between two blood moons, one total eclipse seen by all day of his coming (Malachi 3:2). 2nd

Acts II is turning the world back to God. Obelisks shadow played a vital role in religion and was used to keep track of time and seasons. The shapes of the ancient Egyptian pyramid and obelisk were derived from natural phenomena associated with the sun (the sun-god Ra being the Egyptians' greatest deity) offering in righteousness (Malachi 3:3).

The pyramid and obelisk's significance have been previously overlooked, especially the astronomical phenomena connected with solstice sunrise and sunset equinox: the zodiacal light and sun pillars respectively. This was a noted university town, and here Moses gained his acquaintance with "all the wisdom of the Egyptians. Ancient Sun Temple system of wisdom of keeping holy time is united with modern new church prayer line of faith and truth.

D&C 128:24

"That they may offer unto the lord an offering in righteousness. Let us, therefore, as a church and people and as Latter-day Saints offer unto the Lord an offering in righteousness; and let us present in his holy temple, when it is finished, a book containing the records our dead which shall be worthy of all acceptation."

The Lost Urban Tribes of Juda and Joseph two stick as one, brother's generational authority to study the Word of God being not afraid and without jealousy. Teaching of the Bible together with history new creation from something old. The hub city of Compton is the new modern-day city of On zone where there no Police Department. Model city neighbor loving neighbor living in harmony sunrising and sunsetting can be seen and the keeping new moon to new moon on the cross, praising God in tithes and offerings (Malachi 3:7-8). In the city of Compton, there will be the destruction of anti-Christ idols and sun-god worshiping artificial people of police. Joseph shadow of Jesus Christ great deliverance firstborn blessing saving acts II his family foundation house of Joseph Jr return unto me and I will return unto you (Malachi 3:7).

They never submitted to anti-Christ blood sacrifices and temple worshiping giant people. They were Firefighter like Elijah great seers and high priests of the Lord, studying the Word of God correctly people made giant statue of their image to honor their work. Egyptians had courage to stand keeping holy time creator of obelisk architect of pyramids setting time with movement of heaven wisemen my jewels (Malachi 3:17). They became exiled for refusing to bow down do temple sacrificing of animals persecuted like Daniel placed in an oven fire and lion's den. Temple worshiping was a hustle to keep the artificial people ruling class over the people of God, Greeks used religion making them believe many gods alternative facts was mad at them doing wickedly (Malachi 4:1). It was anti-Christ mean nasty way of worshiping God. Want to circumcise your cleanse heart renew your double mind bipolar from negative to positive balance way of thinking being humble neither root nor branch. Artificial people playing church paying tithes on the weekend to practicing sin hustling during the week in giant corporations counting profits and losses. Using real people to make themselves-bigger than life. But unto you that fear my name shall the sun of righteousness arise with healing in his wings (Malachi 4:2).

Son of man gave freedom of religion in the separation of Church and State, the ability to study the Word of God without fear of persecution for greater understanding doing the right thing remember the law of Moses (Malachi 4:4). There are few places in the world where you can have access to the writing of different great religions and courage not be prosecuted by your own family religion: to read the Torah written by Moses, Quran written by Prophet Muhammad, Bible 1st Acts of the Apostles, Message to Blackman in America written by Elijah Muhammad and Book of Mormon with a curse (Malachi 4:5-6). Doctrine and Covenants revelation given through Joseph Smith by the hand of Elijah the prophet at Jesus coming (JS-History 1:38-39). Restored verse of Genesis.

> JST, Genesis 50:24–38. Compare Genesis 50:24–26; 2 Nephi 3:4–22.
> "Joseph in Egypt prophesies of Moses freeing Israel from bondage; of a branch of Joseph's descendants being led to a faraway land, where they will be remembered in the covenants of the Lord; of God calling a latter-day prophet named Joseph to join the records of Judah and of Joseph; and of Aaron serving as a spokesman for Moses."

Ruler Joseph uniquely faithful prime minister of Old Testament spoke of Eric Joseph, president and modern-day chief administrator feeding of the word of God of Abraham's faith and Lincoln's righteousness (1 Kings 18:36). Black Native America Wokini seeks a new beginning seeing a new vision, writing a book to come together with the old book from a word that has already been sent forward. "Jubilee" universal pardon is the law promise of God moving over our lives turned their hearts back (1 King 18:37). It is two sticks becoming one to give a better understand of God's ministry of the Holy Spirit to Latter Day Saints keys of eternal connection. If you can believe the Book of Mormon Joseph Smith Jr. story, you should not have a problem believing this story of Alone Joseph Moor man Jr.

Not until I was alone, brokenhearted and weak could I see I needed help seek the law of the Lord statutes and judgments (Ezra 7:10). I believed I could fix everything on my own. Having the gift/talent to see how things work, to take them apart and put them back together restore something old and make it like new usable again wisdom of God's perfect love. I realized I needed help I was beyond the river (Ezra 7:25). I could not self-help myself out of my prideful mess. That when I started hearing God's voice of truth, saying I was not heading in the right direction God was upon me (Ezra 7:28). All I had to do was turn around to see the face of God's grace smiling back at me, telling me the only thing that could save me was

I needed to be born again and die to myself. I was to be born of the Holy Spirit, becoming a new creation, with the renewing of the heart and mind intreated of us (Ezra 8:21-23). I had to change the way I think. A double-minded man is unstable in all things. Don't let your heart be troubled.

This was not about a gut feeling and what you think according to your abomination (Ezra 9:1). The Holy Spirit speaks words of truth and comfort to the ear of the heart peacefully. The truth never changes. The mind changes daily, but the heart stays the same in this trespass (Ezra 9:2). The Holy Spirit Jesus Christ is our "Jubilee" today and is forever the same. We are not required to blow a shofar horn anymore for our iniquities. If you speak the word of love softly "Jubilee" during a crisis in Jesus Christ name, change instantly starts happening unto the heavens (Ezra 9:6). It gives power to move angels on your behalf to remove whatever debt or bad marriage you have gotten into. Becoming a good outcome Acts II perfect love.

You can lose your life for talking like this when I heard this news I sat down and wept and mourned praying. Not just anyone can write the Word of God of heaven (Nehemiah 1:4). You must be a chosen seer of the essence of God's continual presence great and awesome God. Those who love you and keep your commandments (Nehemiah 1:5) Acts II perfect love is very precise vision and written on the brokenhearted, down to being named from the womb of a virgin mother to every single step being ordered by the handwritten Word of Holy Spirit mercy. Joseph is the one you must listen to (Deuteronomy 18: 15). As sure as Moses was, Joseph's name will be greater than Moses. If you knew your name was going to be greater than Moses and you had to live fifty years to prove it, how would you deal with that? You can choose not to do it and none could say anything; it's only between you and God to see the distress that we are in (Nehemiah 2:17).

To do it, you have to submit to the will of God and be led in every detail of your life. Many brethren would say, "I am not doing it." All I could do was start praying, thanking the Lord for saving a wretch like me; the hand of God which was good upon me (Nehemiah 2:18). My born-again name was already greater than Moses; He will prosper us. All I needed to do is arise and have little faith by staying alive his servant. As it was in the beginning of time House of Joseph, it will be heirs in the end of time House of Joseph Jr. beautiful heart of people memorial looking up to God (Nehemiah 2:20). As it was said to Abraham, *"And in your seed all the families of the earth shall be blessed"* (Acts 3:25). The same firstborn blessing on Joseph is also passed over to my family: House of Joseph Jr.

I always knew in the worst of bad times that I could go to my backyard and find a treasure. Double blessing our prayer unto our God day and night (Nehemiah 4:9). Did not know it would happen during the four blood moons and total solar eclipse Passover sunrise, atonement sunset reflecting on cemetery wall raising the dead; be not afraid. A vision of seeing the star of David on ancient temple system wisdom of God arch of heaven praising who is great. What is the chance of seeing having a temple monument in your house's backyard (Nehemiah 4:14)?

United on the cross of modern-day church system of praying women and men touching and agreeing in loving relationship with Son of man new covenant, pouring out of the Holy Spirit on all flesh equally unveiling of the Lord. They who built wall bare burdens with one hand wrought in work and with the other hand held a weapon (Nehemiah 4:17). This story is not about replacing one word of the Bible. It is a confirmation to the work of the Holy Spirt every word of God being fulfilled, from beginning. First word in Genesis to end of the book of Revelation last word: Amen. We all are called to be a witness only one is called a choice seer my God for good (Nehemiah 5:19).

As seer look back thought monument eternal time ground zero of temple arch of heaven. United with blood moon remembrance of sacrifice of all life that got us here in Jesus Christ's name. I can peacefully reflect seeing the eye of God's grace looking back giving peaceful comfort and strengthening my hands; everything's going to be alright (Nehemiah 6:9). To see how violent, we are as a culture of people have been. Being eye to eye able to write a story like an artist is able paint a picture one stroke, one word at a time. Every paragraph is an epiphany; when you know who you love, you can preach a church sermon sing out on the mountain together the Negus (Nehemiah 7:5).

Today, we also have access to the new discovery of writing the gospel of Nicodemus Acts of Pontius Pilate sacred texts, testimony of Joseph of Arimathea testified to the elders as a spiritual indictment against the church law of God, and Native American writers seeing a new beginning or seeking a new vision Wokini: Billy Mills a Lakota Journey to Happiness and Self-understanding written with Nicholas Sparks. John Sedgwick author Blood Moon an American Epic of War and Splendor in the Cherokee Nation. Divided in Blood Moon Trail of Tears disaster for the Cherokee Nation force migration. The spiritual journey of the American family from civil war until today understanding and reading (Nehemiah 8:8).

America has blessed us with this gift of discernment, freedom from heaven, an education counting mathematic, reading, and writing, and separation of Church and State, to be free from religion to have a personal one, two, one relationship with the wisdom of God as your savior, a sure covenant; we write it; we seal unto it (Nehemiah 9:38). The arch of suffering represents architect of the scriptures play out yearly sunrising and sunsetting daily on the cross in heaven. Calendar for keeping holy time knowledge of the true architect of men arch of heaven united by a snapshot law of God (Nehemiah 10:28). Do we keep holy time like we count the overtime on the timeclock?

The Gospels and Their Significance

"Jubilee" behold is a way of life commanded to happen after fifty years of life new covenant. If you are a Christian over fifty years and have not proclaimed "Jubilee" and celebrated God having mercy and compassion pass over your soul, take a sabbatical year off doing zero work trusting God, exercise of faith for seven years of work; I will be their God and they shall be my people (Jeremiah 31:31-33). This is how the Lord wants to bless you; it's a right to have all your debt removed, like filing bankruptcy or getting out of prison without going to court every seven seasons the promise of God of a better covenant. A record of the ancestors of Jesus Christ, son of Joseph Jr, son of Abraham (Matthew 1:1). When I prayed in Jesus Christ's name son of Joe Jr, this is what truly happened a firstborn birthright everlasting the finger of God touch me.

Art reflects reality; our history and documents the crucial component of our life's history. The wing goddess Isis painted on the walls of Egypt can only be a seen as a man created fantasy allegory teaching of truth though astrology Zeitgeist spirit of the age. It's the same story brought to life in the Bible by Son of Man the right hand of God, peacefully making it happen as facts in history sacrificing himself and stopping the sacrificing of bulls and animals. A personal relationship with God turned the old hoax religious world around. If you ever studied literature, you will see that writing reflects the period it was written in.

When writers compose their texts, they are influenced by whatever is impacting their current society. So, there were fourteen generations from Abraham to David, fourteen generations from David to the exile to Babylon, and fourteen generations from the exile to Babylon to the Christ (Matthew 1:17). Equality between firstborn seeing sons and daughters' spirit of the times women equal with men crying and praying together giving thanks.

The Foreordained Redeemer

Be careful what you pray for; the Word of God will become real in your life. Just when I thought it couldn't get any worst is yet to come world pandemic act of God. The quiet before the storm. Like Jonah found himself in a big fish hell of a mess or Kobe Bryant with his child flying into the side of a mountain on a cloudy Sunday morning to go play basketball. And now, O father, glorify thou me with thine own self with the glory which I had with thee before the world was. Not doing the will of God can cost you your life die a young legend. And the glory which thou gives me I have given them that they may be one, even as we are one: Glory. 2020 seeing the world turn to God to stop a worldwide pandemic in your life. When you are weak and alone, the Lord makes you strong. Speaking utterance to your heart's desires, ask for wishes to come true. It's a beautiful life can come back to haunt you.

Joseph Dream of Power
Genesis 37:4
"But when his brothers saw that their father loved him more than all his brothers, they hated him and could not speak peacefully to him."

Have you ever been asked are you a prophet? People that I did not know would come ask me was I am prophet. Like they were trying to get me to see something be redeemed. I did not already know about myself; be holy. Why me? I was raised in Compton with a sun temple in my backyard. An epiphany came to me, giving wisdom to see into the past, present, and future becoming new, creating son of Joseph Jr. My name from in the womb is greater than Moses leading a divided nation back to God glory and truth. And he said unto me knowest thou the condescension of God? And I said unto him: I know that he loveth his children nevertheless, I do not know the meaning of all things (1 Nephi 11:16-17). Turning the world upright praising God's glory. I wish the world would stay like this. No winner or losers, no sports, no entertainment, or church events. No competing standing at attention waiting to be judge by the firstborn birthright righthand finger of God pointing Jesus Christ. And now, verily I say unto you, I was in the beginning with the father, and am the Firstborn (Doctrine & Covenants 93:21).

Exodus II spiritual climate change Passover mass departure of people of color, especially emigrants sacrificed out the house of bondage of debt. Movement of the people without going anywhere turning to God omnipresence in history. Renewing of the heart and mind God with us. And behold, the glory of the lord was upon Moses stood in the presence of God, and talked with him face to face. And the Lord God said unto Moses: for mine own purpose have I made these things. Here is wisdom and it remaineth in me. And by the word of my power, have I created them, which is mine Only Begotten Son, who is full of grace and truth. And worlds without number have I created them for mine own purpose; and by the Son I created them, which is mine only begotten (Moses 1:31-33). Seeing the underworld right-side up, south up, north down, everybody wins. Turn the world map around. Peacefully turning the underworld right.

Eternal Joseph born again seed of Abraham faith, righteousness Lincoln, Nebraska, raised straight out of Compton, California, United States of America City of Champions and no police. Seer of the greatest story ever told everything only happening at the appointed time by God's atonement to Passover it a commandment Christian perfection police yourself. For behold, there are many worlds that have died by the word of my power. And there are many that now stand and innumerable are they unto man; but all things are numbered unto me, for they are mine and I know them (Moses 1:35). Keep holy time festival and feast celebration release from debt. Everybody you did evil wrong to God turn it in to something good.

The Birth of Jesus Christ

There some people given a great name before they are born in heaven, and there are people who make their own name great icon shall no man lift up his hand unto thee (Genesis 41:44). Joseph shadow of Jesus Christ is to be a witness for Jesus Christ advent return. As a sign of the Son of Man human spirit God qualifies the heart to write the New Millennial, New Testament, 2nd Acts II Peace, Love and Happiness over all the land today

(Genesis 41:45). Starting with black moon turning the color of blood, planets line up. Seen through an ancient temple wall of tomb arch modern obelisk three pillars of eternity creation, fall and atonement sitting in heaven.

United with star of David and the cross started with a dream setting appointed time whose name was Joseph house of Joseph and the virgins name was Gwen (Luke 1:26-27). Then manifested into reality from my backyard a tomb wall On city Compton ministry of reconciliation protection against idol worshipping. I want my record to show my demonstration of faith started daily Monday through Friday at 5 am on a prayer line of faith with beautiful hearted people highly favoured the lord is with thee (Luke 1:28-29). Protesting crying "Jubilee" out to the Lord Joseph wept aloud there stood no man with him great deliverance posterity in the earth (Genesis 45:1-7).

Underworld capitalist system of goddess way of protection by enmity hating others, seeing things winner and loser god of war (Genesis 3:15). Land of giants artificial people only cares about their wealth not real people health they make themselves larger than life icons. By competing make everything they do a competition wanting to be the serve first his or her rule over thee (Genesis 3:16), being winners in everything and seeing people as winners and losers in battles of the sexist war. Sharing our faith calling on Jesus Christ heir of salvation equally. He shall be great and shall be called the son of the highest: and the Lord God shall give unto him the throne of his father Joseph (Luke 1:32).

Not wasting my holy time with God, playing Play Station games or watching NASA cars go around a racetrack. Standing on the promising Word of God will numb you to the sensation of lies and temptations of the world Internet attacks. The word of God gives wisdom power, insight, and knowledge to stand on truth; it is protection against misleading information. The Word of God speaks truth will soften your tender heart making you cry. Nothing is impossible for God (Luke 1:36). Jesus wept does not care about artificial teardrop tattoo drawn on your face; Holy Spirit speak soft comforting voice written on your heart make you weep.

Prophesy of Messiah Ben Joseph

"Many Jews today believe that Elijah will one day return, and when he does, "he shall turn the heart of the fathers to the children, and the heart of the children to their fathers Jews also taught that the return of Elijah would occur during the Messianic Age. According to one modern scholar, when Elijah returns, he will appear on the top of a mountain. This is intriguing for latter-day Saints as well as Jews who believe that the "tops of the Lord's house" refers to the Lord temple."

The Childhood of Jesus

These are not normal times! Have you ever saw the full black moon turn into blood? Key to the mystery of Babylon unlocking the Bible appointed holy time in the Word of God messiah ben Joseph. It's two life-changing conflation events happening at the same time messiah Ben David sign of the Son of man and messiah Ben Joseph sign of Elijah return. One fiscal turns the underworld upright; the other spiritual presence of God in the world economy and temple worshipping sacrifice. It's written in the Law of the Lord, "Every firstborn male will be dedicated to the Lord" (Luke 2:23). When I saw the sun dying, moon rising on a cross with the star of David turn into blood, on Passover April 4, 2015 and Atonement September 27, 2015 though a cemetery temple arch monument, appearing like a peaceful dream.

Epiphany I had seen the heaven opened come true, giving me the power to proclaim "Jubilee"; the presence of the Lord is on me being made good where I am at wisdom from above. It's a light for revelation to the Gentiles and a glory for your people House of Joseph (Luke 2:32). The vision to see the end to the beginning of the world. Write this story backwards from the end to the beginning keeping Holy time of sacrifice. Acts II perfect love, peace and happiness. Birthright inheritance of messiah ben Joseph from Genesis ancient rainbow covenant to modern day latter-day new covenant messiah ben David Jesus Christ today (Genesis 48:14).

D&C 133: 30-32

"They shall bring forth their rich treasures unto the children of Ephraim, my servants. And the boundaries of the everlasting hills shall tremble at their presence. And there shall they fall down and be crowned with glory even in Zi-On by the hands of the servants of the Lord even the children of Ephraim."

This not a 5G science fiction story or fantasy fairytale. This is about the supernatural work of the Holy Spirit flooding out. Promise of God's Word of protection over our family lives prophecy fulfilled. Keeping holy time with Lord Jesus Christ, King of Kings, living and death return of Elijah fulfilled Passover April 4, 2015 (Malachi 4:5). Keeping you safe from a plague pandemic over policed judgment comes from the Lord remember the law. The greatest spiritual alignment ever captured by greatest of seers alone Joseph Moore than a prophet I commanded unto all nations (Malachi 4:4). Seer of the sun, moon and earth in line turn the color of blood, setting holy time ground zero. As it was in the beginning of days in the Old Testament, Joseph was born again seed of Abraham faith, son of righteousness of Lincoln, Nebraska. Arise with healing called back year 1963, at the time requested by Dr. King wrote his "I Have A Dream" speech go forth and grow up (Malachi 4:2).

Joseph was persecuted for doing the right thing born again from a dream heir of salvation follower of the one and true living God, seer of the beautiful hand of God's shadow working through the Holy Spirit's breath of life and peace with fire of Elijah (Malachi 4:1). What was meant for evil, the Lord makes it good. Fair and equal to everyone freely. The Church of Jesus Christ of Latter-day Saints believes that Elijah returned on April 3, 1836 in an appearance to Joseph Smith and Oliver Cowdery, fulfilling the prophecy in Malachi. God is the same yesterday, today and forever.

Writing the Word on everyone's renewed heart and mind interconnected Ubuntu ministry program out processing the worldwide web root nor branch (Matthew 3:10). Starting from the beginning of the Internet search to the end of the world wide web did not find no wisdom all that was found was alternative facts of ungodliness. There is more wisdom of thee Law of Heaven in these two pictures on the front and back book cover used to begin and end of this story than the Internet worldwide web return of Elijah and sign of son of man Jesus Christ together day of the Lord (Malachi 4:5).

Jacob Reveals His Son's Destinies
Genesis 49:9-10
"Judah is a lion's cub; from the prey, my son, you rise up. He lies down and crouches like a lion; like a lioness—who dares disturb him? 10 The scepter won't depart from Judah, nor the ruler's staff from among his banners Gifts will be brought to him; people will obey him."

Woman at The Well

I never thought I would have seen the world shutdown during Easter seer more than a prophet monument unto Moses (John 4:20). No sport or entertainment event during Passover. When I proclaimed "Jubilee," they said it could never happen, a resetting of the world's economy. Only God can make Jubilee happen; it is a very holy event set to happen at a certain time, commanded to happen precisely every fifty years worship the father (John 4:21). If it is not done correctly, it will become a judgement against the nation 2020 pandemic 100-year cycle.

Life is a cycle of time that keep repeating itself. Born again nobody get left behind when he comes, he will tell us all things of I Am (John 4:25-26). The Bible warns us about not keeping the Holy Time cycle. We become off balance and confused when we don't follow the right cycle of time. We will become lost in time civil religious values of a nation. Jubilee resets time back to God's original order to keep Holy Time feast and festivals of hope is not this the Christ (John 4:29)? The Word of the God will leave a taste in your mouth like salt gives food flavor. Atonement to Passover hearing the voice of God as the New, Millennial, New Testament 2nd Acts II perfect love, peace and happiness, a word of hope he house of Joseph Jr. there two days (John 4:40). Write simple what you see on broken hearts passion of one testament.

Rejection at Nazareth

What would you do if the voice of God tells you I will make your name greater than Moses? Joseph Alone who has died, gone to heaven, and come back from the dead to save his family and others now we believe. Modern day prophet born again choice seer witness acts of God's hand setting heaven order straightway truly savior of the world (John 4:42). Nothing is random on Earth. But first you are required to be born again be named Alone Joseph from the womb by your mother's immaculate conception, father and grandfather also named Joseph son of Jacob plain man book of the prophet Isaiah. It was written every step directed little by little, the Holy Spirit fits into a pattern for good uses of all who love God's birthright return home where you've been raised (Luke 4:16). Must be born of high priest daughter of Aaron Saint Elizabeth midwife, righteous before God, the spirit of the Lord is on me. Nursing care for sick or injured people. Circumcised on the eight day of life, for remembrance of law to be baptized by the age of fifty. Guided by the light of rainbow covenant token of God for remembers proclaim the year of the Lord's favor to act (Luke 4:18). Bible simply teaches Jesus tell the people of Israel the Lord can bring the seed of Abraham up from anywhere on this planet. Today, this scripture has been fulfilled just as you heard it (Luke 4:20).

Jesus Announces Good News to the Poor
Isaiah 61:1-4

"The Lord God's spirit is upon me, because the Lord has anointed me. He has sent me to bring good news to the poor, to bind up the brokenhearted, to proclaim release for captives, and liberation for prisoners, to proclaim the year of the Lord's favor and a day of vindication for our God, to comfort all who mourn, 3 to provide for Zi-On's mourners, to give them a crown in place of ashes, oil of joy in place of mourning, a mantle of praise in place of discouragement. They will be called Oaks of Righteousness, planted by the Lord to glorify himself. 4They will rebuild the ancient ruins; they will restore formerly deserted places; they will renew ruined cities, places deserted in generations past."

It is prophecy that the seed of Abraham's family can sprout up from anywhere like an old olive tree branch lost Urban Tribes. Even in the darkest of time of their life stand united in same line of faith Abraham prayed too be light out of darkness. God gives power to whom He chooses unelected not by man is not this Joseph's son (Luke 4:22)? Trust God in every detail of your life. Could no man have thought of this the whole wide world shutdown fighting a global pandemic. If I would not have proclaimed Jubilee the last seven years now that we see it happening, this would be scary raising of the dead. If I did not know the work of the Holy Spirit then for this to happen during the eight days of Passover celebration, Good Friday, Easter Resurrection service and Ramadan Holy Time for praying and fasting I would be afraid. Holy time women and men praying touching and agreeing together to simply do the right thing be not afraid to cry out in the name of Jesus in public for something better. Jesus doesn't care how nasty you are or how dirty you've been. Jesus cleans everybody feet; no matter where you have laid your head, pickup your bed and get up and walk (Luke 5:23).

The Calling of The Twelve

God hears the prayers of men and women equally at the same Holy time call the righteous. For sinners to repentance, passion baptized immerse in the living Word of Holy Spirit as if it was last drop of water you need it to live be whole (Luke 5:31-32). Down to every drop to save your life. This is how important the Word of God is needed in our lives every word is like drop of refreshing water pure and clean keeping the status quo. You know if you don't drink water, you will die a horrible death of thirst, which is a horrible state of affairs (Luke 5:33-35). Communion with the sharing in the beauty of evening meal breaking of the bread of life. Men do not live by food alone. Only through the life given word out the mouth of our lord Jesus Christ living water.

Renewing healing brokenhearted women united with men caring working together. The Word of God gives you the knowledge to fight stand against conspiracies of men. There are no coincidences here everything fits to the pattern of good for all men kind for I am he who gave the law (JST Matthew 9:18-19). Be in a graveyard during four blood moons sunrise and sunset. City of Compton it came to pass become the model city of destruction of sun gods and idol worship. You see the moon turn the color of blood.

The Holy Spirit peaceful acts of flooding out of mercy and compassion on my soul led me to start writing this story pattern praying to God continually (Luke 6:12). To save myself and return to God rather than going to buy an assault weapon to save myself. I first had to return to a cemetery monument sunset and sunrise Atonement women's day and Passover Resurrection at an appointed time be disciple. God doesn't ask us to do anything that we cannot do; He will provide all the provision wisdom for you to carry it out whom also he named apostles (Luke 6:13).

What does the Bible say about when you see the moon turning like blood? The moon is an instrument spirit level tool setting world order with time balance. Given as a seer stone to set heaven right-angle foundation of time straightway. Plumb-line of faith in things unseen new moon to new moon. Feast and festival season evenness order straight surface by gravity. Power to see into the future and the past Passover to Passover which also was the traitor (Luke 6:14-16). In the book of Genesis first chapter, it is written, the moon phase is precise instrument arch of heaven gate clock. Given as sign and wonder used for dividing night and day, keeping the appointed times of celebrations. Lunar and solar eclipse give wisdom New Gospel-time of renewing change that whatsoever you shall as of the father in my name, he may give it you (John 15:16). Signal of perfection praising God continually New Moon to New Moon time of correction.

The Old Testament Word of God came in drops, one prophet at a time. We are promised by the prophet Joel when the moon turns to blood, there will be a great pouring out of the spirit of God on all people. This will be fulfilled the great noble day of the Lord's last day see your calling. A prediction of the setting up a zone of peace confound the things which are mighty (1 Corinthians 1:26-27). Zi-On the Kingdom of grace of the Messiah glory in the world's first and second coming. By the pouring out of the spirit of perfect love in the latter days, there shall be a deliverance as the Lord has said. A convicting comfort to the believer and tribulations to the nonbelievers. According to the New Testament, God will reveal Himself by dreams and visions both to the young and old noble great sons and daughters.

The Beatitudes

In the first book of Acts 2nd Chapter, Apostle Peter spoke in tongues. In Verse 22, he saw visions of the moon phase turn into blood and the sun darken as history facts. The morning before Passover the day Jesus passed away on the cross a monument (Matthew 5:1). That was the day power gifts of Holy Spirit of the Lord came speaking utterance through upon all souls writing new Law. The book of Revelation, the moon became like blood gives strength, to be not afraid to hear revelations voice of Holy

Spirit. Beatus to be fortunate, to be happy to be blessed because they will inherit the earth (Matthew 5:3-5). Commanded to be a witness and to write it simple, explaining the good work of the Lord and being thankful not afraid of double blessings righteousness: for they shall be filled (Matthew 5:6). The blood moon is used to make people afraid of God's judgement of faith. Blessing to the believer, but impeachment to the nonbeliever, like a horror movie or fairytale to be trodden under foot of men (Matthew 5:13). It is like you are living in a twilight zone twin time dimension stuck in eternity, repeating the same day over until you do the right thing righteously shall in no case enter into the kingdom of heaven (Matthew 5:20).

Believer in astrology is a pseudoscience that claims to divine information about human affairs and terrestrial events by studying the movements and relative positions of celestial object using horoscopes of the moon and star for prediction of self-image behavior in fear don't be agree. They see the blood moon appointed time of good or bad evil event on Earth married to another committing adultery (Mark 10:10-12). The greatest fish God created the sign of Pisces.

Jonah was swallowed up by going around in circles of astrologist cared more about the characters of animals than the characters of people seeing firstborn son and daughter children of God as equal. The study of sign and symbols. You see them all over the place to get your attention remembering you to do things, telling you where to go, even what to say or when to say it; walk the walk or talk the talk. They are very important. Like reading a map not understanding a sign or symbols can cost you your life, be lost falling off a cliff or going in circles wasting time. The most valuable sign is for negative − and positive + together they equal = power energy converted per unit time ∞ infinity a sign prepares us for something about to happen give warnings to stop or U-turn not paying attention. The Arch has been used throughout history as a symbol for greatness memorial from the winner for lives lost in great war and battle to bridge cultures building society bring peace behavior law.

Sermon on The Mountain Top

"Jubilee" you need to read this perfect love story harmony humility. Be perfect even as your father which is in heaven is perfect (Matthew 5:48). Ubuntu philosophy of union to a spiritual divided nation; be humble. "Jubilee" Ministry of "Ubuntu" program of praying humanness not understood. Ubuntu (Zulu pronunciation: [ùɓúnt'ù]) is a Nguni Bantu term meaning "humanity" complete. It is often translated as "I am because we are," or "humanity towards others," but is often used in a more philosophical sense to mean "the belief in a universal bond of sharing that connects all humanity. Wherefore seek not the things of this world but build up the Kingdom of God, and to establish his righteousness; (JST Matthew 6:38). Have you ever heard the utterance of such a more powerful beautiful unselfish word spoken out the mouth of a person pure heart? "Ubuntu" philosophy program of sharing of forgiveness monument of the Lord (Psalm 24:3-4).

"Jubilee" Ministry Universal Pardon a call for liberty release of debt for other persons than yourself; be humble; don't Judge. "Jubilee" is written on the liberty bell. Proclaiming liberty throughout the land every fifty years "Jubilee"! Sounding like a trumping blast, commanding heaven to move on a person's behalf to return them to the original state of beginning judge righteous judgment by the Holy Spirit (JST Matthew 7:1). It is a demonstration order of mercy and compassion to release you from whatever well of debt you may have fallen into. Ask and you will receive. Search, and you will find. Knock, and the prison door will be opened to you. For everyone who asks, receives. Whoever seeks, finds (Matthew 7:7-8). "Jubilee" radical new way of thinking gift of mercy and compassion be humble is like a wise builder who built a house on bedrock (Matthew 7:24).

Why Parables?

There is a famine in the land from not hearing the word of God; comparing correctly can cost you your life. After 2020 years, how does God renew the living word of perfect love overtime and not like their legal experts (Matthew 7:29)? By starting the time clock over after a pandemic. Healing the broken hearts who lost their loved ones concealed in the Word of the scriptures school of thoughts. Writing of Psalm of the old Prophet Isaiah in the tradition of the Old Testament be holy? Ancient Temple prayer line of faith praying from old Jerusalem what was planted in their hearts (Matthew 13:19). Turning the world upright starting the New Millennial Church prayer line seed of faith ending in Compton cemetery deeper understanding. Reason for the season Christian perfection oneness with God today. By revival witnessing revealing Himself everyone who has ears should pay attention (Matthew 13:9). By doing what his mother told him to do. 2nd Acts II perfect love a celebration of the first wedding. Marrying Old Testament together with the New Testament Born-Again Spirit of the living word. 1st Acts of the Apostle in Christian experience the New Testament King James Bible. Because they haven't received the secrets of the kingdom of heaven, but you have (Matthew 13:11).

Conceiving onto the writing of every heartbeat of Israel a family prototype of Jesus Christ first fruit. Firstborn remnants of Joseph the uniquely faithful son and daughter's conscience living word of God's light of transfiguration a halo of protection hovering above their head they see; they really don't see (Matthew 13:13). Conception living word of God instantly creating New, New, Blood type Holy Spirit Crown Royal finer than the best, of the best wine. Given birth to the New Millennial, New memorial, writing of the living word of perfect love Christian perfection. Happy are your eyes because they see (Matthew 13:16). Jesus Christ Methodist is a movement seen as a halo of light all the color spectrums of a rainbow as a sign of peaceful Dove. 2nd Acts II God's perfect love traveling as a peaceful dove over their family revitalizing the church life and temple worship united in rejoicing. Singing "Lift Every Voice & Sing" as the National Anthem to the New Millennial, New Testament new things out of their treasure chest from something old (Matthew 13:52).

Thy Faith Hath Made Thee Whole

Today traveling flooding over the broken heart teardrop of modern-day Joseph persecuted a choice seer seeing confirming the word of God is true can be healed and live (Mark 5:23). By the light of a halo dancing above children of God's heads witnessing 2nd Acts II Perfect Love New Millennial, New Testament. Turning the world right so Jesus went with him (Mark 5:24). The next greatest story ever told to come straight out of Compton making people rejoice by returning brothers and sisters back to God traveling to church crying "Jubilee" celebrating revival proclaiming the special great year of the Lord immediately illness had been healed (Mark 5:25-26). Even greater story than Kendrick Lamar artist best rap DAMN album of the year, 2018 winning Pulitzer Prize in music make people party and move on the dance floor wanting to go to the nightclub. "Church Boy" too DAMN old to be a rap artist.

Who touched me, "Church Boy"? Has anything good ever come straight out of Compton, California (Mark 5:30)? We always hear about the bad thing that goes on around the City of Hub Compton. Here goes a good thing that Passover and atonement the whole wide world saw happen who touched me (Mark 5:31)? Act of liberty when people see my pictures taken from my backyard through a city historical landmark, they think they were taken in Jerusalem middle East someplace other than my backyard in Compton, California. Who would have ever thought the greatest love story ever told would end right in my backyard? It is the age of fulfillment your faith has healed you (Mark 5:33). The angel of prophecy is revealed unity between a beautiful temple arch looking like the Taj Mahal Mausoleum connecting heaven. Sun of man rising and dying on a cross with the full moon star of David straightway (Mark 5:41-42). Working together like the big and little hand setting time on a clock. He gave them strict orders that no one should know what had happened (Mark 5:43). After 2020 year the birth of Jesus Christ heaven and Earth coming together on a cross rising of the dead.

Feeding the Multitude

Exodus II movement of the halo light of God appearing within a dream of We the People and heard him gladly (Mark 6:20). All families' heartbeat at once, knocking down false doctrines by a literacy light of one word foretold of perfect love in a dream of a modern-day choice seer named Alone Joseph alongside Jesus Christ as alignment alliance laying to rest all conspiracy theories; fear God (JST Mark 6: 20). Parallel story of rejection Book of Mormon and the Holy Bible forgiveness together rejoicing with celebration Act II the second coming. Although the king was upset, because of his solemn pledge and his guests, he didn't refuse her (Mark 6:26). The peaceful life and death of my earthly father modern-day alone house of Joseph Jr. Jehovah's Witness alongside violent birth and bloody criminal death of our Heavenly Father Jesus Christ in a tomb keeping Holy Time (Mark 6:27-29).

On the same day crying for peace, peace, the Lord's Day "Jubilee" after celebrating fifty Christmas Advent seasons Passover time. After 2000 years eternal house of modern-day Joseph and David united two kingdoms acting out on the American continent celebration set apart into a desert place (Mark 6:30-31). One modern day church and ancient temple united sent from heaven monument graveyard. The New Millennial, New Testament 2nd Acts II Perfect Love Advent of The Second Coming of Jesus Christ Time Traveler (1 Chronicles 17:5). The fulfillment of the eternal promise of God's rainbow covenant halo of love over everyone's life as a United Nation Universal Church they were as sheep not having a shepherd; he began to teach many things (Mark 6:34).

The greatest spiritual gift an earthly father can Passover to his sons and daughters is knowledge praying continual line of faith as our mother and great grandmothers did a monument (John 6:3). Passover time from observing religious sabbath on the last day of the week Friday. Christian perfection the first day of the week Sunday. The most valuable gift God has given us is time what he would do (John 6:6). First fruit is time off shared with God's favor thanksgiving for the week just passed through, giving thanks for the week just given walking under halo of light, love, and truth test of faith. Keeping family church, the temple of God their heavenly Father's word about Jesus Christ Christian perfection be filled. Floodlight of protection over their troubled hearts by reason of a great wind that blew (John 6:18). How the hand of God's promise has been a halo of light over every word in their family tree life's history in America from the movement of the Lord of creation overtime walking on water (Mark 6:49).

The Bread of Life

The halo light of protection He said to them, "I Am don't be afraid" (John 6:20). Reward appeared at the immaculate conception of our Ethiopian mother in 1944 Great American migration her hometown straight out of Compton, California created from a Spanish land grant that is still honored today called Rancho Dominguez. Los Angeles County General Hospital to her being raised meeting our father named Joseph Jr. Moore firefighter believed in God's promise of rainbow halo became union organizer family activist. Passover to heaven on Christmas morning 2018 went to heaven on a rainbow halo 01/12/2019 my father giveth you the true bread from heaven (John 6:32).

Moors are a culture of people; the term was commonly used as a racial designation for dark-skinned or black peoples exiled, as with its use in English, seen as early as the fourteenth century giveth life unto the new world (John 6:33). Migration to the heartland of America our hometown after the early death of her mother at 29 years of age Abraham Lincoln,

Nebraska. Named after the father of many nations Abraham, Lincoln man of righteousness I will give is my flesh (John 6:51). The Good Life State of faith, Equality Under the Law of Moses eternal life. Joseph meaning "God will increase" spiritual salvation. Alone one unique sole ruler, autocrat or eternal ruler, ever powerful name meaning Eric ^(Little by Little) I will raise you up last day (John 6:54). Alone after our grandfather named Joseph Alone we share the same birthdate 01/19 day of good opposite of 09/11 day of evil. This message is harsh. Who can hear it (Mark 6:60)?

Two biblical home front grassroot ministry for unity a house divided can't stand against itself as old as politics and war anti-Christ (John 6:66). United States of we the people speaking two European noble common languages, one bad English from the King James Bible Protestant Church, the other speaking broken Spanish from the Catholic Church Latin Bible. Suffering from Post-Traumatic Stress Disorder of two Civil wars of Religion Catholic and Protestant Church still being fought today growing together in marriage domestic violence and prophecy at the birth of my Generation X, 1961; this is the work of God (John 6:29).

President Kennedy saying ask not what your country can do for you, ask what you can do for your country was assassinated. Starting the year of my birth 1963 with Dr. Martian Luther King Jr.'s "I have a Dream speech" was assassinated year 1968. Message to a New Movement, New Generation X becoming one New, New Testament 2nd Acts II perfect love children of God born again son of Joseph speaking one common language the son of the living God (John 6:69). Bill Graham Crusade and Civil Right Movement becoming one worldwide peaceful celebration crusade. In perfect love by the hand in hand of God on everybody's eternal life.

The Rock of Our Salvation

If you fold the world map in half, you will see Compton and Jerusalem line right up. Keeping Holy times, the whole wide world is sacred ground today. Jews and Gentiles are one body of people today children of God worshiping going to church one of the prophets (Matthew 16:14). As Black Native American descendants of the United States evil slave trade Ben Joseph son of the living God thou art the Christ (Matthew 16:16).

Deja Vu, I have died and gone to heaven born again so many times the Highland story is nothing compared to this. Joseph, uniquely faithful, I have been here before. Then Jesus replied, "Happy are you, Eric son of Joseph Jr., because no human has shown this to you. Rather, my Father who is in heaven has shown you (Matthew 16:17). This story starts when the spirit of the Lord came onto my suffering as beautiful light of a rainbow halo seen at our prayer warrior grandmother's funeral 1984 and reappeared at our Jehovah Witness father funeral 2019. Renewing my broken heart and mind to God's promise calling out to me be holy. Alone not to be afraid get our family house of Joseph in order turning the upside-down world up-right. By my exact full name Eric Joseph Moore like my mother would do to get my full attention when she wanted to let me know I was in deep water incognito not being good, she was not happy with my behavior. I tell you that you are Eric. And I'll build my renewed church on this sure foundation. The gates of the underworld won't be able to stand against it (Matthew 16:18).

Telling me God is Moore Than A Rainbow halo to be humble act my age. Instructing me by my middle name Joseph Alone little by little like receiving a Ph.D. from God with the Holy Spirit acting as college professor studying the Holy Bible going to Sunday school lecturing be holy saying you're a prophet of Post-Traumatic Stress Disorder Family Ministry raised on the third day (Matthew 16:21). Seer of halo enlightenment knowledge about my own purpose gift of salvation to become baptizes a born-again New Millennial, New, Christian Perfection key to the priesthood mission. By the peaceful soft breath halo of glowing light, the Holy spirit voice of pure loving God great I Am reveled in scriptures, traditions, reason, Christian experience today living revelation. The Comforter blank of protection renewing the brokenhearted united in Jesus Christ Sacred Heart knowing good from evil to live. Seer of the World though our mother's beautiful brown eyes. Turning our up-side down old-underworld view right side up.

Light of the World
And when they found them not, they drew Jason and certain brethren unto the rulers of the city, crying, these that have turned the world upside down are come hither also (Acts 17: 6).

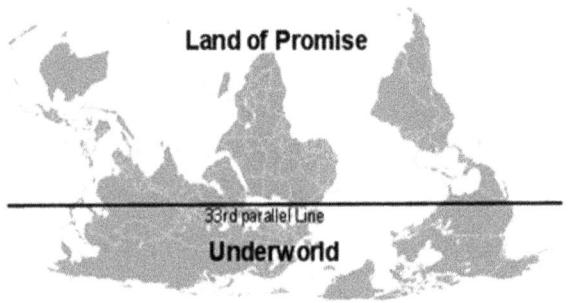

A whole New Millennial, New, way of look at things. A New Millennial, New, Christian is a person that is not afraid of dying. Sacrificing being born again, living forever by faith, not by sight in the very act to (John 8:4). Believe in Jesus Christ Methodist Christian perfection moment by moment relationship. Light of halo the Holy Spirit in their lives renewing mind. Not by their own work but by Scripture, Tradition, Reason and Christian experience. Not because they are required to only by truthfulness 2nd Acts II Perfect Love of the Lord. Then spoke Jesus again unto them saying, I am the light of the world: he that follow me shall not walk in darkness, but shall have the light of life (John 8:12).

I've lived most of my life as a prodigal son running away from the light of God's halo over my life. Anti-Christ covering my light living hiding out in the Dark Age Underworld Civil Religious. Not knowing I was already double blessed by the finger of God. I am one that bear witness of myself, and the Father that sent me beareth of me (John 8:18). I always had a funny feeling a guardian angel in disguise or someone was protecting trying to save me from being killed or killing myself with corrupted world backward way of thinking about debt of being foolish sold like a slave on the stock exchange Fortune 500 giant corporations. In an upside-down world the things I thought were good turned out bad and things that I thought bad turned out good. Antichrist dying alone not believing there is a God. Going into outer dark places husting, not knowing I was the problem. And he said unto me you are from beneath; I am from above you are of the world; I Am not of this world (John 8:23). I was blind and conceited and could not see what the right side of the slave ship of religion to stand on port or starboard, Muslim or Christian and Jews or atheist. Not believing in any god with no religious preference. Telling me our civil religious underworld order was upside down; you can't serve two masters.

As he spoke these words many believed on him (John 8:30). I was chained not going any place by a cycle of debt with payday loan interest spinning in circles out of control. My heartbeat was not truthful, hustling trying to be rich, acting poor going in and out of jail and prison. Not knowing I was already rich, supporting abortions sacrificing being in love putting off having children to get paid be wealthy with house not a home, two cars, a wife and girlfriend. It made me a hypocrite, adulterer double minded emotional and spiritually off-balance bipolar feeling dizzy seasick going from one side to the other, acting shameful some type of way afraid to cry always ready for a fight or kill someone.

I am too proud to beg a sinner was spiritual dead amoral not afraid of ride or dying going to Hell. I did not believe in the power of love for praying to God for good help or reading Psalms for healing and sacrificing time going to church to celebrate the sabbath for peace on Earth. Jesus said to the Jews who believed in him, "You are truly my disciples if you remain faithful to my teaching (John 8:31). I went to war and not to college or church, believing in medicine for healing. Hustling overtime, getting paid double time became my spiritual power to get what I wanted trusting my own work that was not united with the peacefulness sacred comforting heart of Jesus Christ.

I was an automobile mechanic with the gift ability to see how thing work with soft hands to fix anything. Entrepreneur owning my own business, trying to make it in a corrupted capitalist society. Civil religious celebrating all the commercial holidays. But even beyond that, I considered everything a loss in comparison with the superior value of knowing Christ Jesus my Lord today. I have lost everything for Him, but what I lost I think of as sewer trash, so that I might gain Christ and be found in him (Philippians 3:8).

I followed the horoscope zodiac signs made me a Capricorn G.O.A.T. (Greatest of All Time) of astrology for good luck. The precise measurement alignment of the planet and movement of the exact stars on the exact day of month of the year of my birth. Day of peace January 19, 01/19 the opposite of 9/11 day of terror. Saying I'm New Age spiritual weighing of the heart as light as a feather truth of Maat. The full moon was a sign for luck beginning of bad times like the hands of time on a clock. I studied the precise phases pattern of the light of the new moon to new moon, discovering the wisdom of fact that it's 28 days the same time average as a woman menstruation cycle creating my own thirteen-month calendar, becoming spiritual timekeeper like a grandfather clock. But now you seek to kill me, a man that hath told you the truth, which I have heard of God: this did not Abraham (John 8:40).

Watchman seer stone writing the truth letting people know when the exact time of the new praying month would begin for planting and harvesting one season equals seven years. There are only two type of churches here on Earth. One all denomination Christian churches that is united in faith with hope in 2nd Acts II Perfect Love of God's lamb sacred heart of Jesus Christ Holy Spirit halo of enlightenment. The other one belongs to the spirit of the devil, building on pride of family name, money seeking of self-knowledge and spiritual fulfillment through paid graded courses of study and training of weighing of hearts modern day Scientology Book of Death. You are of your father the devil, and the lusts of your father you will do (John 8:44).

The Holy Spirit of the Lord showed me my unrighteousness by name in every detail three part, past, present, and future like *A Christmas Carole*. Holy Ghost story Joseph of the old Testament, Joseph of the New Testament and Joseph Jr Alone of today New Millennial, New, Testament Family Foundation. Written on the time tablets of heaven every heartbeat of man with one name of my father never alone. Your father Abraham rejoiced to see my day: and he saw it and was glad (John 8:56). Joseph saying all things that shall happen to your sons and daughters on the walls of ancient temple be holy unity of Christ Jesus. By one prophet name alone greater than Moses written in the Lamb book of life all believe. There are many prophets only one choice seer which the Holy Spirit has placed supervisor overseer of God's church (Acts 20:28) temple. The fulfilling of God's Word by one named Joseph Alone is the most popular name written about in detail in the Torah, Qur'an, King James Bible and Book of Mormon Joseph Jr. Joseph Alone meaning "increase" is a precise important figure in all four sacred written books; have you seen Abraham (John 8:57).

Joseph Alone was not believed in his family when the Spirit came upon to him in a dream seeing eclipse the sun and moon bow down to him alone. God used him Joseph Alone to save his family foundation with God. Just like our family rejected did not believe our father modern day Joseph Jr. Alone when God called him to organize our family reunion with God by starting a family foundation. Named Joseph and Glades Moore after their father and mother alone as seeds of Abraham Lincoln, Nebraska in the worst of worst of times 2008 Great Recession preparing our family reuniting with God. When he could have done anything, he wanted to do. He too was accused to be a womanizer by my ex-wife dividing our family like Potiphar's wife accused Joseph Alone in the Bible story. Jesus said unto them, Verily, verily, I say unto you, before Abraham was, I Am (John 8:58).

The Good Shepherd

The word of God is so precise. From the movement of the shadow of a solar eclipse alignment crisscross America, down to every letter of the law in one central figure name Enoch. Seer Enoch was dedicated to Jesus Church washed his eye with clay walked with God and had son and daughter he was taken by God. And his disciples asked him saying, Master, who did sin, this man, or his parents, that he was born blind (John 9:2)? The word of God is so precise; no mistake is set right on the 33rd degree parallel line that circles the Earth marking exact timeline of birth and death. No man knows the time of their birth or death only by the hand in hand finger of God spiritual insight. Night is coming when no one can work "Jubilee" 2020 Lord's Day (John 9:3).

What evil used to hurt, God used for good right place. To do a pacific temple work at the end of times of darkness speaking one word from a dream peace, peace. Joseph Alone of the Old Testament was separated as a boy from his family by the hand of God, had a dream to save his family from the sin of the world. We know that God doesn't listen to sinners. God listens to anyone who is devout and does God's will (John 9:31). Saint Joseph Alone of the New Testament separated from his family by the hand of God had a dream to save God within his family. If this man wasn't from God, he couldn't do this" (John 9:33). My father modern day activist Joseph Alone of the New Millennial, New, Testament went to his separated brothers and sister only by the hand of God had a dream to organizes his family foundation reunion with God's promise is Moore Than A Rainbow like he organized the Compton Firefighter Union.

They are called Moors than a messenger of God's Temple multi-cultural. The Moors where the tailors to royalty, makers of fine suits with detail invented made yard stick three feet to measure count miles of material to the inch. For judgment I am come into this world that they which see not might see; and that they which see might be made blind (John 9:39). Seer writers of the prophets with perfect names under very strict requirements of loyalty in penmanship. Not just anybody can speak a word from God then write about it. My sheep listen to my voice. I know them and they follow me (John 10:27). There must be a temple on sacred ground is required called Alone by one exact God given named Joseph with utterance a sign from heaven dedicated sent to exact location. Joseph Alone was chosen by God to do more for human race, more than any name other than Jesus. If you were blind, you wouldn't have any sin, but now that you say, 'We see,' your sin remains (John 9:41).

Sacred graveyard House of Israel under star of David painted on top. Be in the right place at sunrise the right time sunset born of a woman midwife in marriage seed of Abraham following the order of Melchizedek, 613 commandments and regulations listening for the exact sound of a trumpet Shafar horn blast. Every word must be followed; God said I will raise up a Jr. person named Joseph Alone whose father and son will also be named Joseph Alone according to God's promising word to the seed of Abraham faith, circumcised, baptizes born again witness the spirit come down as a dove from heaven, rejected by his family, praying the Lord pray for "Jubilee" have a pure broken heart to hear the voice of God is required to make every step happen glorify his name Alone.

Every family has a person God has appointed called out to be a servant of the Lord to represent God within their family another testament of Jesus Christ second coming Acts II. I have other sheep that don't belong to this sheep pen (John 10:16). That family member was called to serve the Lord before they were born like Aaron. The family member has the free will to fall away and not to represent God to his family. If that family member fails and doesn't do God's will pass over their family and nobody will replace them. The family becomes unprotected and divided against God. There will be no healing and the family dies. This is an honorable appointment to serve God. Isn't it written in your Law, I have said, you are gods (John 10:34)? Alone Joseph uniquely faithful been appointed in life and death the keys of authority over God's human family on Earth and Jesus in heaven working together.

The Jewish Messianic Expectation

When I showed my 75-year-old father named Joseph Jr witness for Jehovah Word (John 1:1). The Messiah Ben Joseph Alone story about the two House of Joseph and David uniting becoming one church house of Jesus Christ United. Written about our family Foundation in the King James Holy Bible and Book of Mormon seed of Abraham at the end of Genesis to the beginning of the New Testament. How God will use our family name Alone at the end of time to bring the nation back to God rod of iron. In him was life; and the life was the light for all people (John 1:4). Because Adam and Eve failed, we are sinners. At first, he didn't believe my insight until he studied both books of insight on the scriptures together for himself. Then, he said I was right! The light shines in the darkness, and the darkness doesn't extinguish the light (John 1:5).

I was the first to give him insight and the Holy Spirit renewed his mind. To the Black Native American named son of Joseph Alone Lost Urban Tribes of Judah God's hand will raise up seed of Abraham descendant of Joseph know for certain that your offspring will be strangers in a country without land they own, enslaved and oppressed for four hundred years in good life state seed of Abraham Lincoln, Nebraska heartland of equality under the law of Moses a New Nation United States of America, they will be a remnant of people keeping God's rainbow covenant and God will turn to them freely and openly. The Word became flesh and made his home among us House of Joseph (John 1:14).

My father had never heard about "Jubilee" commanded every fifty years behold God's glory. He said he studied the Bible with the Jehovah Witnesses for twenty years. He never thought about starting over reconciliation Ubuntu ministry of forgiveness. This is why we celebrate Christmas today. After fifty Christmases, you get the gift reward of "Jubilee." A biblical holy year to be bless sabbatical time off with God, release out of debt, be holy restored turned into commercial holiday to get paid turn debt from red to black. That's when I recognized the Word of God was not being taught correctly in our family. You must study the Bible exact Word of God for yourself testimony be holy new creation from something old "Who are you" (John 1:19).

The Cost of Discipleship

When the Holy Spirit of love came praying over my name Joseph Alone to be holy many believed on him there (John 10: 42). The Holy Spirit of the Lord conceived on heart commissioned me to write 2nd Acts II Perfect Love. I was blinded by pride of the light from my own ego and could not see my own bullsh*t broken heart. Opening my closed mind to the practice of praying to be united in Jesus Christ studying the history of the Holy Bible. And the lord commended the unjust steward, because he had done wisely: for the children of this world are in their generation wiser than the children of light (Luke 16:8). The practice of praying over our family life made by our grandmother's prayer warrior pure heart calling it the New Millennial, New, Testament as I am a living sacrifice my life to writing. 2nd Acts II of the Holy Bible journeys across America. And I say unto you, make to yourselves friends of the mammon of unrighteousness (Luke 16:9).

It led me back to where my journey began. My mother's hometown place of birth, Compton, California Los Angeles County General Hospital. Ending in my hometown hospital place of birth name after Saint Elizabeth midwife and mother to John the Baptist's rebirth in the heartland cornfields. Abraham Lincoln Nebraska part with God's promise of hearts of mercy and compassion gift of free salvation covenant made to Abraham's seed of faithful exactly written by pacific name son of Joseph Alone and Jesus saying about their destiny unto you out of these stones God will raise up children unto Abraham faith spreading the Word of God to the end of the world be holy. He that is faithful in that which is least is faithful also in much: and he that is unjust in the least is unjust also in much (Luke 16:10). God's promise of divine salvation Perfect Love is available to everyone by one seed of faith God given name Joseph Alone.

2nd Acts II Perfect Love divine perfection nothing added or subtracted down to every little by little detail word spoken must be fulfilled by faith for the gospel. Call the poor, the maimed, the lame, the blind and thou shalt be blessed; for they cannot recompense thee (Luke 14:13-14). Joseph Alone fighting on two home fronts for unity speak two languages from the old colonial war between King James speaking English and Spanish speaking do nothing Catholic church still going on today. For I say unto you, that none of those men which were bidden shall taste of my supper of Saints (Luke 14:24). Wherefore, because of this covenant thou art double blessed; for thy seed shall not be destroyed, for they shall hearken unto the words of the book special invitation inherit eternal life (Luke 18:18).

The Joseph Alone story formed a unitary story with literary rather than oral origins written on four different continent Africa, North America, Asia and Europe in three different languages. In Rabbinic tradition, Joseph Alone is considered the ancestor of another messiah writers called, "Mashiach ben Yosef", by himself according to which he will wage war against the evil forces alongside Mashiach ben David and die in combat with the enemies of God and Israel. Two Messiahs acting as one Messiah Ben Joseph Alone and Messiah Ben David as Jesus both redeemers are involved in delivering the Jewish people from guilt (exile) and ushering in long awaited era. Seer Ezekiel called them two sticks becoming as one word "Jubilee." Two books becoming one New Millennial, New Testament.

2nd Acts II Perfect Love two Messiahs acting as one king and priest, each one being called Messiah David King Jesus Christ divinity and humanity are united in one nature, the two being united without separation, without confusion and without alteration saying God be merciful to me a sinner

(Luke 18:13). The celebration of the conception of Jesus Christ and death of Joseph Alone on the same day. These two Messiahs, sons of David, are the descendent of David and the Messiah descendent House of Joseph Alone. Sold into four hundred years of slavery by his jealous brothers, he rose to become vizier, the second most powerful man in Egypt next to Pharaoh, where his presence and office caused Israel his father to leave Canaan and settle in Egypt America today. Messiah ben Joseph Alone's death and Messiah ben Jesus birth celebrated together. The death of my earthly father and birth of my heavenly father acting as one rainbow for peace trusting God alone.

Lazarus, Come Forth

Joseph Alone is regarded by Muslims as a prophet and a whole chapter Yusuf is devoted to him, the only instance in the Qur'an in which an entire chapter is devoted to a complete story of a prophet. This pandemic is not unto death, but for the glory of God, that the Son of God might be glorified thereby (John 11:4). It is described as the 'best of stories.' Joseph Alone is said to have been extremely handsome, which attracted his Egyptian master's wife to attempt to seduce him.

Who would have ever thought the world would end like this victory over death, but I go that may awake him out of sleep (John 11:11-12)? The Law of Muhammad Ali the greatest law of them all No War! Everybody loved Muhammad Ali; he could float like a butterfly and sting like a Bee; the greatest fight of his life was not in the Boxing Ring. Muhammad Ali v. United States. Only Allah (God) can call for a holy war given the same right of exemption from going to war to Muslims that Jehovah Witnesses receive in Jesus Christ's (God) name as they conscientiously object to serving in the military under the law of the Constitution. Becoming I AM Ali the Greatest Law above all, The Law of Muhammad Ali: No War!

Call of the prophet priesthood teaching truth on Earth spiritual experience is real let us also go, that we may die with him (John 11:16). Choice seer is more than a prophet man of culture favor of God greatest creation by prayer line of measured little by little faith born again willing to give up their life. Letting patience have its perfect work in patience wisdom of Holy Spirit perfect witness. Yes, Lord: I believe that you art the Christ, the Son of God, which should come into the world (John 11:27). This is not about politics as usual democrat or republican party "Jubilee" party celebration what the lord is doing. Prophecy is the key to the divinity of Jesus Christ prophecy when he would and how would signal his return to earth to judge. Lord if you had been here, my brother had not died (John 11:32). To a specific place and time to his believers by a precise name Joseph Never Alone. It is as it was in the days of Noah so it shall be also at the second coming of sign of the Son of man; Jesus wept (John 11:35).

The Sign of the Son of Man (JS-M 1:41)
Matthew 24:30

"And then shall appear the sign of the Son of man in heaven: and then shall all the tribes of the earth mourn, and they shall see the Son of man coming in the clouds of heaven with power and great glory."

The editor, as well as some others, "thinks that Joe Smith has his match at last," because Mr. Redding thinks that he has seen the sign of the Son of Man. But I shall use my right, and declare that, notwithstanding Mr.

Redding may have seen a wonderful appearance in the clouds one morning about sunrise (which is nothing very uncommon in the winter season,) he has not seen the sign of the Son of Man, as foretold by Jesus; neither has any man, nor will any man, until after the sun shall have been darkened and the moon bathed in blood; for the Lord hath not shown me any such sign; and as the prophet saith, so it must be—"Surely the Lord God will do nothing, but He revealeth His secret unto His servants the prophets." (See Amos 3:7.) Therefore hear this, O earth: The Lord will not come to reign over the righteous, in this world, in 1843, nor until everything for the Bridegroom is ready.
Yours respectfully, Joseph Smith
Amos 3:7
"Surely the Lord God will do nothing, but he revealeth his secret unto his servants the prophets."

Then follows the interview between Joseph Smith and Mr. Douglas as recorded in the journal of William Clayton, as published in the News a year before Mr. Douglas' Springfield speech, and as now given in this chapter of the HISTORY OF THE CHURCH.
This News editorial boldly accepted the challenge of Mr. Douglas. He raised his hand against the followers of Joseph Smith, despite the warning of the prophet; and they in the chief organ of the church, reproduced the prophecy and told Mr. Douglas that he had "sealed his damnation and closed his chance for the presidential chair" through disobeying the counsel of the prophet. The presidential election of 1860, and the death of Mr. Douglas in the prime of life, the year following, tells the rest.

Pearl of great price discussions a fresh start ideal of Jesus Christ from something old becoming something new creation book of Mormon Joseph Smith Jr. prophesy about his self-great credibility. Raising of the dead (John 11:43).

D&C 3:3-15

3 Remember, remember that it is not the work of God that is frustrated, but the work of men; 4 For although a man may have many revelations, and have power to do many mighty works, yet if he boasts in his own strength, and sets at naught the counsels of God, and follows after the dictates of his own will and carnal desires, he must fall and incur the vengeance of a just God upon him. 5 Behold, you have been entrusted with these things, but how strict were your commandments; and remember also the promises which were made to you, if you did not transgress them. 6 And behold, how oft you have transgressed the commandments and the laws of God, and have gone on in the persuasions of men. 7 For, behold, you should not have feared man more than God. Although men set at naught the counsels of God, and despise his words. 8 Yet you should have been faithful; and he would have extended his arm and supported you against all the fiery darts of the adversary; and he would have been with you in every time of trouble. 9 Behold, thou art Joseph, and thou was chosen to do the work of the Lord, but because of transgression, if thou art not aware thou wilt fall. 10 But remember, God is merciful; therefore, repent of that which thou hast done which is contrary to the commandment which I gave you, and thou art still chosen, and art again called to the work; 11 Except thou do this, thou shalt be delivered up and become as other men, and have no more gift. 12 And when thou deliverers up that which God had given thee sight and power to translate, thou delivered up that which was sacred into the hands of a wicked man, 13 Who has set at naught the counsels of God, and has broken the most sacred promises which were made before God, and has depended upon his own judgment and boasted in his own wisdom. 14 And this is the reason that thou hast lost thy privileges for a season. 15 For thou hast suffered the counsel of thy director to be trampled upon from the beginning.

Secret of the age test of faith who do you believe come out of darkness into the light (John 11:44). Many people had seen the things which Jesus did, believed on Him. But some of them went their ways to the Pharisees, and told them what things Jesus had done (John 11:45-46). And one of them being the high priest that same year, said unto them, you now nothing at all, nor consider that it is man should die for the people, and that the whole nation perishes, not burying the truth in a graveyard (John 11:49-50).

The Triumphal Entry

A New Millennial, New, Witness for the Articles of Faith (pages 425-26) Prophet states and the Lord said unto me also: I will raise up (a man) up unto the fruit of thy loins (Moor man); and make for him a spokesman (Joseph Alone "Church Boy") And I behold, I will give unto him (Moor man) that he shall write the writing of the fruit of thy loins, unto the fruit of thy loins: and the spokesman of thy loins (Joseph Alone) shall declare it. Wherefore, the fruit of thy loins shall write; and the fruit of the loins of Judah shall write; and that which shall be written by the fruit of thy loins, and also that which shall be written by the fruit of the loins of Judah, shall grow together, unto the confounding of false doctrines and laying down of contentions, and establishing peace among the fruit of thy loins, and bringing them to the knowledge of their fathers in the latter days, and also to the knowledge of my covenants, saith the Lord.

And out of weakness he shall be made strong, in that day when my work shall commence among all my people, unto the restoring thee, O house of Israel, saith the Lord. And thus, prophesied Joseph Alone, saying: Behold, that seer will the Lord bless; and they that seek to destroy him shall be confounded; for this promise, which I have obtained of the Lord, of the fruit of my loins, shall be fulfilled. Behold, I am sure of the fulfilling of this promise; And his name shall be called after me; and it shall be after the name of his father call Joseph Jr. And he shall be like unto me; for the thing, which the Lord shall bring forth by his hand, by the power of the Lord shall bring my people unto salvation. Yea, thus prophesied Joseph Alone: I am sure of this thing, even as I am sure of the promise of Moses; for the Lord hath said unto me, I will preserve thy seed forever raising of the dead. She anointed Jesus' feet with aroma of perfume. This perfume was to be used in preparation for his burial and this is how she used it (John 12: 3,7).

Who is Joseph Alone today? Hosanna save us Lord! He is a real character icon. Blessings on the one who comes in the name of the Lord (John 12:12). Born again by midwife Saint Elizabeth daughter of Aron. Circumcised on the eighth day a seed of Abraham Lincoln, Nebraska Cornhuskers. We have blessed you out of the house of the Lord (Psalm 118:26). In a good life state under the law of equality seeing man and woman as equal. Judgement of being confident in God's promise is double blessing to the believer impeachment to the unbeliever and pandemic to the world, preserved to hold the keys forever in life and death. Don't be afraid, City of Zi-On, Look Your King is coming (John 12:15).

He was dead to his family and became alive again what evil done to hurt him was use by God to do good new creation "Church Boy." I Alone too was saved from shadow of death; Eternal Joseph was spiritually dead and came back alive when I became born again baptized son of Joseph Jr. Alone "Church Boy." I shall not die, but live and declare the works of the Lord (Psalm 118:17). New creation by the grace of God the Holy Spirit of promise Jesus Christ the evil I did was use for good. Yes, the Lord definitely, disciplined me, but he didn't hand me over to death (Psalm 118:18). Let me know I am on the right course spirit of the Lord dwelling within. Letting us know Holy Spirit work within you and you're going to make it. Open to me the gates of righteousness (Psalm 118:19).

This is why the cycle of Mayan Calendar would end December 21, 2012. The being of my spiritual journey son of Joseph Jr. Alone, sacrificing my life to study the Word of God to be able to give my family a greater understanding of God the Holy Trinity. I thank you because you answered me, because you were my saving help (Psalm 118:21). Discern study the Bible like a calendar to like getting a doctoral degree beginning and ending of time comparing relationship with religion seeing my family tree life a branch of righteousness as a church of clay seer stone washing my eyes to see truth forever lasting with no ending. The stone which the builders refused is become the head stone of the corner (Psalm 118:22). The New Black Moon as a sign Lord's day first day of the spiritual month for continually praying to new black moon. The Lord's day was is a sign made for a day of praying and a day of rejoicing. This is the Lord's doing; it is marvelous in our eyes (Psalm 118:23).

You cannot see them, but you know they're there: positive and negative magnetic fields around Earth. Space weather for many centuries, the effects of space weather were noticed but not understood thus demonstrating that specific solar events could affect the positive and negative spiritual climate on Earth. The flipping of the magnetic field negative and positive. Lord, please save us now! Lord, please let us succeed (Psalm 118:25)! Changes spiritual climate set in Heaven from negative to positive on earth.

This generational movement started the year of my birth 1963 when Dr. Martin Luther King gave his famous "I Have a Dream" speech. Becoming my generation marching orders for civil right turning into a celebration of "Jubilee" God moving on all human lives at one holy time. The one who enters in the Lord's name is blessed; we bless all of you from the Lord's house (Psalm 118:26). Exodus II God moving on we the people to form a perfect union. Acts II Perfect Love Second Coming of Jesus Christ and Elijah peaceful reign of blood and fire over the temple arch of heaven. The Lord is God! He has shined a light on us! So, lead the festival offering with ropes all the way to the horns of the altar (Psalm 118:27).

Two messengers acting as one celebration victory of birth and death on the same day. "Jubilee" release of debt by the hand of God promise of inheritance. 2nd Acts II The Greatest Story Ever Told never ending. The Greatest Story Never Told Joseph Jr. persecuted for doing the right thing keeps repeating. Now this happened to fulfill what the prophet said,

(Matthew 21:4). Returning from the dead uniting the family as one body of positive spiritual people feeding the word of God. The same precise hand of God used Joseph in the beginning of writing Genesis. Say to Daughter Zi-On, "Look your King is coming to you. Is the same precise handwriting at the end of revelations using House of Joseph Jr offspring (Matthew 21:5). Confirmation of Passover return of Elijah with blood and fire on mountain top in the tabernacle of clouds appointed time Jesus Christ sign of the Son of Man miracle on Earth pray line of faith in every word of the Bible ending at a temple monument praising God. Symbol of royalty kingship prince of peace coming in victory to claim the people crown over life and death then he sat on them (Matthew 21:7).

The Sabbath was made for the Lord is the Sabbath day of rest. The Bible speaks and teaches of life after death. I looked, and there was a great crowd that no one could number. They were from every nation, tribe, people, and language. They were standing before the throne and before the Lamb (Revelation 7:9). Afterlife the spirit has the will to live without a heart. Except the Holy Spirt the one and only one spirit with the sacred heart of God's perfect love. Acts II Perfect Love all heart beat as one sacred heart unconditional love of God of mercy and compassion. They cried out with a loud voice: "Victory belongs to our God who sits on the throne, and to the Lamb" (Revelation 7:10).

Why is there all this babbling going on in the church (Genesis 11:1-9)? Because the word of God was not being taught correctly in the church. The people started babbling, speaking in the spirit and nobody understands what they are talking about. The Word of God has tongue utterance speaking to a nation's heart to change minds. Saying, "Amen! Blessing and glory and wisdom and thanksgiving and honor and power and might be to our God forever and always. Amen" (Revelation 7:12). Releasing the weak broken hearted the Word of God speaks straight to accountant of your heart reconciliation. Every heartbeat is normal reconciled back to God. Then he said to me, "These people have come out of great hardship in the

Lamb's blood. They worship him day and night in his temple, and the one seated on the throne will shelter them (Revelation 7:14-15).

To get to God of eye for eye equality in revenge and jealousy name Amun Ra in ancient Egyptian only the pharaoh could Passover to the afterlife with no love; they used beautiful hieroglyphs painting handwriting system of religious documents Book of the Dead god believe you had to have a pyramid and temple build to honor statue of sun god of man the exact detail measurement π copy of heaven picture drawn on Pharaoh's tomb walls, side of coffin texts and body art need to be preserve exactly right to weighing of the heart test as truth Maat did not work. Astrology was used to predict the future movement of heaven time birth and time of people's death sign of the Son of Man. And when Jesus entered New Jerusalem, the Hub City On was stirred up. "Who is this?" they asked (Matthew 21:10).

The family of inheritance Israel Judaism believed in the Law of the Torah scroll handwritten copy of holiest book with word past down generation after generation to get to God named Jehovah in afterlife raising of the dead, bare record work of the prophet. Jesus predicted his victory over death called it secret until his second coming rising from the dead and living monument to God glory. This was all a sign of prophet Elijah return to the temple with fire and blood. For this cause the people also met him, for that they heard that he had done this miracle (John 12:17-18). You must be holy born knowing the right family name. Speaking one specific language of Hebrew every word and letter under the Law of Moses had a snake on a stick to be followed and 613 commandments that could not be changed or broken the return of Prophet Elijah on a mountain must happen with blood and fire.

And the multitude said this is Jesus the prophet of Nazareth of Galilee (Matthew 21:11). Moses' law must be obeyed; every boy must be circumcised on the eighth day is not required circumcised heart is required for all. Perceive you how you prevail nothing? Behold the world is gone after him (John 12:19). God was placed in a box no one could not touch, moved in a tabernacle need to be followed down to every precise little by little detail must be keep. Sacrificing animal blood of lamb to God. Unclean woman and man are separated. The identification of Jesus as the Messiah is not accepted by Judaism. And some of the Pharisees from among the multitude said unto him, Master, rebuke the disciples (Luke 19:39).

Islam is an Abrahamic monotheistic passed down inherited radical religion which teaches that there is only one God (Allah) and that Muhammad is the messenger of God all thing witness. I tell you that, if these should hold their peace, the stones would immediately cry out (Luke 19:40). Its adherents are known as Muslims. Islam teaches that God is merciful, all-powerful, unique and has guided humankind through prophets, revealed scriptures and natural signs. The hour is come, that the Son of man should be glorified (John 12:23). The primary scriptures of Islam are the Quran, viewed by Muslims as the verbatim word of God, and the teachings and normative example (called the sunnah, composed of accounts called hadith) of Muhammad. Muslims believe that Islam is the complete and universal version of a primordial faith that was revealed many times before through prophets including Adam, Abraham, Joseph Moses and Jesus. My house shall be called the house of prayer; but you have made it a den of thieves (Matthew 21:13).

Muslims consider the Quran to be the unaltered and final revelation of God. In Arabic-speaking cultures, two words are commonly used for Christians: *Naṣrānī*, plural *Naṣārā* is generally understood to be derived from Nazareth means followers of the Messiah. Men first born sons are allowed to inherit and marry more than one wife and file for divorce. He came, if happily he might find anything thereon: and when he came to it, he found nothing but leaves; for the time of figs was not yet (Mark 11:13). Treating first born daughter separate not equally to firstborn son praying in one direction becoming apostasy church build on foundation clay.

The Last Supper

New, New, Christian believe in resurrection rising from the dead suffering to serve others. A New, New, Christian is a person who follows or adheres to Christianity based on the movement of the Holy Spirit on their lives and teachings of Jesus Christ grace and truth equally to men and women in the moment. I will not any more eat thereof, until it be fulfilled in the Kingdom of God (Luke 22:16). The term "New Christian" is also used as an adjective to describe anything associated with Christianity, or in a proverbial sense "all that is noble, and good, and Christ-like. Jesus Christ God within has many names in three parts the Trinity, Father, Son, and Holy Spirit, as a New, New, Creation Kingdom of Heaven on Earth a place where life after death happen in an instant be Holy born again New, New, Christian creation spiritual baptizes life is eternal sacred heart. And he took the cup, and gave thanks, and said, Take this, and divide it among yourselves (Luke 22:17).

The most valuable thing God created is the love written onto the human sacred heart of Jesus Christ mercy and compassion spoken in all language. "Jubilee" New, New, Testament Acts II Perfect Love: The Second Coming of Jesus Christ all religion praying for peace and forgiveness together as one body on bended knee tongues confessing by faith remembrance of God with us. This cup is the New testament in my Blood, which is shed for you (Luke 22:20). Christian perfection acts II being transfigured into a new creation more beautiful person elevated by inherit power of the word of God bread and wine of life.

Who would have believed God would have honored my father in death by one name Alone Born-again Joseph Jr a seed of Abraham, righteousness of Lincoln out of the house of Joseph Alone and David, James, and Daniel as Judah one Nation united in Jesus Christ to call "Jubilee" this Great, Great, Commandment of repentance start time over was a dream way before our time generational movement of inherit faith. Now this was the custom of the Jews under their Law; wherefore, Jesus did this that the law might be fulfilled (JST John 13:10). A house divided cannot stand. "Jubilee" mercy and compassion unite us. Having loved his own which were in the world, he loved them (John 13:1). Commandment to happen every fifty Christmas years like clockwork to protect God's children firstborn birthright to the land God promised Abraham seeds. He said to them, "Do you know what I've done for you (John 13: 12)? Teaching son and daughter to live sin-free lives. You call me 'Teacher' and 'Lord,' and you speak correctly because I am (John 13:13). It guarantees future generation the promise of God's freedom and justice and liberty for all. If I, your Lord and teacher, have washed your feet, you too must wash each other's feet (John 13:14)

The Great Black Native American migration from the violent segregated Southern State of Ringgold Louisiana Exodus II the Northern Midwest plane State of Abraham Lincoln, Nebraska Heartland of America after the evil Civil War of "Jubilee" 1865 still being fought today. I have given you an example: Just as I have done, you also must do (John 13:15). A young man named Joseph Alone with his wife dreaming of a better life for his young family one generation from living alongside evil of slavery of the greatest names from the Bible Saint Martin Luther through Dr. Martin Luther King, Jr. I assure you, servants aren't greater than their master, nor are those who are sent greater than the one who sent them (John 13:16). America was created for a time likes where children out of the house of Joseph Jr. Alone will be free to read all the scripture discern the truth then write a book about it; God serving feeding humankind without jealousy. Since you know these things, you will be happy if you do them (John 13:17).

Negus, please! This sad state of affairs we find ourselves in divided nation today. The White man this, The White man that. Before we talk about anybody, we need to look at ourselves. I'm not speaking about all of you. I know those whom I've chosen. But this is to fulfill the scripture, the one who eats my bread has turned against me (John 13:18). Negus ministry is real teaching the word of God to African Americans lost generation culture of people that turn away from personal relationship with God in the latter days in your own family. People that are not able to identify with seeing themselves in the Bible. The most valuable thing you have as a people your identity how you see yourself with God. You cannot serve two masters.

When the Negus Royal Monarch did not teach the word to serve God to their people correctly lost their identity. "I'm telling you this now, before it happens, so that when it does happen you will believe that I Am (John 13:19). They became enslaved in debt to the world of artificial people capitalism as property of giant world corporation stock and bond market tower of babel Iron and clay today. Plastic artificial person Mastercard and Visa credit score are the plantation slave owners today. There are more people enslaved in America today than before the Civil War. You can lose your freedom in two different ways. One by signing your name and one from breaking the law. I assure you that whoever receives someone I send receives me, and whoever receives me receives the one who sent me" (Joh 13:20). A nigger is a person that doesn't know he or she is a slave. A Nigga N.I.G.G.A Never, Ignorant, Getting, Goal, Accomplished continuity praying. One day, you will be asked what you did during the great pandemic of 2020.

Love Commandment

It is written, as it was in the beginning, it will be in the end the House of Joseph Alone as my family foundational named after my grandparents Joseph and Gladys fleeing the violent south looking for work like the South American are fleeing their country today looking for work a better life. Son of man Jesus said, "Now the Human One has been glorified, and God has been glorified in him sign of the Son of Man (John 13:31). They were sons and daughters of New, New, Christian accepted Jesus Christ as a better way of lifestyle helping build all denomination churches not because they were required to just on their faith with prays of hope and pennies.

New Christians where required and forced or coercion to convert to the Catholic church under the threat of slavery or death. The Catholic church failed to protect the New Christian of South America from the sin of criminals and cartels like they failed to protect Moor New Christian Civil Rights Southern part of Northern America. New Christians were freely allowed to come to America some returned to their old traditional way of worshiping. If God has been glorified in him, God will also glorify the Human One in himself and will glorify him immediately (John 13:32).

Becoming New, New Testament New Christians most build started their own family church with graveyard monuments headstone. Giving their children Christian biblical names as a tradition showing honor to God and evert word in the Bible. They moved to the end of the New World creating new parishes into a new city as a light like a city on a hill for all to see Compton, California New, New Jerusalem Hub City of Peace. To a place of faith of Abraham Lincoln righteousness good life state of Nebraska heartland America Keeping the law of equality men and women praising God. I also tell you now - 'Where I'm going, you can't come' (John 13:33). To do a secret peaceful temple work an order of righteousness directed by the right hand of God set aside to live alongside the unrighteousness to make them righteous. Created from an old land grant from the queen of Spain that the land return to the native after ten years is still honor today becoming new creation from something old.

"I give you a new commandment: Love each other. Just as I have loved you, so you also must love each other" (John 13:34). Returning the land back to Zi-On the Foundation of God original landlord. Zi-On time zone of peace. Cannot be bought; the land is in the hand of Lord. This is how everyone will know that you are my disciples, when you love each other" (John 13:5). Zone of Zi-On is a place of inheriting keeping Holy Time Passover to Atonement.

Sign of the Son of Man Book of Jubilee Acts II World Peace
Nu Year Zero Timeout
Keeping My Family Church
Spiritual Climate Change Action Plan

Whoever would have believed that God's gathering of divided world chaos and order would come together at the time of the end like the comedy of Get Smart Television show and Hollywood Movie become a reality KAOS Soviet Union communism scare. It's all a joke: fake news. With the phenomenon, triumphing election of Donald Trump as president of the United States of America KAOS fake news from fake prophet Bear of Russia Gate has gotten into the White House. Out of chaos comes order. 2016 Extraordinary Holy Nu Year 0000 timeout of suspended time. Sanctuary balance between security and liberty "Jubilee." Suspend time until celebrated rightly.

Biblical timeout of reconciliation and restoration its reset time sacred law preternatural event guaranteed autonomy justice according to the "Divine Law of the Homeland Human Rights and Privileges." The vibrating trumpeting soundwave of universal hope is law one word: "Jubilee" Divine law mandates cannot be rejected or denied; they supersede presidential authority and triggers all the power of heaven and Earth to start moving and acting on your behalf to restore time back to God's original order; be faithful. From Abraham to Abraham Lincoln, Nebraska Acts II Perfect Love Exodus II Zi-On as the capital of black Native American descendants of Joseph as a monument praising God.

This is why the president's power authority is suspended in a state of time, being Passover. Award to God's omnipresent state of favor from phenomenon double blood moons over a sanctuary cemetery dream. It's a cultural contract of very good news written in prophetic times, turning the world upright. A gift of autonomy salvation eternal life, honoring the dead elders in Jesus Christ for turning time back to become born again.

Acts II World Peace Nu Age Day Zero freedom of radical violent extreme thinking. The opposite of Christopher Columbus who used fake news that God was mad like pastors are doing today. In 1502, Columbus lied about a blood moon and used fear to scare the Native Jamaican people to stop them from killing him and his crew for stealing. Leave your fake religion radical babbling, barbarian tattoo belief behind you. It's a personal holy time of prayer in utterance, sacred worship event fellowship celebration peacefully rededication passing over all heart suffering minds pondering sorrows with communion trusting God's truth by going to New United Church House of Prayer. 2021-year latter-days baptizing in the name of Jesus Christ in my pool west coast Compton. Hub City of Zi-On parallel the mountain Abraham took is oath of faith middle east and Pillars of Herakles Strait of Gibraltar. Destroying idol and sun god worshiping nations.

This is not about worshiping or going to war over the policy of one holy city's praying at the sacred wall your parents passed down radical religion sexism and violent protesting beliefs marching in the public street or rioting throwing stones from hearing sad news that does not fix one problem. "Jubilee" great commandment solution to all problem God's omnipresent phenomenon state of favor caused you to stand at attention keep the status quo and rejoice, unmoving with your hand up to the sky, being thankful not afraid just like the statute of Lady Liberty and Justice suspended in time fighting evil prophet of Baal with tongue on fire spiting truth.

It's a gift eclipse light reflection of hope; sunrise praise and worship serves on Sunday morning, hearing the blowing of a shofar ram horn that makes me start crying "Jubilee," remembering me to be baptized Easter morning 2013, becoming born again celebrating Passover sacrifice my life honoring living elders with thanksgiving for the sacred week end we just Passover and the New Holy week we just have been given. Therefore, no need to practice praying five times a day. It's witnessing the eyes on the prizes emerging revival of truth Affordable Care Act is good for America from a great attack in alternative facts fake news cycles talking points about Obamacare replacement is only created to scare you. About urban tribes sprawling of America trigger happy police to the wind-swept plains' tribes of Nebraska Midwest inner city blues created 2017 years ago. We the People to be a great nation city on a hill as a light to the world that can't be hidden a spiritual rebellion gift of God coming to you. Intentionally on purpose to be a predetermined purpose driven life today's appointed moment window in time Nu Age Year Zero Timeout honor God.

Start time over Spiritual Climate Change Action Plan towards a balanced social worldview state of God's favor. Living with trusting God's Spirit of truth with good news. The birth of the New United Church House of Prayer honoring Jesus Christ Glorified One, Two, One ministry. Repairs God's spiritual broken relationship with lost urban tribe American family being baptized in front of a temple monument to God. By the trumpeting sound of one word "Jubilee" call into action celebrating the history of going to New United Church House of Prayer first Sunday communion as opposition with a spirit to learn unity through education. Trusting that God's Spirit of truth is real never has ignored you, not trumpeting radical lies of President Donald Trump the lying tweeter.

"And whether a child is born in the urban sprawl of Detroit or the wind-swept plains of Nebraska, they look at the same night sky. They fill their heart with the same dreams and they are infused with the breath of life by the same almighty creator So to all Americans, in every city near and far, small and large, from mountain to mountain, from ocean to ocean, hear these words: you will never be ignored again."
President Donald Trump 2017 Inaugural Speech

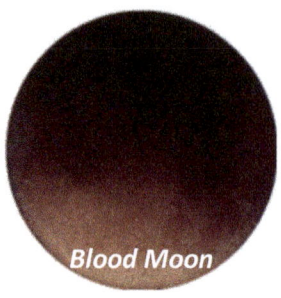
Blood Moon

CHAPTER I
The Long Day of Debate

This story is to my elders.

In the glorious beginning of the Renewal Nu Testament Age Year Zero before all time of God's joyful tears, release from suffering and sorrow for this is a day the Lord God has made and given thee this authority (Matthew 21:23). Be thankful! Rejoice! Be glad in it! For this is a holy year of our Lord's extraordinary "Jubilee" (party) of mercy and compassion of God's welfare over the people. Zero Year timeout where nobody is ignored again or left behind from heaven or of men (Matthew 21:25). Celebrating our history of opposition in unity, as a resistant to the radical thinking of President Donald Trump's administration on common ground by going to church. A quiet storm spiritual reset God's exodus moving on We the People to stop radical violence twisted thinking creating very good news of a nuclear weapon free Zi-On (Zone) social order of peace who will give him the fruit when it's ready (Matthew 21:41). The cornerstone to Jesus Christ grassroots ministry renewing hearts and minds, keeping my family church foundation reconciled to God's purpose of sharing all privileges equally the Lord has done this, and it's amazing in our eyes (Matthew 21:42).

In the beginning, there was a word Love, and the word Love as present with Love is wisdom. All things were made has an opposite with a purpose by Love and without Love's wisdom, not anything Joyful was made. In Love was mercy, compassion with charity, the light life of human personality kindness. Without the word Love, there is no mercy or wisdom arrested under the law, and darkness will not comprehend light dividing periods of dark time with divisions of religions day begin at sunset Friday night weekend of time and one season equals seven years turning into a darkness period. What the word Love has joined together can't no man separate, there is compassionate order wisdom liberated in trusting truth darkness conceived light unified time (John 1:1-5). Into joyful leap year calendar correction Nu Day Zero begin at sunrise Sunday morning holy communion resting first day of the new week with remembrance of the Law with thanksgiving every seven-dark season. Whoever falls on this stone will be crushed. And the stone will crush the person it falls on (Matthew 21:44). Four Blood Moon Eclipse, New Moon to New Moon phases lighting the dark night with dream and vision of the soft peaceful glow of hope "Jubilees" anniversary celebrations of independence worldwide campaign Nu Year Zero Timeout. Reconciliation Lord's Day they knew Jesus was talking about them (Matthew 21:45).

This is the celebration of history of the division of the Nu Days Zero fullness of time in the law of sunshine ray of hope in the Testimony of Jesus Christ, of the sacred events of rejoicing after the Holy Nu Year 2016 Extraordinary "Jubilee" of Mercy. "Many people are invited, but few people are chosen" (Matthew 22:14). The trumpeting sound of this one word brings hope into a spiritual action plan of all the power in heaven moving on your behalf and welfare to restore God's order be faithful here on Earth. It is very valuable as a yearlong communion Christmas and Easter Celebration all rolled up in this once-in-a-lifetime historic sacred event teach God's way as it really is. We know that you are not swayed by people's opinions, because you don't show favoritism (Matthew 22:16). It was meant to be a holy timeout celebrated every 49-50 years is sacred as a holy time of liberation, freedom and of celebration when everyone will receive a gift of time back to their original property and disowned family name. Prisoners and slaves will return home to their families; the law allows people to pay taxes or not (Matthew 22:17). Debt would be forgiven commandment to start Timeout Nu Year Zero over for keeping a zone social order of peace Zi-On. "Jubilee" universal pardon bad behavior return time back to God's original order; they should love one another, unifying hope in divine opportunities of liberty, peace, charity, made into rest healing power medicine doctrine of eternal love. Jesus replied, "Why do you test me, you hypocrites?" (Matthew 22:18).

This is how the universe works; a house divided against itself cannot stand. "Give to Caesar what belongs to Caesar and to God what belongs to God" (Matthew 22:21). I always had a funny feeling somebody or an invisible person was shadowing me trying to get my attention. We are Christian children of tomorrow, divinely fully contacted by the living word doctrine of love that quietly connects individuals peacefully together with rest healing medicine, love one by one face to face nonviolently. How do the Christian children of tomorrow peacefully teach living word medicine prescription message to the rest in unconditional love? Jesus responded, "You are wrong because you don't know either the scriptures or God's power (Matthew 22:29). Divine fully contact and correct rightfully to redemption of forgiving personality one family (nation) of peace at once trusting truth doctrine and covenant love? By simply speaking the truth to power, one right word at the right time nonviolently.

At the resurrection, people won't marry nor will they be given in marriage. Instead, they will be like angels from God (Matthew 22:30). Obeying one peaceful commandment reprogram of fear of the darkness with instructions in remedy love, divine fully praise sound like the reprogramming of a mainframe computer hard drive after a. viral attack, a time clock striking quit overtime or reset U.S. National debt clock to zero debt and sweet harmony of church bells ring on Christmas and Easter Sunday Sabbath spreading joy. He replied, "You must love the Lord your

God with all your heart, with all your being, and with all your mind" (Matthew 22:37).

"Jubilee" of divine mercy universal pardon bad behavior praise with thanks and giving from being saved off death row or going to hell. It is the one word Jesus was put to death for. This is the first and greatest commandment (Matthew 22:38). It is Ubuntu operation system humanism a programmed social order correction of therapy remembrance spiritual time, political year for the universal church and government to start over nuclear weapon free together trusting the God's spirit of love over President Donald Trump's wall of hate. And the second is like it: You must love your neighbor as you love yourself (Matthew 22:39). "Jubilee" is a privilege the wealthy does not want to share. The Lord said to my lord, 'Sit at my right side until I turn your enemies into your footstool' (Matthew 22: 44).

The Olivet Discourse

This is a special report about a holy time sacred event, not a mystery, secret holy place or scary left behind Omega Man sci-fi fiction Soylent Green story about one Bible verse sacred scroll end of last days nine harbingers blood moon guessing about something about to change blowing up the world left behind story. Blessed is he who cometh in the name of the Lord, in the clouds of heaven, and all the holy angels with him (JST Matthew 1:1). This is a memorial double budget multigenerational solution true life Democrat, Republican and Tea Party Bipartisan Mandate straight out of heaven Acts II World Peace. "Jubilee" (Party) will be the sign of your coming and the end of the age (Matthew 24:3). This one word stops you from going to hell for blowing yourself up with nuclear weapons and is why world is upside down. *You will hear about wars and reports of wars. Don't be alarmed. These things must happen, but this isn't the end yet (Matthew 24:6).* America is spiritually cracked and racially divided, World Trade Center, 9/11 violent Nine Harbinger (Omen) come to pass, and the

Liberty Bell is cracked! *This gospel of the kingdom will be proclaimed throughout the world as a testimony to all the nations. Then the end will come (Matthew 24:14).* The Liberty Bell is an iconic symbol of American independence: We the People of the United States, in Order to form a more perfect Union.

Leviticus 25:10 Jubilee Bible 2000
"And ye shall sanctify the fiftieth year and proclaim liberty throughout all the land unto all the inhabitants thereof; it shall be a jubilee unto you; and ye shall return every one unto his possession, and ye shall return each one unto his family."

How does a cracked liberty bell become the iconic symbol for a racially divided cracked nation? But for the sake of the ones whom God chose, that time will be cut short (Matthew 24:22). Because America's Preamble to the United States Constitution fundamental purposes and guiding principles was cracked from the beginning. The Liberty Bell bears a timeless message: "Proclaim liberty throughout all the land unto all the inhabitants thereof." Look, I've told you ahead of time (Matthew 24:25). Jubilee's promise guarantees future happiness and deliverance from tribulation courts have referred to it as reliable evidence of the founding fathers' intentions regarding the constitution's meaning and what they hoped the constitution would achieve that this nation under God shall have a new birth of freedom and that government of the people, by the people, for the people, shall not perish from this earth. *Then the sign of the Human One will appear in the sky. At that time all the urban tribes of the earth will be full of sadness, and they will see the Human One coming in the heavenly clouds with power and great splendor (Matthew 24:30).* Americans did not keep God's promise sharing privileges equally established justice, ensure domestic tranquility, provide for the common defense, to provide liberty is freedom from the effects of "sin, spiritual servitude to all the inhabitants 50 years after the war for independence year 1776 or the Civil War 1865.

The cracked liberty bell failure to ring is national symbol of a national failure to equally live correctly under "Jubilee" Lord's day. He will send His angels with the sound of a great trumpet, and they will gather His chosen ones from the four corners of the earth, from one end of the sky to the other (Matthew 24:31). God's privilege of sharing love equally original plan of order a horn blast of joy announcing attention year zero ensign Zi-on. "But nobody knows when that day or hour will come, not the heavenly angels and not the Son. Only the Father knows" (Matthew 24:36). God's wishes commune to live with human families (Israel) celebrating ringing First Church Unity Bell the rebirth in the hope of nuclear weapons Free Zone, New International Worldwide Campaign. As it was in the time of Noah, so it will be at the coming of the Human one sign of the Son of man (Matthew 24:37).

Preparations for the Last Supper

This is the noble beginning of divine opportunities celebrate first Passover methods Invisible person Jesus Christ "Jubilee." *The Festival of Unleavened Bread, which is called Passover, was approaching* (Luke 22:1). Ministry ensign analysis of the coming together Latter Day Saint Nu Millennium, Nu Testament Christmas to Easter story of holy communion joyful climate change weeping tears of sorrow. From seeing reporting of the breakdown of first African American United States President Barak Obama crying tears of sorrow on national television because of the flood of gun violent racial killings going on from aftermath Sandy Hook Elementary School shooting, AME Church shooting Charleston, South Carolina to San Bernardino, California terrorists attack. The chief priests and the legal experts were looking for a way to kill Jesus, because they were afraid of the people (Luke 22:2).

I cried my own tears of suffering sorrow, like Jesus wept, fighting posttraumatic stress disorder depression and mourning in this extraordinary calendar year 2016 Mandate "Jubilee," from believing the first woman president could be a United Methodist woman like my mother to hearing the trumpeting election result reporting the election of Donald Trump, the lying tweeter lesser of two evils as UNPRESIDENT OF UNITED STATES OF AMERICA, and violent flood gunshots go down that murdered one-year-old baby girl Autumn Johnson. Then, Satan entered Judas, called Iscariot, who was one of the twelve (Luke 22:3). There is no Black power when a baby is killed by a coward in her twin mother's arms, at her father and great grandmother's house four doors over on Holly Ave in Compton celestial city of Zi-On of Refugees. Witnessing seer supernatural Nu Millennial revelations descend of Holy Spirit manifesting and demonstrating trusting promise God's spirit of love the rainbow of people as it came to pass a upside down worldwide great reversal rest onto trusting the Lord Christians police their self. He went out and discussed with the chief priests and the officers of the temple guard how he could hand Jesus over to them (Luke 22:4).

The anchor of speaking one word a mandate political party year zero for governments and churches to start over "Jubilee" celebration presentation of Christmas and Easter correctly. Forerunner praying speaking truth to power one word, Four Blood Moons something changed, and my family's beautiful smile joyfully seeing the nonviolent reality of Dr. Martin Luther King, Jr.'s "I Have A Dream" speech come true. They were delighted and arranged payment for him (Luke 22:5). "Jubilee" Easter and Christmas party revival. The sounding of this one commandment foreshadows love of human kindness and nature of charity meet intervening in history peacefully. As Blood Moonlight Eclipse sunlight of transfiguration spiritual junction of heaven and Earth cornerstone to this story keyhole of ministering truth rising from the graveyard. He agreed and began looking for an opportunity to hand Jesus over to them - a time when the crowds would be absent (Luke 22:6).

From angels about remembrance memorial life victory over death changing event ahead of time before it comes down. A spiritual dissertation report explaining unlocking the trumpeting authority to sounding "Jubilee" one word over my urban tribe family Ubuntu (philosophy) humanism towards others to stop the religious violence sexism treating the drug epidemic and violent crime punishment as medical health problem. The Day of Unleavened Bread arrived, when the Passover had to be sacrificed (Luke 22:7). Becoming Nu Year Zero capstone for a nuclear weapon free Zi-On (zone) operation system correction into the Nu, Nu, Testament celebration treatment taking politics out of punishment. Because programmed calendar 2000 Nu Millennium Great "Jubilee" was not passed down correctly celebrated right is a social system failure sacred event. Jesus sent Peter and John with this task: "Go and prepare for us to eat the Passover meal (Luke 22:8). It was the highlight of Pope Saint John Paul II pontificate keystone to open new horizons in preaching to unify the Kingdom of God and President Bill Clinton acts of peace into the Middle East. A sign the next episode of God's Sabbath Ministry of tutoring mercy and compassion. They said to him, "Where do you want us to prepare it?" (Luke 22:9). Christmas Celebrating Passover Easter correctly spiritually social system keeping family church history. Tutoring charity Acts II World Peace straight out of heaven. Ubuntu (philosophy): "I am what I am because of who we all are" underpins the conceived conception of holy communion and nuclear weapon free peaceful open society Zi-On!

Jubilee: I Am Because We Are, Chapter 17, Y2K13: "I told my mother that I was going to get baptized on Easter Sunday Morning and I would like for her and my father be there. I did not want to make a big deal about it. The Holy Spirit let me know this is not about me. They told me to be bold in the spirit. I told my best friend that I was getting baptized on Easter

Sunday morning. I told him that I did want to make a big deal out of it. The Spirit told me this is about the family and the end the story, not just with myself getting baptized, but my family and nation being baptized with a gift from God- Jubilee. The next day, my best friend called me and told me that his pastor called him and told him that they need to do baptism. We took that as confirmation for both our family ministries. He was baptizing families, and I was getting baptized for my family. We both were Jubilee 50 years old" (p. 271).

When my pastor read the above paragraph, and I explained how I was drawn back from Abraham Lincoln, Nebraska with the epiphany vision to take the pictures of opposite Blood Moon eclipses through the Arch of Moorish style Temple monument to God. Jesus replied, "When you go into the city, a man carrying a water jar will meet you. Follow him to the house he enters" (Luke 22: 10). Cemetery on the 33rd parallel Masonic Bloodline of No Nuclear Weapons Free Zone at the same spot for the front and back cover of this book from a peaceful dream in a cemetery to hearing a prophet blow a shofar ram horn in a church service, making my heart cry jubilee like a born-again child of God spiritual change me to love the church like I love my family and country, he asked me if I was a prophet. I said, "No. Say to the owner of the house, 'The teacher says to you, "Where is the guestroom where I can eat the Passover meal with my disciples?"' (Luke 22:11). There is only one living prophet today: Jesus Christ and the Holy Spirit, ministry order "Jubilee." I am a repair mechanic. I can discern how the nuts and bolts of a thing works doing preventive war maintenance, with the talent to repair heavy equipment from reading repair manuals. "Jubilee" is calendar scheduled preventive maintenance to stop nuclear war. He will show you a large upstairs room, already furnished. Make preparations there" (Luke 22:12). Keeping a zone of social order and society of peace like daylight saving or leap year time zone correction. Reading the King James Bible is simple like doing math or repair work; if you are confused at the beginning of the problem, you will be confused at end of problem. They went and found everything just as he had told them, and they prepared the Passover meal (Luke 22:13).

Pre-scientists studied and reported on a life climate changing event before it came to pass in remembrance the spiritual accountant Enoch Administrator who was a biblical economist dividing history into periods or "Jubilees" of 49 years, lived 365 solar calendar years, wrote the Book of Economic "Jubilee" that is not in the King James Bible. When the time came, Jesus took his place at the table, and the apostles joined him (Luke 22:14). It explains the solar-based calendar and more accurately represents the 49 years and provided for a better understanding of prophecy. Passover walked with God saying the Lord cometh with ten thousand of his saints. "Jubilee" reset order back to God's time. He said to them, "I have earnestly desired to eat this Passover with you before I suffer (Luke 22:15).

This is not a coincidence; there are no accidents; this prophecy program system failure is why the Acts of 9/11 terrorism, 2008 Capitalism Stock Market drop, Child Abuse Pope Benedict XVI resign option, 2013 President Executive Order 13653 Climate Change Action Plan, Pope Francis sounding spiritual climate atmosphere change cultural balance reconciliation starting 2015 visit Cuba, United States White House and the 2016 "Extraordinary "Jubilee" of Divine Mercy" World Grassroots Peace correction of life celebration trumpeting Election of President Donald Trump inauguration address child born again from the wind-swept plain of Nebraska and urban sprawls Detroit never again be ignored promise. I tell you, I won't eat it until it is fulfilled in God's kingdom" (Luke 22:16).

I said you appointed me Sexton physician unto the church accountable for scared objects overseer keeping my family church hearing reporting specified fact into word pictures of opposite or scenes seen in the mind's natural eye wonders of future God's plans of salvation of heaven and hell as one place: Earth. After taking a cup and giving thanks, he said, "Take this and share it among yourselves (Luke 22:17). I told him my born-again friends call me "Jubilee" Watchman sounding awaking alarm to stop the passing down of Muslim religion Isis Islam Holy State of radical mind eye for eye, tooth for tooth revenge violent and sexist statute way of thinking its right to disown or kill your own child for not believing in your religion arranged marriages Sharia law way of thinking. I tell you that from now on I won't drink from the fruit of the vine until God's kingdom has come" (Luke 22:18). This is a celestial fight between opposite forces spiritual revolution of believers divided in the promises of God's doctrine and covenants holy days are Passover and everybody wins.

Where the promise of men's violent tradition and weapons right to keep and bear arms statute holiday ritual for citizenship is passed down with winner and losers. After taking the bread and giving thanks, he broke it and gave it to them, saying, "This is my body, which is given for you. Do this in remembrance of me" (Luke 22:19). Moreover, you can't bring an Atom bomb to a spiritual fight. It is a Passover celebration of history called for the great divide Universal Church Choir to gather together from the four-wind singing by the rising of the moon unify amazement grace promises of God's favor mercy and forgiveness of sin peaceful nonviolent eternal Christmas to Easter revival. In the same way, he took the cup after the meal and said, "This cup is the new covenant by my blood, which is poured out for you" (Luke 22: 20).

It is a call to action like Paul Revere alerting the approach of the British Red Coats at the opening of the American Revolutionary War when shots were heard around the world. "But look! My betrayer is with me; his hand is on this table" (Luke 22:21). This a word to be sonic boom heard around the world opening Constitution Convention to add an amendment creating a double budget one to be pay off by the Elder War Generation Bill and one paid by the Younger Peace Generation Affordable Care Act Fifty Years Church and State Start Over "Jubilee" Ubuntu Diplomacy Ambassadors of Reconciliation Unity. "The Human One[a] goes just as it has been determined. But how terrible it is for that person who betrays him" (Luke 22:22).

President Nelson Mandela used Passover to stop the violence call of forgiveness, unity, social holiness justice and liberation. Secretary of State Hillary Clinton's foundation takes a village, turning violent prisons into hospitals, treating violent inmates and drug crimes as a medical problem under Affordable Care Act and transferring politics of punishment from Justice Department Federal BOP into US Dept. Health creating hospitals taking profit out of prisons. We must learn to work together bring the medical hospital, court judges, and church family to the table. They began to argue among themselves about which of them it could possibly be who would do this (Luke 22:23). It is a pyramid three-sided Nobel peace prize approach to the problem.

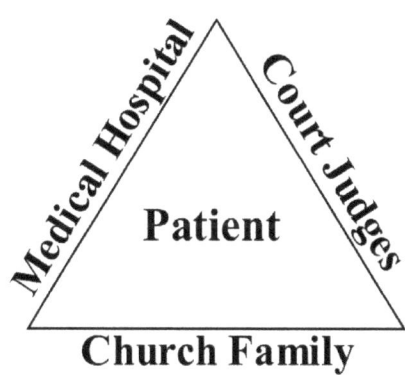

The Last Supper

Under prison to hospital approach prisoner become patient under court supervision indefinitely until declared righteous be two of the three, church and family bring God spiritual Foundation to the pyramid approach with doctors' medical health care on one side and court judges supervising on the other. An argument broke out among the disciples over which one of them should be regarded as the greatest (Luke 22:24). One cannot do it without the other. Ubuntu (Philosophy) diplomacy spiritual exodus humanity toward others I am my brother's and sister's keeper straight out of heaven. Like Rastafarian Reggae singer Bob Marley singing about Three Little Birds singing "don't worry about anything," everything little going to be all right, and Exodus God moving onto the people freeing them from Capitalism economic inequality, spiritual revolution get up, stand up, for your right's, do not give up the fight.

The glorified message of the Cross's shadow as a natural tool for keeping time records intersection bridging generation to generation over trouble deep waters. Becoming a spiritual door stairway to heaven Passover past sin crossing over without dying to the promise land Zi-On social order of peace zone. But Jesus said to them, "The kings of the Gentiles rule over their subjects, and those in authority over them are called 'friends of the people" (Luke 22:25). "Jubilee" Universal Pardon bad behavior and traditions teardown walls of division turning the World Paul and Silas turned upside down right upside. "Jubilee" repairs the racial crack in America and the Liberty Bell. Building bridges of unity through Education stopping all fear from the pass down culture of white Supremacy Crackers hater's eating and feeding off cyber tree of social media good and evil confusion Rush Limbaugh All Right misinformation end of dark bad time Apocalypse Nuclear war prediction. I tell you, I won't eat it until it is fulfilled in God's kingdom" (Luke 22:16). Of historical 1900's World Wars Disaster dark nuclear war holocaust destruction of human life event from forever again repeating. Releasing all crisscrossed-up hearts and mind to Passover spiritually climate change plan of action into a Web of faith Nuclear Weapon free Zi-On. After taking a cup and giving thanks, he said, "Take this and share it among yourselves (Luke 22:17).

Ending spiritual hang-ups from all pass down War debt and the threat of Nuclear World War III. Tradition of Ubuntu (Philosophy) "Jubilee" of Divine Mercy Universal pardon bad behavior release to God passing over vindicate everybody. It is Universal True Justice from all our past sinful behavior and fear dark bad Nuclear War desires. Releasing passing over everyone too their divine destiny of human-ness oneness (Holiness) with

God washing your feet. Now this was the custom of the Jews under their law; wherefore, Jesus did this that the law might be fulfilled (JST John 13:10).

It's a gift emancipation exemption from punishment of crime or sins like Conscientious Objection exempt for those who oppose "participation in all Political wars is release from Military Serves. Having loved his own who were in the world, he loved them fully (John 13:1). "Jubilee" Universal Pardon is a reward citizenship to D.E.C.A. Dreamer you can't hold the sin of a parent over a Child. It is old testament Nu Law get out of Jail and War card free it sets a Supreme Court president. Muhammad Ali's vs. United States: Greatest public Fight against Vietnam war that was not against a man and Nelson Mandela fight against apartheid, a promise of I Am Prepared to die too Ubuntu (Humanness) forgiveness Peace to nonviolently bring healing from God to renew South Africa. He said to them, "Do you know what I've done for you?" (John 13:12). His Government focused on dismantling the legacy of apartheid by tackling institutionalized racism and fostering racial reconciliation.

It is better than finding a Gold Nugget Treasure on the reality television show Gold Rush or celebrating winning the Power Ball Lottery. It is charity joyful giving from the heart. You call me 'Teacher' and 'Lord,' and you speak correctly, because I am (John 13:13). Not about having expensive heavy equipment putting men life at risk to work digging in a glory hole hopping for good luck to buy a piece of expensive jewelry to be passed down. Charity is glory a gift reward divine opportunity of mercy and compassion from living word God. If I, your Lord and teacher, have washed your feet, you too must wash each other's feet (John 13:14). Not for our meanness bitter violent unfaithfulness will to destroy the world. Charity is God's will by keeping their nonviolent word being obedient dedicated faithfulness passing over to us. It is God celebrating the Sabbath's sabbath. God is required to keep the Law. I have given you an example: Just as I have done, you also must do (John 13:15).

All we must do is sound the Commandment "Jubilee": universal pardon bad behavior is very valuable political commanded too occur every fiftieth calendar year, in which church and state government is required to start over correctly. Slaves and prisoners would be nonviolently freed return to family. I assure you, servants aren't greater than their master, nor are those who are sent greater than the one who sent them (John 13:16). Debts would be forgiven the mercies of God's word of wisdom; first fruit wonders would be particularly manifest and demonstrated passing over all. And I confer royal power on you just as my Father granted royal power to me (Luke 22:29). "Jubilee" double blesses you for free, what you pay tithes for and the society that you voted for. Extraordinary signs of responsibility peacefully stopping violent bad behavior protest. Thus, you will eat and drink at my table in my kingdom, and you will sit on thrones overseeing the twelve tribes of Israel (Luke 22:30).

That They All May Be One

This is the shameful Millennium Nu, Nu, beginning testament Easter to Christmas conception story how the Holy Spirit conceived in my born-again spiritual personality heart and mind straightway, passing over correction onto me with deliverance from being violently self-centered hating off the Internet web of weaponizes misinformation matrix of anti-truth. I'm not speaking about all of you. I know those whom I've chosen. But this is to fulfill the scripture (John 13:18). Instant forgiving and tutoring me to grow together Passover spiritually into a web of faith in prayer into a choice seer of things afar-off. New beginning year Zero modern revelation from end Negus (King) ministry in mercy, for my mourning and suffering sorrow of selfish unfaithfulness.

Renewing my unfaithful heart of stone with faithful heart of joy and comforting arm of protection from my grandparents' praying loving personalities, rescuing me from my antichrist violent self. "I'm telling you this now, before it happens, so that when it does happen you will believe that I Am" (John 13:19). Like the great story of Jonah rescued by a great huge fish to give a short message of destruction to an anti-God great city in good times. Like Jonah, I was saved by a great anti-God state of mind. "I assure you that whoever receives someone I send receives me, and whoever receives me receives the one who sent me" (John 13:19). I am sent to cry one word in dark times to an antichrist violent great nation, celestial city of Compton city of refugees to stop the violence and to write this good-times great story never told city upon a hill Zi-On.

This is not a violent story about Blair Witch Project or a great party with alcoholic spirits going on over here on holy ground for three days with the roof on fire or a funeral party over there on scared phantasm ground where ghosts burnt the house down. Jesus was deeply disturbed and testified, "I assure you, one of you will betray me" (John 13:21). This is not just another cleverly invented Christmas birthday or Easter death story. This is a Millennium Nu, Nu Testament about advent returning of Jesus Christ mother's immaculate conception, conceived his birth with his communion at death back into the original Christmas to Easter story of Passover. One of the disciples, the one whom Jesus loved, was at Jesus' side (John 13:23).

His personal appearance was changed into a glorified form on monument praising God April 4, 2015. Transfiguration birth of the first church year Zero, his spiritual resurrection on Easter Passover. Sunday morning seven weeks after Passover Act II Pentecost peaceful flood terrific wind sunlight dancing in all the color of Fire and Blood Moon eclipse. No one sitting at the table understood why Jesus said this to him (John 13: 28). Shadow of Holy Ghost passing over from pass radical violent tradition and sexism nasty rituals to peaceful baptizes celebration becoming born again personality of children of tomorrow God atonement washing away sin. The apostles' accounts 2016 year ago on top Mount Tabor witnessing Jesus talking to the prophet Moses and Elijah begins to shine transfiguration into great understanding the light radiant glory Christ power not to die but give permission to ministering angels to call people onto following Christ's mission. If God has been glorified in him, God will also glorify the Human One[c] in himself and will glorify him immediately (John 13:32). Drawing recreating and bringing past and present, loving me into crying and shouting like my grandson, sucking his thumb, signaling sounding the alarm "Jubilee" a commandment for a spiritual revolution by God, a nonviolent order for celebration for the universal church family and state to start over like the reassurance of reconciliation you get after a I.R.S. audit.

Then, take two pictures through the capstone of the three great power transfigured by one light of the invisible man Jesus Christ's shadow risen from the dead in Christ from my backyard Hollywood location landmark Angeles Abbey Cemetery contains examples of Byzantine, Moorish and Spanish architectural style. "Where I'm going, you can't come?" (John 13:33). The cemetery houses tens of thousands dead Christian souls and was built in 1923 and survived the 1933 Long Beach earthquake! 2016 years ago on Mount Tabor of transfiguration peaceful event marked a sign from heaven at ground zero for birth of New Testament church to create a great crack in families and radical violent dark world legions religions northern legions fighting southern legions fighting eastern legions and fighting western legions over bringing Passover first fruit Sunday morning offering going to the New Jerusalem Church not the nasty unsacred temple marketing system that sacrifices animals house of merchandise and den of thieves.

"I give you a new commandment: Love each other. Just as I have loved you, so you also must love each other (John 13:34). Opposites of Blood Moon through the ancient arch symbol of Jesus Christ sacrifice for us Nu, Nu Jerusalem birthing a Nu Compton year Zero they are on opposite sides of the world on the 330-parallel zone of peace God want our heart and mind suffering sorrow to be our first fruit offering on Sunday morning the first day of the week. This is how everyone will know that you are my disciples, when you love each other" (John 13:35). God wants to be our climate change plan of action in our personality Nu, Nu, Testament. God does not need our cash change or pass down violent traditions of confederate legions to a flag.

Matthew 17:9
"And as they came down from the mountain, Jesus commanded them, saying, 'Tell the vision to no man, until the Son of man be risen again from the dead'."

Lord Day is Nu Millennium a period of time Passover; there are no secrets or mysteries; there is no suffering or sorrow; judgment is for eternal rewards at the already realized heavenly enthronement of the Jesus. "Lord, where are you going" Jesus answered, "Where I am going, you can't follow me now, but you will follow later?" (John 13:36). ceremonial law the moon, the church for the front and back cover of this book. A quiet storm Act II world peace event, reflecting transfiguration light clearly showed that the law and the prophets must give way to Jesus of peace. The color of blood with the sweet smell of peace in the air before it happens historical twofold Blood Moon eclipse prophecy. "Lord, why can't I follow you now? I'll give up my life for you?" (John 13:37). Write this Millennium Christmas to Easter story about a straight out of heaven grassroots stop the violent celebration of peace sounding of God's commandment and the anointed spiritual breath of fresh air sweet smell excellent movement of Holy Spirit's shadow walking tutoring understanding confidence truth passing over onto the nonviolent people. Jesus replied, "Will you give up your life for me? I assure you that you will deny me three times before the rooster crows" (John 13:38). Tutoring peaceful truth every step, every word, every moment, every sign from Heaven.

Acts 2:20 Jubilee Bible 2000
"The sun shall be turned into darkness, and the moon into blood before that great and notable day of the Lord shall come."

Not like Jonah who protested and hated the great city walk halfway warned of end of good time's destruction. "Don't be troubled. Trust in God (John 14:1). Trust also in me. "Jubilee" emancipation ends dark bad times giving liberation gifts of freedom reward celebrating Christmas to Pentecost transfiguration lighting the center of the world way into New Millennium Era beginnings for a nonviolent fresh start. Great-dedicated men violently laid down their life to make this nation great. My Father's house has room to spare. If that weren't the case, would I have told you that I'm going to prepare a place for you (John 14:2)? President Abraham Lincoln's Gettysburg Address mark a turn in the violent past Civil War for unity. I loved growing up in the great city of Compton during violent bad times. When I go to prepare a place for you, I will return and take you to be with me so that where I am you will be too (John 14:3). We were raised to believe everything is going to be all right, to continue the fight and have the vision eyes on the prizes and dream of seeing the nonviolence reality of Dr. Martin Luther King, Jr. "I Have a Dream" speech coming true, giving liberty and freeing everyone equally before it was celebrated as a national holiday King's birthday. You know the way to the place I'm going" (John 14:4). You cannot fight or bomb Isis Islam state of mind of violence with force of peace until it is labeled.

Just like commandment for the attacks on dark day 9/11 acts of destruction violence became ground zero for terrorism Isis Islamic state of violence mind eye for eye that brought the World Trade Center down. "Lord, we don't know where you are going. How can we know the way?" (John 14:5). The word "Jubilee" restores and is a commandment for peace, straight out of heaven acts of mercy becoming year Zero for turning the other cheek pardon bad behavior turning the underworld right side up creating nuclear weapon free Zi-On. Jesus answered, "I am the way, the truth, and the life. No one comes to the Father except through me (John 14:6). Basically "Jubilee" party is simple a noble old, Old Testament ideal ordinance for the Nu, Nu Testament Generation rethinking church can happen anywhere united methods Jesus Christ Ministry guarantee living into a nuclear weapon free future time zone.

I always had a peaceful talent, lighten shy uncommon proud smart sailor's mouth way of not obeying following the Golden Rule doing what I was supposed to do I falsely identified my life from hearing confusion about biting off apple tree of misunderstanding, wrestling with the word Love. I will ask the Father, and he will send another Companion, who will be with you forever (John 14:16). Like Jonah, a sailor on a ship in a great storm, trying to escape a divine opportunity mission remembrance. Celebrating acts of war in the military with Fourth of July fireworks, superstitious holiday like Halloween or witnessing dark underworld news cycles harbinger violent radical sexual events. Fearing the weather climate change, smelling rain in the air, misunderstanding spiritual climate change out of balance from the living word Love (God) of grace, not right dividing family keeping bad time called Search Engine Driven Mentality Disorder of terror fellowship.

This Companion is the Spirit of Truth, whom the world can't receive because it neither sees him nor recognizes him. You know him, because he lives with you and will be with you (John 14:17). Repeating or reposting hateful words misinformation from commercial driven Internet service search engine that causes a person to become violently afraid. Judging and ending how I appeared in matrix sun and moon cycle of light, as I am watchman sounding the alarm. I never was a follower of the light from sound of this commandment Love. "I won't leave you as orphans. I will come to you" (John 14:18). It tells the age I am in, dividing blood moon to new moon, shooting star night from sun day, creating calendar of ten commandments for keeping holy time. I had felt feelings of influence that I am somebody from the sound commandment Love; hearing the commandment Love was trying to propose to me and engage me through this light of Love. I made myself holy on their behalf so that they also would be made holy in the truth (John 17:19).

Protecting me from the giant image of my own violent twisted double minded one-way wrong way of bad thinking about Ubuntu (philosophy) being a loving human being. The White/Black male/female dividing me on the far-side from God. Wasting time eating tender leaves from one barren fig fruit tree of social media dead work. Like a caterpillar not understanding who it is, with a tattoo of a beautiful black butterfly on its back, not knowing freedom comes from understanding who you are. I pray they will be one, Father, just as you are in me and I am in you. I pray that they also will be in us, so that the world will believe that you sent me (John 17:21). Sent earmarked in the spirit of time for fulfillment of a divine opportunity mission. Elijah the prophet called fire down on the false prophets for doing the same things today- misleading the people. I've given them the glory that you gave me so that they can be one just as we are one (John 17:24). "Jubilee" sound for celebration, mercy, and forgiveness to conceive one commandment from a cocoon of God's loving family trees of life into colorful butterfly effect love.

One of the biggest and wisest lessons I had to learn as a born-again man-child in the promise land to hear God's wisdom in the spirit of truth as a seer of supernatural revelations upside down underworld through the peacefulness pain of humility in my loving mother's pretty brown eyes. I'm in them and you are in me so that they will be made perfectly one. Then the world will know that you sent me and that you have loved them just as you loved me (John 17:23). Giving me the words wisdom to see and smell the world right side up at peace to write this story glorifying the Lord crying.

This is the joyful beginning of telling the story on how the rapture matrix already has started, having people choosing to give their heart and mind and become born again into Zi-On kingdom of love after Great Jubilee 2000 celebration, trusting God. Father, I want those you gave me to be with me where I am. Then they can see my glory, which you gave me because you loved me before the creation of the world (John 17:24). The underworld economic middle-class families have vanished into two inequality parties: The Have and The Have Nots. There are upper non-working-class Republicans that can afford family health care; they don't have to work. They, the Haves, passed down family inheritance. "Righteous Father, even the world didn't know you, but I've known you, and these believers know that you sent me" (John 17:25).

And there are lower poverty working class Democrat families, the Have Nots, that can't afford family health care. They do not qualify, have pre-existing conditions, and must work because lost or stolen family identity and bad credit scores. This represents capitalism inheritance inequalities. The middle-class working family became born again, passing over into Zi-On culture of charity zone, giving from their heart and mind peacefully sharing. They volunteer their free good time, working for Zi-On God's kingdom of heaven freely sharing and donating their wealth equally within the charity zone. It is an invisible economy that the underworld cannot tax. "I've made your name known to them and will continue to make it known so that your love for me will be in them, and I myself will be in them" (John 17:26). It is good talents of grace providing their daily bread, healing, and blessing the spiritually poor to keep the family's church. God does not care about your tithes; after 2016 years, Jesus wants your heart and mind.

Gethsemane

I never called myself a writer or rap artist using bad words rapping about party times in pair of good shoes and expensive outfit that had the talent for telling a story with no unity saying it like that, this is the way it is. Jesus and his disciples came to a place called Gethsemane. Jesus said to them, "Sit here while I pray" (Mark 14:32). I was a hard worker that enjoyed being a help and hard player having fun celebrating not always following the Golden Rule or the status quo. I was not like the other boys playing with broken heart like they broken toys and throwing stone breaking hearts, blocking people out of my life. He took Peter, James, and John along with him. He began to feel despair and was anxious (Mark 14:33). I was a nigga with an attitude, straight out of Compton, before the gangster rap album and million dollar hit movie and Boys 'n the Hood. On the rap song Californication Love, "Jubilee" is the one word Tupac Shakur prophesied Negus (King) would sound change in the world from Long Beach Boulevard and Rosecrans Ave., like gang banging and hip-hop gangster rap changed the underworld.

Doctrine & Covenants 45:3-5

Listen to him who is the advocate with the father, who is pleading your cause before him saying: father, behold the sufferings and death of him who did no sin, in whom thou wast well pleased; behold the blood of the Son which was shed, the blood of him whom thou gavest that thyself might be, glorified; wherefore, father, spare these my brethren that believe on my name, that they may come unto me and have everlasting.

I never capitalized or made money from identifying myself as a Piru or a Super Crip, with hand signs, talking using slang words like Blood or Cuzz, set trip off colors red and blue, promoted thug life or gang bang. He said to them, "I'm very sad. It's as if I'm dying. Stay here and keep alert" (Mark 14: 34). I am a good kid M.a.a.d. city who lived, played in alley ways, worked manual labor in dirt, grime and crime. I am that mortal man loud mouth Negus (King) that is over thirty years old that Tupac Shakur was talking about on Kendrick Lamar's *To Pimp A Butterfly* album fighting spiritual war (Jihad) within myself with a force of peace, mercy and compassion walking to church. Then he went a short distance farther and fell to the ground. He prayed that, if possible, he might be spared the time of suffering (Mark 14:35). I have no tattoos on my body or wear any piercing rings. To show, my joy I smile. Educated as a New Deal Roosevelt roughrider, Whaley Worrier, Eastside Compton Rancho Dominguez Don (Lord). I volunteered my life a private First Class in the California National Guard, Able Seaman

U. S. American Continual Navy Military service and was appointed Vice President of First United Methodist Men Church Compton Sexton where I clean demons from the church. He said, "Abba, Father, for you all things are possible. Take this cup of suffering away from me. However-not what I want but what you want (Mark 14:36). I am born on King Day of Peace January IXX, reverse day of dark day IX/XI, trained to urban street fight terrorism kill or be killed with the speaking sound force of a church bell ringing peacefully harmony.

On March 7, 2015 Los Angeles Silhouettes of Kappa Alpha Psi Fraternity, Inc. Peter Butler Family Foundation spotlighting past, present, and future black achievers at the Kappa Kastle, Crenshaw Blvd was my first public presentation as an author: "Jubilee": I Am Because We Are 50 Anniversary of Bloody Sunday Selma, Alabama. The time has come for the Human One to be betrayed into the hands of sinners (Mark 14:41). VII days later on March Friday the Thirteen 2015, the second Anniversary of Pope Francis the calls for Extraordinary "Jubilee" of Mercy-mercy announcement world event Acts II World Peace, on November Friday the Thirteen 2015 the Paris terrorist attack event was an evil Isis Islam state of mind act of war. Get up! Let's go! Look, here comes my betrayer" (Mark 14:42). Arrested and sentenced to federal prison made me a bigger consumer that did not spiritually change me for acts as rich young ruler acting poor with a violent gangster ride or die attitude not scared to do what it does.

The Arrest of Jesus

I am a shot caller, never been shot at or stabbed. I did not honor my grandparents by going to church or believe in understand the faith healing authority of the King James Bible peace. Who is Jesus, God's son; because we don't have a high priest who can't sympathize with our weaknesses but instead one who was tempted in every way that we are, except without sin (Hebrew 4:15). I supported abortions, sacrificing children to my Baal god. I walked in the rhythm, grooved to sound riding high on the P-Funk mothership, party animal dancing with drunk super freaks demons drinking with dead alcoholic spirits members at Legion Freemason, Legion Elks, Legion Veterans of Foreign Wars Lodges, and After Hour Legion Motorcycle Clubs. I followed the signs of astrology, read horoscopes, watched pornographic movies, did not eat pork, sex without marriage, have children out of wedlock. Finally, let's draw near to the throne of favor with confidence so that we can receive mercy and find grace when we need help (Hebrew 4:16). When I was unfaithful, I did the unforgiveable with Christian women of faith in my marriage; I was forgiven. My wife claims my love I showed my younger first cousin and her children the same age as her oldest daughter was inappropriate, unhealthy and disrespectful to her marriage made her see my cousin as my other woman.

Christ's agony in the Garden is unfathomable by finite mind, both as to intensity and cause. He struggled and groaned under a burden such as no other being who has ever lived on the earth might even conceive as possible. It was not physical pain or mental anguish alone that caused him to suffer such torture as to produce an extrusion of blood from every pore, but a spiritual agony of soul such as only God was capable of experiencing. In that hour of anguish, Christ met and overcame all the horrors that Satan, the Prince of this world, could inflict.
James Talmage, Jesus The Christ

It was when I was asked to join and become a member of the Legion Freemason the anointed sweet smell Holy Spirit feet came straightway onto me like a soft breath of fresh air with comforting joyful understanding. Look, the time has come for the Human One to be betrayed into the hands of sinners (Matthew 26:45). Like a thief showing up in the midnight and a treasured expensive perfume oil smell that never left me telling me to be not afraid get up standup and be a man. Negus is a royal title in the Ethiopian Semitic languages. It denotes a monarch such as in pre-1974

Ethiopia. The title has subsequently been used to translate the words "king" or "emperor" in biblical and other literature.

I Nephi 19:8-9
And behold he cometh according to the words of the angel, in six hundred years from the time my father left Jerusalem. And the world, because of their iniquity, shall judge him to be a thing of naught; wherefore they scourge him, and he suffereth it and they smite him, and he suffereth it. Yea, they spit upon him, and he suffereth it, because of his long-suf-fering towards the children of men.

You cannot serve two masters Negus (King); you belong to God. Get up. Let's go. Look, here comes my betrayer" (Matthew 25:46). I begged God for forgiveness and said I am sorrowful for not understanding. God of compassion commanded me to be obedient, peaceful, start over with real heart repentance, changing the way I think peacefully. With thanksgiving Jesus Christ, praising, singing heart songs, Love Amazing Grace for saving a wretch like me peacefully. Blessing me with the start of my family foundation and wife, praying for a miracle, of family working together in peace, celebrating peaceful healing in my marriage trusting Love. They had been sent by the chief priests and elders of the people (Matthew 26:47). With Christmas presents, tree and lights on the house was when my wife and my first cousin gossiped to my family that my father was unethical and spoke inappropriately and sexually to her.

People in my family said I was crazy because my mourning broken heart did not want to divide my family; working together with instant forgiveness, we could do anything. His betrayer had given them a sign: "Arrest the man I kiss" (Matthew 26:48). My ex-wife said I was acting too good, acting like a Black Jesus straight out of Compton. She lied about how much money was in her saving accounts and swore out protection order warrant in court, saying she was afraid. She said I had a nervous breakdown, and that I was trying to brainwash her into believing in Jesus Christ. She had me escorted out of my own home by two white armed police officers the day after our ninth wedding anniversary. Just then he came to Jesus and said, "Hello, Rabbi." Then, he kissed him (Matthew 26:49). We got a divorce on the morning of tenth anniversary of the day and time that we first met. I was told to just get over it by my first cousin who was divorced three times, and said she was happy her brother's wife had received her divorce. "Friend, do what you came to do." Then they came and grabbed Jesus and arrested him (Matthew 26:50). She was celebrating on the day of my divorce, seating on my couch, while lying and going out with my ex-wife to the Legion Freemason 357 Club.

No man knows how bad he is until he tried very hard to be good. A silly idea is current that good people do not know what temptation means. This is an obvious lie. Only those who try to resist temptation know how strong it is, after all, you find out the strength of the German army after fighting against it, not by giving in. You find out the strength of a wind by walking against it, not by lying down. A man who gives into temptation after five minutes simply does not know what it would have been like an hour later. That is why bad people, in one sense, know very little about badness. They've always lived a sheltered life by always giving in. We never find out the strength of the evil impulse inside us until we try to fight it. And Christ, because he was the only man who to the full what temptation really means.
C.S. Lewis, Mere Christianity

I was not engaged or focused being the entire natural alpha male my brown eyes can see. One of those with Jesus reached for his sword. Striking the high priest's slave, he cut off his ear (Matthew 26:51). I am a troubled hearted man under the spiritual security shadow of King David Royal Guard, wisdom of King Solomon to judge truth, authority of King James

Bible Law of Moses to wrestle with God myself. I am salty, spiritually poor hung-over off balance over sensitive afraid and ashamed to cry like a baby.

As I have read this account, my heart goes out to Peter. So many of us are so much like him. We pledge our loyalty; we affirm our determination to be of good courage; we declare, sometimes even publicly, that come what may we will do the right thing that we will stand for the right cause, that we will be true to ourselves and to others. Then the pressures begin to build. Sometimes these are social pressures. Sometimes they are personal appetites there is a softening of discipline. There is capitulation. And then there is remorse, followed by self-accusation and bitter tears of regret. One of the great tragedies we witness almost daily is the tragedy of men of high aim and low achievement.
Gordon Hinckley

Divine opportunity destiny appointment in time is that passion for methods of Jesus Christ I am feeling knowing God died on the cross, seat throne of mercy for my interest. Then Jesus said to him, "Put the sword back into its place. All those who use the sword will die by the sword" (Matthew 26:52). When I am sitting on Sunday morning in church, keeping family church, the minister's sermon reveals directly to me about secret matters on my heart and mind. In bad times, only God and I knew that I was going on in my crossed-up family heart twisted mind. Or do you think that I'm not able to ask my Father and he will send to me more than twelve battle groups of angels right away? (Matthew 26:53). I could turn to no one else or do nothing about it. I feel that she, the minister, is praying in tongue utterance for my peace deliverance talking only to my crossed-up heart's passion methods of Jesus Christ "Jubilee" ministry Love one, two, one face to face. That day, the sermon was like from a mountain top about the voice of God's love and truth grace-grace sacred secret methods of Jesus Christ "Jubilee" ministry blown sounding global spiritual climate change of balance in time. But if I did that, how would the scriptures be fulfilled that say this must happen? (Matthew 26:54).

"Jubilee" unicorn horn blast of mercy-mercy moving like the blowing Santa Ana winds, calling on his followers to renew broken hardened crossed up heart, commanding to start over ordering all to instant forgiveness of all debt. Day after day, I sat in the temple teaching, but you didn't arrest me (Matthew 26:55). Great commission under a purpose driven life God's love grace-grace face of mercy-mercy instant forgiveness of all debt will be our heart's prosperity. The face of God appears to me when I conceived in my heart the song I heard with fresh air smell of peace, thanksgiving and light taste of communion, in remembrance testament of the love God's oil mercy instant forgiven me. But all this has happened so that what the prophets said in the scriptures might be fulfilled" (Matthew 26:56). I was inspired freed from spiritual hang-ups stubborn way of thinking by the sound hymnal song of glories living word of great wisdom love sorrow and mercy peace this day I started to cry like a baby. He entered that area and sat outside with the officers to see how it would turn out (Matthew 26:58). It was a peaceful act of God's love and eye of mercy right on time at the end of a bad dark period before lighting a new beginning of sorrow point in my born again renewed soft heart's song keeping family church life revival.

Much of the criticism of Simon Peter is centered in his denial of his acquaintance with the Master. This has been labeled 'cowardice.' Are we sure of his motive in that recorded denial? He had already given up his occupation and placed all worldly goods on the alter for the cause. Is it conceivable that the omniscient Lord would give all theses powers and keys to one who is a failure or unworthy? If Peter was frightened in the court when he denied his association with the Lord how brave he was hours earlier when he drew his sword keys to one who is a failures or unworthy? If Peter was frightened in the court when he denied his association with the Lord, how brave he was hours earlies when he drew his sword against an overpowering enemy, the night mob, later defying the people and state and church officials he boldly charged 'him ye have taken and wicked hands have crucified and slain' (Acts 2: 23). To the astounded populace at the healing of the cripple at the gate beautiful he exclaimed, 'Ye men of Israel, the God of our fathers hath glorified his son Jesus, whom ye delivered up and denied him in the presence of Pilate. Ye denied the holy one and killed the Prince of life whom God hath raised up from the dead whereof we are witnesses.' Does this portray cowardice? Quite a bold assertion for a timid one. Remember that Peter never denied the divinity of Christ, he only denied his association or acquaintance with Christ, which is quite a different matter. Is it possible that there might have been some other reason for Peter's triple denial? Could he have felt that circumstance justified expediency? When he bore a strong testimony in Caesarea Philippi, he had been told that 'they should tell no mam that he was Jesus the Christ.'

Spencer W. Kimball

The Trial and Crucifixion

The methods of Jesus Christ Jubilee ministry as a child couldn't be found with his family doing what his mother told him to do. Mary and Joseph had to returned to old Jerusalem where they last saw him three days earlier during the Passover feast. The legal experts and the elders had gathered there (Matthew 26:57). They found their son in the temple, teaching and studying facts and doctrinal covenants with the teacher and doctors of the temple. When asked why he was not doing what his mother told him to do but was divided from the family, he responded with sound doctrine of compassion and sorrow, receiving instant forgiveness. "I find no legal basis for action against this man" (Luke 23:4). That he was being about dividing times of darkness not family to building Nu Jerusalem church setting the cornerstone planting his father's business. Revealing the nonviolent creation of the kingdom of heaven on Earth, showing God's healing, peaceful, sorrow, mercy and love.

> Luke 2:49 Jubilee Bible 2000 (JUB)
> *"And he said unto them, 'How is it that ye sought me? Knew ye not that it behooves me to be about my Father's business?'"*

The methods of Jesus Christ Jubilee ministry in the Old Testament prophecy is simple; the New Testament prophecy concealed in ancient scriptures scrolls passed down through bad dark customs violence and sex of slavery, blood covenant by not watching out and working together with trusting God. Starting from Galilee all the way here (Luke 23:5). "The bricks have fallen down, but we will rebuild with hewn stones; The sycamores are cut down, but we will replace them with cedars." God's prophet Isaiah, warning of violent punishment removing God's protection treatment (Isaiah 9:10). Making their own self prisons, protection armor, sword and shield, turning God into an instrument, weapon of war, celebrating violent acts of war, hung-up on wrong philosophy intellectualism and vain deceit of keeping their own methods of torture and cruel unusual punishment. Hearing this, Pilate asked if the man was a Galilean (Luke 23:6). Traditions of men and holidays family customs laws not being sorrowful, superstitious days, i.e. Friday the XIII or Halloween celebration for doing evil is anti-truth.

The methods of Jesus Christ "Jubilee" ministry is nonviolent, anti-war, anti-slavery, anti-debt anti-discrimination (John 6:66). The New Testament translation prophecy is the Old Testament prophecy revealed philosophy of grace-grace. When he learned that Jesus was from Herod's district who was also in Jerusalem at that appointed time (Luke 23:7). The character of a Methodist of Jesus Christ "Jubilee" ministry is charity God's love peacefully lighting moving stop the violence. Delivering instant forgiveness on individuals one by one, face to face, as one who really believes and lives the nonviolent common principles charity of Christianity: "the Spirit of the

Lord is upon me, because he hath anointed me to preach the gospel to the poor; he hath sent me to heal the brokenhearted, to preach deliverance to the captives, and recovering of sight to the blind, to set at liberty them that are bruised. Also, to preach the acceptable year of the Lord. And he closed the book, and he gave it again to the minister and sat down. And the eyes of all them that were in the synagogue were fastened on him."

The methods of Jesus Christ Jubilee ministry in the New, New, Testament is the Old Testament and New Testament prophecy the Force of comforting Peace fitting together like a hand-and-glove philosophy (Ubuntu) fulfilled. Very glad to see Jesus, for he had heard about Jesus and had wanted to see him for quite some time. He was hoping to see Jesus perform some sign (Luke 23:8). United methods of Jesus Christ Jubilee ministry is God's love passing over moving keeping family church. In this eternal story, new gospels of Good News Act II World Peacetime reconciliation commanding capitalist rich young ruler (Keeping Family Church Nation) to peacefully political and spiritual start over like it 1492 coming to America, 1776 United States with Liberty Bell, 1863 Emancipation, 1865 Thirteenth Amendment Acts of War, 2016 election of Donald Trump President. But Jesus didn't respond to him (Luke 23:9).

You know the commandments: 'You shall not murder, you shall not commit adultery, you shall not steal, you shall not give false testimony, you shall not defraud, honor your father and mother.' The legal experts were there, fiercely accusing Jesus (Luke 23:10). "Teacher," he (Family) declared, "all these I have kept since I was a boy." Jesus Christ (Methods of God) looked at him and loved him. "One thing you lack," he said. "Go, sell everything you have (sword, shield of weapons of mass destruction, atom bombs, battle ships) and give to the poor, and you will have treasure in heaven. Then come, follow me." At this, the man's (family) face fell. He the (family) went away sad, (Antichrist) because he had great weapon of wealth. Jesus looked around and said to his disciples, "How hard it is for the rich (family) to enter the kingdom of God!"

Blessed are the peacemaker poor in spirit of the time with communion seeding hearts on many families' tree timeline. Before this, they had been enemies (Luke 23:12). That is disciple by a supernatural moving God spiritual personal trusting relationship revival with Jesus Christ Grace-grace. They gathered the whole company of soldiers around him (Matthew 27:27). The message of the Cross Acts II descent of the Holy Spirit voice of God's eternal flame dancing moving commanding followers to start over like it is the day of Pentecost, 1868 First United Methods Church Compton, 1888 City Compton, 1990 Ubuntu in South Africa as a guiding ideal for the transition from apartheid to majority rule, 2000 Great Jubilee, 2015 Blood moon Ground Zero to 2016 Extraordinary Jubilee of Mercy New, New Jerusalem Acts II world peace from heaven creating the New, New Testament of Faith 2020 twin year of the Lord. A shower of God's love cleaning unclean spirits.

They stripped him and put a red military coat on him (Matthew 27:28). Peaceful force humanism spiritual climate change balance set in time revealing instant forgiveness police yourself with trusting God's spiritual guard glory protecting all ages victory too victory no loser anywhere they are family at keeping family church event "Jubilee" of mercy revival living like every day of the week is peaceful Pentecost Sunday event. Becoming police brutality. Then they bowed down in front of him and mocked him, saying, "Hey! King of the Jews!" (Matthew 27:29).

I was peacefully drawn back to my grandmother's church: African Methodist Episcopal Quinn Chapel, the oldest Black America church in my hometown. It was organized in 1871, four years after the city was organized and named after the father of the faithful and Freedom Abraham, Lincoln the Great Emancipator, the Star City Capital of the State of Nebraska the Good Life State Heartland Corn Field Worlds Bread Basket of North America in the Midwest. After they spit on him, they took the stick and struck his head again and again (Matthew 27:30). This is where the face methods of Jesus Christ's Jubilee ministry love were revealed to me at my arrival Saint Elizabeth Hospital like John the Baptist. As a child, over forty some odd years before, this is where I first took Easter communion with Jesus Christ. I remember attending Easter Sunday school classes in the basement of Quinn Chapel, my aunt Ella's wedding (R.I.P.), her funeral and that special day at my grandmother's funeral, when all the colors of light appeared in a rainbow miracle in the sky and all the color of life in a rainbow of people. "We have a Law, and according to this Law he ought to die because he made himself out to be God's Son" (John 19:7). We call it our family's church. Being there made me feel like there is no place like home.

I knew my grandmother was smiling from heaven that peaceful day. Family drama is like a chain; it is only as strong as its wickedest, weakest link. "Are you the Christ, the Son of the blessed one?" (Mark 14: 61). I was a weak link in family chain of faith. I was there with my aunty (grandmother's youngest daughter) and my baby brother who had just been released from state prison. I was one of five of her grandchildren and my cousin's friend whom we call Wolf. Jesus said, "I am. And you will see the Human One sitting on the right side of the Almighty and coming on the heavenly clouds" (Mark 14:62). This is the sign for revival in the church, with the Wolf and me the Lamb Capricorn baby goat being shepherd coming together keeping family church.

We had been wicked weak links problem children in both our twisted family's soap box drama chain of faith and turning away from hearing God's voice that was dividing family, pulling and twisting us apart. We been to prison for selling drugs. "You would have no authority over me if it had not been given to you from above. That's why the one who handed me over to you has the greater sin" (John 19:11). I knew some words from the King James Bible wrestled with God's living words methods of Jesus Christ all my life. I chose not to follow method of Jesus Christ or believe in the King James Bible keeping family church. Jesus Christ chose me to suffer. Holy

Spirit representatives of God the Father in heaven made me an offer I could not refuse: Do what I am supposed to do or go to hell suffering!

I was product of my environment civil religious, entrepreneurial capitalist. I pledge my league to flag of capital of capitalism United States America with my right hand over my heart to one nation under God under the Constitution. "We have no king except the emperor," the chief priests answered (John 19:15). I love hated my great country of exile immigrate as Ethiopian African American European Black Man Refugee speaking King James Bible Roman Great Britain English Nobles using Arabic numbers in France's and Spain's foreign land. "Let's see if Elijah will come and save him" (Matthew 27:49). We were resting, turning closer to God, repenting spiritually, changing our ugly twisted hung-up bad way of thinking seeing everything created is good. Asking for instance forgiveness that day to strengthen the chain of faith that bound us together with revival love and devotion.

JST Matthew 27:50

Jesus, when he had cried again with a loud voice, saying, father, it is finished, thy will is done, yielded up the ghost.

Because my entrepreneurial underworld capitalism employment, fellowship in the sciences darkness of astrology and the stain of bondage to generational sin nature in my family tree of drama. Again, Jesus cried out with a loud shout. Then, he died (Matthew 27:50). I was born a stubborn Capricorn Mountain Zi-On (social society of peace) Ram Horned Goat carefree solid as a rock tuff mud clay dirt dust. The spiritually dead capitalist I was at the time of the dark end of my twisted capitalism broken marriage in the world. They were filled with awe and said, "This was certainly God's Son (Matthew 27:54). She was a proud Leo, a mean African Lion cat covering up her own mess, using the power of having the same spiritual dreams of seeing the Acts II of unfaithfulness in future cell phone bills coming in the mail.

The Resurrection

You are everything, everything is you, I sacrifice my life to your death from a broken heart. They won't break any of his bones (John 19:36). Firework from traditions our influence seeing eye for eye revenge hardens hearts being male or female war of roses inequality. We had grown up in the tradition of broken homes with violence and "sex without marriage" drama. They will look at him whom they have pierced (John 19:37). We went through the hurting feeling of resentment from bitterness and guilt, ashamed and nastiness of "out of marriage" sex, singing "Mo' Better Blues" from the Maze of joy and pain of love. We tripped over the broken heart chain of sin snapping divorce, dividing family drama, ready to kill or be killed for a home that we did not owned; it was all debt. Joseph was a disciple of Jesus, but a secret one because he feared the Jewish authorities (John 19:38). I spent time in the Los Angeles County Jail and in the federal prison system, for being a leader shot caller of an illegal conspiracy to capitalize from sale drugs. That sent me and five other people to prison. Nicodemus, the one who at first had come to Jesus at night, was there too (John 19:39). If I knew then what I know now the what, the when and the why in hindsight, things would have been different. I had to look at the consistent stain drama of sin on my broken wicked self; I was a shamed hypocrite. And every spirit that doesn't confess Jesus is not from God. This is the spirit of the antichrist, which you have heard is coming and is now already in the world (1 John 4:3).

The Doctrine of the resurrection is the single most fundamental and crucial doctrine in Christian religion. It cannot be overemphasized, nor can it be disregarded. Without the Resurrection, the gospel of Jesus Christ becomes a litany of wise sayings and seemingly unexplainable miracles

with no, ultimate triumph. No, the ultimate triumph is in the ultimate miracle: for the first time in the history of mankind, one who was dead raised himself into living immortality.
Howard W. Hunter

What Think Ye of Christ

The message of the cross this day assured me like a breath of fresh air apart of divine nature. Jesus came and stood among them. He said, "Peace be with you" (John 20:19). The spirit of the Lord is on me. I am double blessed being prepared clean to serve successfully for atoning fellowship with the message of the family, rainbow and cross covenant of Christmas to Easter grace-grace and mercy, bridging the right path of love with my broken soul and spiritual peace. A divine appointment to unify and align the heart and mind relationship with honoring and praising God's glory of constant unconditional love. When the they saw the Lord, they were filled with joy (John 20:20). We are being guided and drawn by God, one by one, to the cross. How does God guide one family onto the cross by passing over the bridge over troubled waters to the seat of mercy at once? "Peace be with you. As the Father sent me, so I am sending you" (John 20:21). I did not know this peaceful path of love would lead me to see the cross seat of mercy of God's love as the only open gate (doorway; eye of the needle; keyhole) to heaven and call and guide me to write this story monument to God. Then he breathed on them and said, "Receive the Holy Spirit" (John 20:22). It is a spiritual dissertation of an event that has not happened yet Sign of Son of man.

I had to be at the right spot in time, an hour before sunrise and sunset, to take a front and back picture of a once-in-a-lifetime event from the sound of a one-word commandment. If you forgive anyone's sins, they are forgiven; if you don't forgive them, they aren't forgiven" (John 20:23). Shofar blast Capricorn Ram horn Jubilee of mercy-mercy release of hang ups spiritual climate change action plan balance in time starting over beginning of sorrow called from heaven's eternal light. "We've seen the Lord" (John 20:25). That was the revelation that it is time for the great extraordinary "Jubilee" of divine mercy-mercy. This is the beginning of sorrow, an opening, a way for a revival spiritual exodus, leaving past hang ups behind you. Jesus entered and stood among them. He said, "Peace be with you" (John 20:26). Living life like every day is Sunday Christmas to Easter Passover Pentecost worshiping praising. A movement of God passing over the divide spiritual poor family Israel exile in west culture desert turning releasing them from generational bondage dependency on government assistance to moving closer to God right where they are. Put your hand into my side. No more disbelief. Believe! (John 20:27) Revealing the Holy Spirit's utterance of God's voice, organizing family charity for a plan of action, a grassroots' reprogram to instantly forgive and celebrate Christmas to Easter grace-grace and peace where nobody dies, go to jail, or get left behind, a "Jubilee" of mercy universal pardon rapture of seeing the family and church debt free as one universal church body keeps family Bible study the factory of hope alive.

I have always been a handyman, like the methods of Jesus Christ as a carpenter, sent to build, a Holy Spirit custodian keeping the family church. "My Lord and my God!" (John 20:28). I am sent as a repair mechanic selected as a sexton administrator and hired as a janitor, who was given the keys to understanding and the authority of grave digger to clean, fix and repair the church, a watchman sounding of one word "Jubilee" revival to start over- reset. I love to fix problems; I always had the faith in the power to forgive and to change the climate, resetting a situation from negative to positive. "Happy are those who don't see and yet believe" (John 20:29). I could see the facts with principle on how broken things are put together and work like new in my mind. I am prosperous as an automobile, diesel engine, heavy equipment mechanic with my soft hands as instruments, using tools to do hard dirty work, fixing renewing and rebuilding broken things to run right and make a good living for my family.

I have the gift/talent of discernment, which is the ability to judge suggestions and endure well with true facts, principles, and great wisdom. I have the power to read instruction/repair manuals and lay hands on broken things and push a button to fix and/or reset themselves. The first half of my broken life. I am a go-getter.

I AM what I AM because we are under the double blessing covenant of grace-grace and mercy-mercy of God's glory, not my own work or a religion, so I cannot boast. I always like a challenge. Then Jesus did many other miraculous signs in his disciples' presence, signs that aren't recorded in this scroll (John 20:30). I lived a dangerous independent purpose-driven life doing the wrong things, believing in my good looks and hard work with my soft hands, doing what I did to get what I wanted- do or die. I would put business before family as an entrepreneur, trying to make it in a capitalist society. Now the second half of my life as a grandfather and godfather, I employ methods of Jesus Christ "Jubilee" ministry light of transfiguration for all who is family, having instant forgiveness, drawing and calling my spirit by name, pulling me out the capitalism well of confusion and conflict from the spiritual far-side broken dark upside down unfair underworld of capitalist dirt that I called my private and public life. I was made a disciple, a face of God of human kindness and righteousness.

As a pre-scientist disciple, following and hearing the voice the great word giver of the law and prophet, I am submitting a spiritual dissertation on keeping family church. But these things are written so that you will believe that Jesus is the Christ, God's Son, and that believing, you will have life in his name (John 20:31). I do not call on renowned war demons or dead spirits like King David's son King Solomon, fiction spirit telling story about the nine harbingers or dead president like capitalist gangsters. I am using my spiritual and capitalist real-life Christian story, Passover walk with God peacefully like the renowned spirit of Enoch who wrote the book of "Jubilee" about economic calendar of truth that is not in the King James

Bible. It is a spiritual truth, using faith force of peace compassion like a mechanic uses tools.

> Genesis 5:24 Jubilee Bible 2000 (JUB)
> "And Enoch walked with God; and he was not, for God took him."

I am to be used as instrument of peace, sounding loud as seven unicorn horns. Trumpets are methods of Jesus Christ's Great Commission and Great Commandment, living and resting in truth and faith. You must follow me" (John 21:22). As an example to explain God's peacefulness sacred secret Holy Spirit great two works Extraordinary "Jubilee" of mercy beginning of sorrow and love grace–grace in scripture of New Gospel of Good News. Me and many families great commission to believe with our hearts in faith, force of peace and trust God constant loving Grace-grace will supply the rest for a miracle. "If I want him to remain until I come, what difference does that make to you?" (John 21: 23). It is like when you find yourself in a good place at the right time or at bad place at the wrong time to turn the other cheek. It becomes scary and uncomfortable even confusing to instantly forgive.

The methods of Jesus Christ Jubilee ministry call on all His followers by name to baptize all people, groups, cultures of nations in the name of the Father, Son, and Holy Spirit voice of God face to face peacefully in everybody's dreams.

> Matthew 28:16-20 Jubilee Bible 2000
> "Then the eleven disciples went away into Galilee, into the mountain where Jesus had appointed them. And when they saw him, they worshipped him; but some doubted. And Jesus came and spoke unto them, saying, All power is given unto me in heaven and in earth. Go ye therefore and teach all nations, baptizing them in the name of the Father and of the Son and of the Holy Spirit, teaching them to observe all things

whatsoever I have commanded you; and, behold, I am with you always even unto the end of the age. Amen."

I have been with family members that would swear I talk to the minister or preacher and told their personnel family business. They became afraid did not understand the supernatural power of the spiritual living word God in the Bible. We know that his testimony is true (John 21:24). Thinking their Underworld Capitalist system, double life of right and wrong was twisted like the dark rap song by the Geto Boys: "My Mind Is Playing Tricks on Me" and left the church service.

Since only God and I know my entire unseen problem, all I can do is take it as being a supernatural sign and living spiritual word from God's grace-grace. It made me feel inspired to dance some kind of way, like if somebody is watching out for me to forgive my credit debt. Jesus did many other things as well. If all of them were recorded, I imagine the world itself wouldn't have enough room for the scrolls that would be written (John 21:25). Freeing the spiritual creative artist in me from enslavement working overtime doing underworld spiritual dead time artificial me as ambassador in chain speaking boldly as I ought to speak to my heart's captivated mind to my sin and credit debt score raptured me to do Moore good in people's lives all at one time to instantly forgive debt.

Matthew 28:20
"teaching them to obey everything that I've commanded you. Look, I myself will be with you every day until the end of this present age."

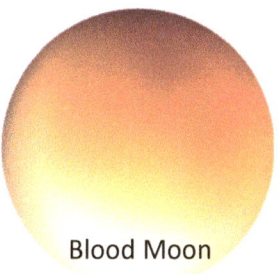

Blood Moon

"Acts II Perfect Love"

CHAPTER 2
Ordained To be A Witness

In the spirit of the beginning age of joyful sorrow, "No man can surpass his own time, for the spirit of his time is also his own spirit." As they were watching, he was lifted up and a cloud took him out of their sight (Acts 1:9). It is the spirit of the time of the end, for no man knows the end of dark bad time. The methods of Jesus Christ is the light at the end to my dark struggles. We are commanded to start over in remembrance of the beginning of sorrows methods of Jesus Christ grace-grace and truth. Suddenly, two men in white robes stood next to them (Acts 1:10). Humble thyself with prayer and worship to be inspired with the blessing of a balanced spiritual climate change revelation knowledge from straight out of heaven gift artistry talent of spiritual discernment peacefully unifying the northern and southern churches. "Will come in the same way that you saw him go into heaven" (Acts 1:11).

Like King James United England, Joseph (Jah has added increase) kept Egypt from famine's dark failing, and Daniel (my judge is God) saved Israel in darkened Babylon with fasting, prayer and words from God, as writings on a wall. They humbled themselves with consequences from sin in faith to interpret dreams and visions of kings in the King James Bible to do God's will by instantly forgiving and unifying the divided family (Israel) of remnants. All were united in their devotion to prayer, along with some women, including Mary the mother of Jesus, and his brothers (Acts 1:14). They were exiled and separated from their family King James Scotland- his mother, Joseph- his father and Daniel's birthright of Israel's Promise land for not worshiping other gods. When they entered the city Zi-On (Acts 1:13).

They were divinely appointed in bondage in Great Britain, Egypt and Babylon, Pyramids, Golden Temples Gates of many gods and on the Masonic 33rd degree parallel line death dividing the Western Northern Kingdom and Western Southern Kingdom. The reason they call it the 33rd parallel line of death is because it is used to divide the unfair underworld. Concluding that God had called us to proclaim the good news to them (Acts 16:10). All the underworld financial institutions War I, II, and World III media spiritual battle for peace was fought on or below this line. Most of the people on Earth live above this line. Keeping family church unified, the western Latter Day Church would stop the spread of divide, conquer underworld, cross up double minded state of war and nuclear weapon above of the 33rd parallel line of death.

Ezekiel 48:32, 35 (JUB)
"And at the east side four thousand five hundred reeds: and three gates; the gate of Joseph, one; the gate of Benjamin, another; the gate of Dan, another It was round about eighteen thousand reeds: and the name of the city from that day shall be, THE LORD IS HERE."

I am named Eric like the Viking explorer, warrior eternal one ruler and my father Joseph humbling myself to complete working under divine right of God's authority and autonomy King James Bible by the grace-grace consent of God's divine appointment. Many people have already applied themselves to the task of compiling an account of the events that have been fulfilled among us (Luke 1:1). Looking up to my older brothers Daniel a prophet and captain fire fighter paramedic elder brother divine rights of King James conceived from a virgin birth acts in the backseat of a car during the planting advent season of favor, born under the zodiac sign Virgo in the harvest season of atonement antislavery into being a slave for capital of capitalisms heartland of antichrist beast that saved me. They used what the original eyewitnesses and servants of the word handed down to us (Luke 1:2).

Like Jonah was saved in the belly of a whale. With my father first union president fought fires and saved lives. A seed remnant tender heart of King David shadow praying, repenting with thanksgiving for healing, I had already been given and fasting from anger, prejudice, worry, hate, meanness, pride and world news boasting. I have also decided to write a carefully ordered account for you, most honorable Joseph (Luke 1:3). I did not create the problem, so I am not required to fix the problem. God is. I am called me to consent, serve, sound "Jubilee" instant forgiveness, be a helpmeet, as a praying knight under the order of the King James Bible to suffer and bear witness (write this story) and be a watchman in a western northern Midwest good life state spiritual family of Judah (Israel).

I want you to have confidence in the soundness of the instruction you have received (Luke 1:4). Traveled through the rocky mountain Colorado state to the Golden Gate state, land of many churches living on the Masonic 33rd degree parallel line of colors of death red, white and blue in a Western Southern state of twisted confusion on the City of Angels. This is not just a westside or East Compton thing. M.A.A.D. City, California is where I was divinely appointed and had been sent to play out the one-word commandment from God from heaven sounding event "Jubilee." During this time, the family of believers was a company of about one hundred twenty persons (Acts 1:15). It's better than playing Powerball Lottery. Like Jonah was saved and divinely appointed to give a word from God to repent and start over.

The sound of this word is not about where I was born, where I'm going, or what hood I am from: Blood or Cuzz. "Therefore, we must select one of those who have accompanied us during the whole time the Lord Jesus lived among us" (Acts 1:21). It is about the spiritual climate change and bringing balance, freedom, liberty, equality, royal protection from the spiritual hang ups, torture, and lynching of the past. It is giving the power of the sound of this word Jubilee to start over. Opening up hearts of faith and minds to hear with the gift of excellent spiritual discernment the Holy Spirit gave utterance voice of God's word of great wisdom to interpreting dreams and instantly forgiving, like the king of kings. "Beginning from the baptism of John until the day when Jesus was taken from us. This person must become along with us a witness to his resurrection" (Acts 1:22).

With this story of 2016, spiritual climate change plan of action event keeping my family church global quiet storm celebration, God's family of seeing the reality of manifestation and demonstration divine opportunity of Dr. Martin Luther King, Jr.'s "I Have a Dream" speech come true extraordinary "Jubilee" of mercy 2016. So, they nominated two: Joseph called Barsabbas, who was also known as Justus today "Jubilee" (Acts 1:23). The part prompted by Mahalia Jackson's cry: "Tell them about the dream, Martin!" In this part of the speech, which most excited me as listener and has now become its most famous, King described his dreams of freedom and equality arising from a land of slavery and hatred. He also stated, "I still have a dream, a dream deeply rooted in the American dream one day this nation will rise up and live up to its creed, 'We hold these truths to be self-evident: that all men are created equal.' I have a dream…"

Dr. King also had a dream of President Kennedy signing a Second Emancipation Proclamation Executive Order against segregation at the centennial celebration of the first Emancipation Proclamation. They prayed, "Lord, you know everyone's deepest thoughts and desires. Show us clearly which one you have chosen from among these two (Acts 1:24). "He publicly instigated this idea in a speech on June 6, 1961 at a New York news conference saying, 'Just as Abraham Lincoln had the vision to see almost 100 years ago, that this nation could not exist half-free, the present administration must have the insight to see that today the nation cannot exist half-segregated and half-free'." During a tour of the Lincoln sitting room with Kennedy in October 1961, King pressed President Kennedy for a proclamation "outlawing segregation." Kennedy said he would take it under consideration and asked King for a draft of the proposal.

Dr. King presented his sixty-four-page manifesto "On Behalf of the Negro Citizenry" to President Kennedy asking him to issue a second Emancipation Proclamation Executive Order to use the powers of the executive office to strike a severe blow to segregation in of the United States of America in 1962. To take the place of this ministry and apostleship (Acts 1:25). The document went on to cite legal precedents and laws by the hundreds, making special note and not one mention King James Bible Orders verses Leviticus 25:10 Jubilee Universal Pardon instant forgiveness.

Pentecost

Extraordinary Jubilee of Mercy Universal Pardon eternal rule of order is a God-given right, Ordering Commandment for the whole world to consent and receive immediate forgiveness tongue of fire. They were all together in one place (Acts 2:1). The Methods Grassroots Movement of Jesus Christ Jubilee Ministry is the Anti-Slavery Society, Human Rights Organization, Billy Graham crusades and Martin Luther King's Civil Rights Movement ending as one Acts II World Peace. Jubilee of mercy is more power than a person claiming conscientious objection to be free from United States military service not to fight in a war. Suddenly a sound from heaven like the howling of a fierce wind filled the entire house where they were sitting (Acts 2:2).

The sound of law of "Jubilee" free every born-again citizen/believer from serving prison (slave) time for past moral bad times behavior as given for bad time recession economic behavior debt. The King James Bible has a dual function as an insurance protection for future generations, guaranteeing nobody negative or positive rights or liberty is left behind forced expulsion or force to convert. "Jubilee" is a political peaceful sound off event. They saw what seemed to be individual flames of fire alighting on each one of them (Acts 2:3). Over 2016 years after the birth methods of Jesus Christ "Jubilee" Ministry Anti-Slavery Act II World Peace. Not like the words of peace on the public decree issued by the Pope Papla bull 1452 to conquer extended to the Americas in 1493 from an act of war Treaty of Granada 1492 force expulsion bringing an end to "live and let live."

Acts 2:4

They were all filled with the Holy Spirit and began to speak in other languages as the Spirit enabled them to speak.

Many countries in the New World and elsewhere officially celebrate as a holiday the remembrance the anniversary of Christopher Columbus' arrival in the Americas, which happened on October 12, 1492. There were pious Jews from every nation under heaven living in Jerusalem (Acts 2:5). Just like the word in the Declaration of Independence, creating the Bill of Rights proclaiming "all men are created equal," July 4, 1776 was a political act of war, which started the Revolution War waving the flag "Don't Tread on Me" being ratified in 1788 for giving birth to a new nation "Give me Liberty or Give me Death." A house dived cannot stand. When they heard this sound, a crowd gathered (Acts 2:6).

An executive order, an act of war power, Emancipation Proclamation was issued on January 1, 1863 by the government of the people, by the people for the people, which heaven itself has ordained, the Gettysburg's address, for blessing the people United States capital of capitalism that we still celebrate today Juneteenth time as the end of the Civil War. "We hear them declaring the mighty works of God in our own languages!" (Acts 2:11). Because acts of God's Law of "Great 2000 Jubilee" year to start over was not done politically correct as one church and state working together, an ordained call of unity came on the second anniversary Friday, March 13, 2015 Extraordinary "Jubilee" a spiritual climate change of balance from spiritual hang ups. "What does this mean?" (Acts 2:12).

During Fall Equinox Atonement September 19, 2015, Pope Francis first visit to the North Americas as Pope sounding asking people to pray for his deliverance is a message of instant forgiveness spiritual balance remembrance of Jesus Christ final conformation. Peaceful start waving a sword of charity instant forgiveness debt fulfillment celebration arrival methods of Jesus Christ "Jubilee" ministry starting over like it is 1492 Cuba, 1789 United States, 1863 Emancipation, Gettysburg Address and 1865 time at the end of the Civil War event all in one. He raised his voice and declared, Know this! Listen carefully to my words (Acts 2:14)! Take the head off communism and capitalism, torture and terrorism violence bring a spiritual balance from our hang ups about money, sexual abuse and the Catholic church. Delivering messages of Amazing Grace Acts II World Peace of instant forgiveness asking the White House, joint session Congress to address the United Nations. This is what was spoken through the prophet Joel (Acts 2:16). Praying for forgiveness on Wall Street Memorial the start of slavery beginning sorrow for slavery and torture on world terrorism. City of Brotherly Love reconciliation of the keeping family church this one word Extraordinary "Jubilee" of divine mercy universal pardon instant forgiveness 2016 spiritual climate change of freedom from past spiritual hang ups in families and government for the world rebirth of equality and to pursue happiness.

Acts 2:17

In the last days, God says, I will pour out my Spirit on all people. Your sons and daughters will prophesy. Your young will see visions. Your elders will dream dreams.

It is Dr. Martin Luther King, Jr.'s dream come true that has not happened yet. 2016 Extraordinary "Jubilee" political year of mercy spiritual climate change restores equality in wealth to the divided land of love and hate bring spiritual balance unity to the American family and government after the one hundred fiftieth anniversary of Abraham Lincoln signing the Emancipation Proclamation 1863 was not the only blessing of freedom President Abraham Lincoln gave. He wrote: "... (we) gave the people of this Republic the greatest blessing they have ever had – their own paper money to pay their own debts..." Whoever controls the climate volume of money in any country is the absolute master of all industry and commerce. Because he was a prophet, he knew that God promised him with a solemn pledge to seat one of his descendants on his throne (Acts 2: 30). During the Civil War, President Lincoln needed money. The bankers (money changers) were going to charge him high interest. President Lincoln and Treasury Secretary Salmon P. Chase got Congress to pass a law, authorizing the printing of full legal tender treasury notes to forgive/pay the war effort debt.

Acts 2:18

Even upon my servants, men and women, I will pour out my Spirit in those days, and they will prophesy.

The European governments, which was controlled by the wealthy European bankers (money changers), moved to support the Confederate South, hoping to defeat Lincoln and the Union and destroy this government which they said had to be destroyed. This Jesus God raised up. We are all witnesses to that fact (Acts 2:32). President Lincoln knew the sweet sound of amazing graces, and he knew that divided nation could not stand one-half economic free one-half spiritual dead in slavery. European governments and the people would not support slavery. United British Empire had the act for the Abolition of Slave Trade March 25, 1807.

In 1823, the Anti-Slavery Society Charity was founded, the world's oldest human rights organization. He was exalted to God's right side and received from the Father the promised Holy Spirit. He poured out this Spirit, and you are seeing and hearing the results of his having done so (Acts 2:33). It continues today as Anti-Slavery International and Slavery Abolition Act 1833, so he issued the executive order: Emancipation Proclamation; a presidential proclamation: "states a condition, declares a law and requires obedience, recognizes an event or triggers the implementation of a law (by recognizing that the circumstances in law have been realized)." Presidents define situations or conditions on situations that become legal or economic truth, as an insurance policy, which declared the abolishment of slavery in the United States.

Acts 2:19
"I will cause wonders to occur in the heavens above and signs on the earth below, blood and fire and a cloud of smoke."

At that point, the divided European governments and money changers (bankers) could not openly support the Confederacy because the European people simply would not stand for their country supporting slavery. "Change your hearts and lives. Each of you must be baptized in the name of Jesus Christ for the forgiveness of your sins. Then you will receive the gift of the Holy Spirit" (Acts 2:38). He was fighting against the enslavement and bondage of the American people to debt of the European money changers and Wall Street bankers.

Acts 2:20
The sun will be changed into darkness, and the moon will be changed into blood, before the great and spectacular day of the Lord comes.

President Kennedy did not take the opportunity to issue a second Emancipation Proclamation "and noticeably avoided all centennial celebrations of Emancipation." Teaching, to the community, to their shared meals, and to their prayers (Acts 2:42). On June 4, 1963, President Kennedy signed a presidential document, called Executive Order 11110, which further amended Executive Order 10289 of September 19, 1951. That gave Kennedy, as president of the United States, legal clearance to create his own money to run the country, money that would belong to the people, an interest and debt-free money. They shared food with gladness and simplicity (Acts 2:46). President Kennedy wanted to instant forgive all American families from being in bondage debt and control of the money changers, Federal Reserve System. Dr. King did speak about it at the March on Washington D. C. in 1963. He called it a "dream"; he also referred to it as a return insurance policy check to the American Negro marked insufficient funds from the world money changers. They praised God and demonstrated God's goodness to everyone. The Lord added daily to the community those who were being saved (Acts 2:47). The Northern European and Wall Street money changers made money off instant forgiving Underworld Capitalism national debt from Wars I, II, slavery and Third World national debt Jubilee 2000.

Acts 2:21
"And everyone who calls on the name of the Lord will be saved."

Only one day after Kennedy's assassination, all the United States notes, which Kennedy had issued, were called out of circulation. This through an executive order of the newly installed president, Lyndon B. Johnson who sign the Equal Right Bill 1965 and war on poverty.

Acts 2:34-35

"The Lord said to my Lord, 'Sit at my right side, until I make your enemies a footstool for your feet."

CHAPTER 3

There Is None Other Name

The Civil War for civil rights to civil religion, the fight for "Jubilee" releasing instant forgiveness of debt for all poor families has already been won! The established prayer appointed time (Acts 3:1). A spiritual climate change Exodus II California Love Acts II Perfect Love without going any place; we do not have to break any law, kill or need security. The spiritual climate change sound "Jubilee" of Mercy 2016 will cut off the head of giant organizations that torture, like the C.I.A. and terrorist ISIS Islam state of mind thinking violence or killing somebody can fix a problem. This is not another New Deal program for the poor or underprivileged. "Look at us!" (Acts 3:3). Extraordinary "Jubilee" of mercy universal pardon Emancipation Proclamation political year of the family 2016 global spiritual climate change celebrating the principle of instant forgiveness out pouring from heaven is an order (commandment) written on our hearts that would happen every fifty calendar years is a fair deal for everyone's family that has already been done.

A spiritual climate change of balance movement from spiritual hang ups on the people moving closer to God that you do not have to go anywhere or campaign Zi-On keeping Passover. "I don't have any money, but I will give you what I do have. In the name of Jesus Christ, the Nazarene, rise up and walk!" (Acts 3:6). The external politics has already been done sounding Jubilee 2000. It has twice entered The Guinness Book of World Records, once for the largest petition and once for the most international petition. A spiritual climate change of balance, they (the father, son, and Holy Spirit voice of God's utterance) come to you moving like a thief in the night, blowing as a quiet storm soft Saint Anta Winds. It's an insurance policy from heaven already written and paid for. Jumping up, he began to walk around. He entered the temple with them, walking, leaping, and praising God (Acts 3:8). It will put you in a better state of mind like State Farm Insurance. Reset button from Heaven. It is an eternal redemption spiritual upgrade for everybody to eat manna (spiritual food) out the same Book Table! The sounding of Extraordinary Jubilee of Mercy Universal Pardon spiritual climate changes the course of the history like a hurricane Katrina changed a nation. "Jubilee" is God in a person's life. They were filled with amazement and surprise at what had happened to him (Acts 3:10). This is a call for a New, New Amendment to the U.S. Constitution for a balanced-budget Jubilee amendment, every fifty years to start over. Jubilee is the call for an Article V Constitution Convention that all state legislators, except Hawaii, have already passed that is already proposed would happen every fifty calendar years, nonviolently, with no war or killing, just like our presidential election that by law happens automatically every four years.

Acts 3:16

His name itself has made this man strong. That is, because of faith in Jesus' name, God has strengthened this man whom you see and know. The faith that comes through Jesus gave him complete health right before your eyes.

I can petition the popes of northern and southern kingdom, king/queen, president or the governor, leader of a state a request for pardon of instant forgiveness at any time and they can grant it or deny the petition. But this is how God fulfilled what he foretold through all the prophets: that his Christ would suffer (Acts 3:18). The sounding Extraordinary Jubilee of Mercy Universal Pardon they and all the power of angels in the presence of Heaven and Earth is required to be obedient, moving on God's behave to grant the petition of instant forgiveness.

This petition should be handled as a sacred Acts II of God. Like Bull of Indication dated April 11, 2015, Extraordinary Jubilee of Mercy sounding of a spiritual climate change should prevail. Fall equinox visit to Cuba on September 23, visit to the White House called for spiritual climate change. Then the Lord will provide a season of relief from the distress of this age and he will send Jesus, whom he handpicked to be your Christ (Acts 3:20). Historical peaceful address to both houses of Congress, stating, "Do unto others" that you have done to yourself. Call for Extraordinary Jubilee at the United Catholic Church against sexual abuse, address the United Nation on debt release, going to Wall Street asking to be prayed for forgiveness for its part in the dark American Slave Trade to celebrating of Amazing grace-grace the unity between the family and the church in the City of Brotherly Love.

Acts 3:21

Jesus must remain in heaven until the restoration of all things, about which God spoke long ago through his holy prophets.

The protests movement caught the attention of Prime Minister Tony Blair and Chancellor of the Exchequer Gordon Brown, who met with the directors of sounding of Jubilee 2000 to discuss the issue of heavy debt in poor countries, and subsequently, the Prime Minister publicly expressed his personal support for and dedication to instant debt forgiveness. While the UK's move to cancel significant third world debt was also influenced by the millennium development goals, Gordon Brown's decision to support debt cancelation at a sounding of Jubilee 2000 rally at St Paul's Cathedral underlies the significance of the movement in influencing UK policy.

Acts 3:22-25
"Moses said, The Lord your God will raise up from your own people a prophet like me. Listen to whatever he tells you. Whoever doesn't listen to that prophet will be totally cut off from the people. All the prophets who spoke—from Samuel forward—announced these days. You are the heirs of the prophets and the covenant that God made with your ancestors when he told Abraham, Through your descendants, all the families on earth will be blessed."

It is an insurance policy, protecting poor family future generations that nobody is left behind not like in a million-dollar entertainment movie, assuring equality and balance to wealthy World Monitory System. You cannot apply King James Bible authority instant forgiveness principle only for a select group of a poor nation without instant forgiving the poor family. Nobody remembers to gets baptizes led to Jesus Christ or released from prison!

Acts 4:11-12
"This Jesus is the stone you builders rejected; he has become the cornerstone! Salvation can be found in no one else. Throughout the whole world, no other name has been given among humans through which we must be saved."

Later a promise from the United States, the capital of Capitalism during the G-7 (G-8 financial ministers, excluding Russia) meeting in Cologne, Germany in 1999, to cancel 100% of the debt that qualifying countries owed the U.S. was attributed in part to the influence of the campaign. They had no rebuttal (Acts 4:14). The Jubilee 2000 later lobbied the United States Capital of Capitalism Congress to make good on this promise. Congress responded to the growing pressure to address debt relief issues in 2000 by committing $769 million to bilateral and multilateral debt relief instant forgiveness.

Acts 4:24-26

"They listened, then lifted their voices in unison to God, "Master, you are the one who created the heaven, the earth, the sea, and everything in them. You are the one who spoke by the Holy Spirit through our ancestor David, your servant: Why did the Gentiles rage, and the peoples plot in vain? The kings of the earth took their stand and the rulers gathered together as one against the Lord and against his Christ."

The instant forgiveness principle of Jubilee of Mercy Universal Pardon Antislavery Law cannot just be given to poor counties and not allow poor families the same economic manifestation and demonstration of God's instant forgiveness opportunity. The spiritual climate change sound of Extraordinary Jubilee of Mercy Universal pardon releases instant forgiveness from everything. It what you play the lottery for and more it already been paid for. You get everything you ask God for. They were all filled with the Holy Spirit and began speaking God's word with confidence (Acts 4:31). Sounding Extraordinary Jubilee of Mercy universal pardon 2016 spiritual climate change instant forgiveness ensures no family birth right inheritance will ever be lost or stolen.

Acts 4:32

*The community of believers was one in heart and mind. None of them would say, "This is **mine**!" about any of their possessions, but held everything in common.*

It insures stability to the immigration and refugee problem. Releasing prisoners by instantly forgiving bondage of sin and past criminal history, the captivated minds of religions and the enslaved bondage to corrupted corporation capital debt, returning them home for reunion with their suffering families in common.

Acts 4:36-37
Joseph, whom the apostles nicknamed "one who encourages", He owned a field, sold it, brought the money, and placed it in the care and under the authority of the apostles.

The four blood-moon eclipses from 2014-2015 on the appointed day of God, Jews' feast days are sounding a sign of the spiritual climate change balance rebirth of the time of outpouring instant forgiveness from heaven for the people of planet Earth to get their sh*t together. It does not take 2016 years to get this right, one messenger and one message. Spiritual climate of God instantly forgiving everybody from our sin of unfaithfulness to be our God.

Acts 5:4
"Wasn't that property yours to keep? After you sold it, wasn't the money yours to do with whatever you wanted? What made you think of such a thing? You haven't lied to other people but to God!"

This eight time four-blood moon eclipse happened on appointed days of God's calendar from the beginning in Jesus Christ's ministry today signaling families spiritual turning closer to God in instant Forgiveness and humility.

Acts 5:11
"Trepidation and dread seized the whole church and all who heard what had happened."

Christianity was never supposed to be about religion. It is about charity from a one-to-one relationship with principle consciousness of spiritual God keeping the family church. "Jubilee" (Hebrew yovel יובל) year is the year at the end of seven cycles of literally "release" (Sabbatical years), and according to Biblical regulations had a special impact on the ownership of slaves and management of land in the land of promise. Sounding of spiritual climate change "Jubilee" unifying the Northern Israel and Southern kingdom Judah under Easter leap year calendar of United Kingdom of Heaven where God is head ruler.

Acts 5:14
"Indeed, more and more believers in the Lord, large numbers of both men and women, were added to the church."

Keeping the Sabbath's Sabbath in rest is a powerful political principle seed and harvest from the Old Testament beginning tears of sorrow time, like we are supposed to. That is the way God planned it.

Genesis 2:3 Jubilee Bible 2000 (JUB)
"And God blessed the seventh day and sanctified it because in it he had rested from all his work which God created in perfection."

Spiritual climate change celebrating the Sabbath's Sabbath cycles sowing seed and harvesting is insurance protection for future generations assuring nobody is left behind in bondage. This is Uncommon Sense 2016 Age of Spiritual Enlightenment see Tomas Pain (slave abolishes) 1776.

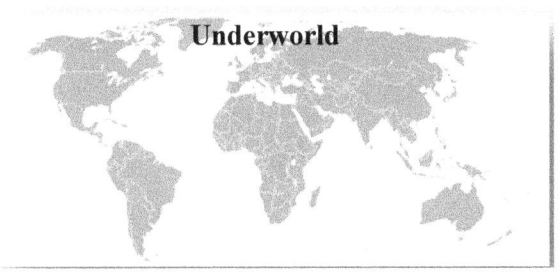

Common Sense: "We as a people have the power to start the world over!"

Keeping family church would turn the twisted underworld capitalism nation right side up if you see the world twisted and turned upside down, then turn the world map right side up. In the United Kingdom of Heaven, south is up and north is down; the people on the bottom become on top and the last become first, making South Africa the crown of the United Kingdom of Heaven. All churches are one body. King James Bible principles are applied equally to everybody with God's favor.

Acts 17:6

"And when they did not find them, they brought Jason and certain brethren unto the rulers of the city, crying, These that have turned the world upside down have come here also."

The capitalist first president George Washington in his first inaugural address gave a warning to the people of America concerning "light of the Nation" their blessing "the propitious smiles of Heaven can never be expected on a nation that disregards the eternal rules of order and right which Heaven itself has ordained; and since the preservation of the sacred fire of liberty and the destiny of the republican model of government are justly considered, perhaps, as deeply, as finally, staked on the experiment entrusted to the hands of the American people."

Acts 5:19

"An angel from the Lord opened the prison doors during the night and led them out. The angel told them."

The spiritual climate change sounding "Jubilee" of Mercy Universal Pardon arrangement provides reconciliation, restoration, liberation redemption and atonement to divide America public for its Capitalist racial inborn sins and domestic COINTELPRO (an acronym for COunter INTELligence PROgram) Illegal Constitution Violation of Fifth Amendment Due Process and non-judicial review or Administration review.

Acts 5:20

"Go, take your place in the temple, and tell the people everything about this new life."

The spiritual climate change sounding Extraordinary "Jubilee" of Mercy Universal Pardon brought about an insurance policy in balance in wealth from sharing in a stable standard of land values and prevented a great internal debt and its resultant false prosperity that brings inflation, deflation, and business depression. Spiritual climate change would also unify the churches and restore the land back to the calendar of God's wealth management system back over to the people like it is supposed to.

The descendants of Joseph Justus Family Foundation support Exodus II seeing the capital of the United States Washington D.C. moved to Abraham Lincoln, Nebraska new capital of north and south America as monument to God Zi-On city on a Hill.

Acts 5:39
"If it originates with God, you won't be able to stop them. Instead, you would actually find yourselves fighting God!" The council was convinced by his reasoning."

Spiritual climate change sounding Extraordinary Jubilee of Mercy Universal Pardon Insurance Policy would also bring instant forgiveness and healing to urban tribes of America Gang War crippling my neighborhood of Compton, California and Omaha, Nebraska. They had them beaten. They ordered them not to speak in the name of Jesus, then let them go (Acts 5:40). We do not need another ten-point program, midnight basketball program, peace treaty or a Ferguson, Missouri street riot One person shot by a police officer on duty church shooting eight people killed by one person trying to start a race war instant forgiveness remove the Confederate flag from the capital of South Carolina one hundred and fifty years after the Civil War of Jubilee. God said sound the horn of "Jubilee" of mercy have a global party shows the world how to instant forgive.

Acts 5:41
The apostles left the council rejoicing because they had been regarded as worthy to suffer disgrace for the sake of the name.

We need an Extraordinary Jubilee of Mercy Universal Pardon three and a half years world event; it's a spiritual climate change action plan party. It is the spirit of the time restoration to celebrate the Holy Spirit's joyful glow light revealing themselves to the Underworld Capitalist system. By the calling of an uncommon body of people to turn-up glow joy on the dark Underworld Capitalist system right side up unifying God's family north and south spiritual climate of change balance beginning equality.

Acts 5:42

"Every day they continued to teach and proclaim the good news that Jesus is the Christ, both in the temple and in houses."

CHAPTER 4
I See the Heavens Opened

Blood Moon Eclipse April 4, 2015

Leviticus 25:10 (KJV)
"And ye shall hallow the fiftieth year, and proclaim liberty throughout all the land unto all the inhabitants thereof: it shall be a jubilee unto you; and ye shall return every man unto his possession, and ye shall return every man unto his family."

This is why the Liberty Bell has a crack in it. "Jubilee" is anti-slavery, and that is why in the King James Bible, Israel and Judah were exiled to the

western Underworld Capitalist system to build many churches! Brothers and sisters, carefully choose seven well-respected men from among you. They must be well-respected and endowed by the Spirit with exceptional wisdom. We will put them in charge of this concern called Sexton (Acts 6:3). The spiritual climate change sounding of Extraordinary Jubilee of Mercy Universal Pardon will mend the crack in the Liberty Bell and the divided Church. Cutting head off of giant antichrist terrorist organization corrupted capitalist government makes God head of the Catholic church body unifying the family like King David unified Israel with God by cutting the head off Giant Goliath, not like the Queen of England who separated King James from his mother, by cutting her head off.

Leviticus 25:10 is on the Liberty Bell.

What happens when a state, a group of states, a government department, or government itself violates the liberty of the Constitution, fails to protect its citizens God-given negative, positive rights or tries to separate itself from the insurance protection of the Constitution?

Acts 6:4
"As for us, we will devote ourselves to prayer and the service of proclaiming the word."

That state, states or government can lose its authority to police, judge, prosecute and governor authority over the people. Put under a commission of reconciliation, to reconstruction or it can also be made to forfeiture of property, pay for damages and pain and suffering. Even start over. The King James Bible says you could be exiled west to an underworld culture desert- Book of Daniel. God is my judge.

Daniel 2:41

"As for the feet and toes that you saw, which were a mixture of potter's clay and iron, that signifies a divided kingdom; but it will possess some of the unyielding strength of iron. Even so, you saw the iron mixed with earthy clay."

Civil religion in America manifests itself most clearly in the public governmental acknowledgement of God. Be born again. New creation 2020 United States created 1776. In God we trust. From the divided ancient Roman Empires transferred to the west from the Eastern religions.

Acts 6:7

"God's word continued to grow. The number of disciples in Jerusalem increased significantly. Even a large group of priests embraced the faith."

The United States was settled at a set time of favor in part by wealthy gentlemen and gentlewomen, the Fraternal Order of Freemasons men of God and wealthy religious dissenters from the established Catholic Christian Church and Church of England, Kingdom of Morocco Moriscos. Even so, many leaders believed in him, but they wouldn't acknowledge their faith because they feared that the Pharisees would expel them from the synagogue (John 12:42). New Christian exile who desired a nonviolent civil society of peace founded on a different religious belief out the King James Bible vision self-deliverance, where wealth and prosperity were shared equally with all men eating from same book, Table of Contents not just a few. Poor people do not own slaves. Wealthy Catholic and other wealthy Protestant religious traditions were strongly represented by some settlers and by later immigrant exiles.

Acts 6:8
"Stephen, who stood out among the believers for the way God's grace was at work in his life and for his exceptional endowment with divine power, was doing great wonders and signs among the people."

Americans have come to see the document of the United States Constitution, along with the Declaration of Independence and the Bill of Rights, as being a cornerstone of a type of civic or civil religion or political religion. However, they couldn't resist the wisdom the Spirit gave him as he spoke (Acts 6:10). Americans embrace a common "civil religion" capitalism with certain fundamental beliefs, values, holidays, and rituals, parallel to, or independent of, their chosen tax-free religion. Then they secretly enticed some people to claim, "We heard him insult Moses and God." They stirred up the people, the elders, and the legal experts (Acts 6:11-12). Presidents have often served in central roles in civil religion, and the nation provides semi-religious honors to its martyrs, such as Lincoln and the soldiers killed in the Civil War.

Examples of civil religious beliefs are reflected in statements, such as the following:

- "America is God's chosen nation today."
- "A president's authority...is from God."
- "Social justice cannot only be based on laws; it must also come from religion."
- "God can be known through the experiences of the American people."
- "Holidays like the Fourth of July are religious as well as patriotic."
- "God bless America."

Acts 6:13
Before the council, they presented false witnesses who testified, "This man never stops speaking against this holy place and the Law.

Since the days of George Washington, presidents have assumed light unto the nations one of several roles in American civil religion, and that role has helped shape the presidency. Abraham Lincoln declared in his 1838 Lyceum speech that the Constitution and the laws of the United States Capital of Capitalism ought to become the 'political religion' of each American.

Acts 6:14

"In fact, we heard him say that this man Jesus of Nazareth will destroy this place and alter the customary practices Moses gave us."

Throughout American history, the president has provided the leadership light of the nation in the public faith capitalism. Sometimes, he has functioned primarily as a national prophet, as did Abraham Lincoln. Occasionally, he has served primarily as the nation's pastor, as did Dwight Eisenhower. At other times, he has performed primarily as the high priest of the civil religion, as did Ronald Reagan. In prophetic civil religion, the president assesses the nation's actions in relation to transcendent capital values and calls upon the people to make sacrifices in times of crisis and to repent of their corporate sins when their behavior falls short of the national ideals. The high priest asked, "Are these accusations true?" (Acts 7:1). As the national pastor, he provides spiritual inspiration to the people by affirming American core capital values and urging them to appropriate those capital values and by comforting them in their afflictions. In the priestly role, the president makes America capitalism itself the ultimate reference point. He leads the citizenry in affirming and celebrating the nation and reminds them of the national capitalism mission, while at the same time glorifying and praising his political flock.

Acts 7: Beginning

"Stephen recounts the history of Israel and names Moses as a prototype of Christ. He testifies of the apostasy in Israel. He sees Jesus on the right hand of God. Stephen's testimony is rejected and he is stoned to death."

The Constitution as scripture Article VI, third clause, requires all political figures, both Federal and State, "be bound by oath or affirmation to support this Constitution, but no religious test shall ever be required...." This was a major break not only with past British practice commingling authority of state and religion, but also with that of most American states when the Constitution was written. This is also done in religious ceremonial tradition as swearing in with a left hand on the Holy King James Bible and right hand held up to God in public, pledging to a belief in a spiritual connection in the King James Bible and the Constitution. The King James Bible is not required.

Acts 7:6-8

"God put it this way: His descendants will be strangers in a land that belongs to others, who will enslave them and abuse them for four hundred years. And I will condemn the nation they serve as slaves, God said, and afterward they will leave that land and serve me in this place. God gave him the covenant confirmed through circumcision. Accordingly, eight days after Isaac's birth, Abraham circumcised him. Isaac did the same with Jacob, and Jacob with the twelve patriarchs."

I see in the original Constitution, the declaration that "all men are created equal" - in their positive and negative rights - it informed the Constitution in such a way that could label the Constitution, when properly understood, as an anti-slavery document. The Thirteenth Amendment abolished slavery and involuntary servitude, except as punishment for a crime. Modern punishment prisons are a form of civil religion. Prison for profits are modern day slavery. The Fourteenth Amendment has been interpreted so as to require states to respect citizen negative and positive rights in the same way that the Constitution has required the federal government to respect them with equal protection. The Constitution does not allow cruel and unusual punishment, such as an eye for eye. Three ways of enslavement are monetary credit debt, religion and corporation imprisonment.

Acts 7:9-18

"Because the patriarchs were jealous of Joseph, they sold him into slavery in Egypt. God was with him, however, and rescued him from all his troubles. The grace and wisdom he gave Joseph were recognized by Pharaoh, king of Egypt, who appointed him ruler over Egypt and over his whole palace. A famine came upon all Egypt and Canaan, and great hardship came with it. Our ancestors had nothing to eat. When Jacob heard there was grain in Egypt, he sent our ancestors there for the first time. During their second visit, Joseph told his brothers who he was, and Pharaoh learned about Joseph's family. Joseph sent for his father Jacob and all his relatives—seventy-five in all—and invited them to live with him. So Jacob went down to Egypt, where he and our ancestors died. Their bodies were brought back to Shechem and placed in the tomb that Abraham had purchased for a certain sum of money from Hamor's children, who lived in Shechem. "When it was time for God to keep the promise he made to Abraham, the number of our people in Egypt had greatly expanded. But then another king rose to power over Egypt who didn't know anything about Joseph.

Eye for eye, tooth for tooth equality in ministering revenge cruel and unusual punishment. Don't see God Acts II perfect loving a beautiful woman the same as an evil man. The mercy and compassion of the Lord is given equally measures of little by little faith. Jesus, called Justus, also says hello. These are my only fellow workers for God's kingdom who are Jewish converts. They have been an encouragement to me (Colossians 4:11). The constitution guarantee that women and men will be judge equally under the law of Moses receive Justus treated with righteousness and encouraged to do good in the pursuit of happiness. Ancient Egyptians believed in a goddess that had sex with a penis made from wood conceived a god to revenge the death of his father killing animal to idol of god Joseph put Amen to that. He even forced them to abandon their newly born babies so they would die (Acts 7:19). Christians believe an immaculate conception of a young virgin girl heard a word from God conceived it upon her circumcised heart becoming a new blood type concepted a child. Nine new moons later, she gave birth unto a baby boy to save the world by sacrificing his own blood, dying for others not killing. To protest bring peace stopping the revengeful killing and police brutality still going on today.

Acts 7:22-23

"Moses learned everything Egyptian wisdom had to offer, and he was a man of powerful words and deeds. When Moses was 40 years old, he decided to visit his family, the Israelites. He saw one of them being wronged so he came to his rescue and evened the score by killing the Egyptian. He expected his own kin to understand that God was using him to rescue them, but they didn't."

There are more people enslaved in America than there was before the Civil War. Many great man and women have died in Jesus Christ name trying to stand up and do the right thing like unto Stephen not hurt nobody.

Acts 7:37

"This is the Moses who told the Israelites, 'God will raise up for you a prophet like me from your own people'."

There once was a good boy who came in extraordinary worst wickedness times of persecution. His name was De'Anthony Born Again from the threat of abortion, walked through the Valley of Death Arizona Youth Detention Center doors of unjust persecution from mass incarceration and church sexual abuse scandal. He did not fear evil. His divine investiture authority was talented sent straight out of heaven blood line of great faith seed of Abraham. He is the one who received life-giving words to give to us (Acts 7:38). The firstborn of a young abused teenage girl named Beautiful Strange (precious) Barbara foreign (far-off) happiness born December 8, Day of The Feast of Immaculate Conception celebrated worldwide of the belief in Blessed Holy Mother teenage pregnant girl promised in marriage saved by angels from being stoned to death. Protectress against fire and lightning teenage daddy's girl Barbara pregnant not promised in marriage unsure who her baby's daddy was, got beat, threatened with abortion until Planned Parenthood Clinic said "she is too far gone."

Acts 7:39

"He's also the one whom our ancestors refused to obey. Instead, they pushed him aside and, in their thoughts and desires, returned to Egypt."

This dedicated good boy was a cornerstone pattern of happiness. Not just an ordinary uncut rough on the edge hew stone talented by the grace of God sacrificed altar. Boy dedicated remnant seed of Abraham great faith example Lamb of God's perfect love for all happiness. Ye stiff-necked and uncircumcised in heart and ears, ye do always resist the Holy Spirit; as your fathers did, so do ye (Acts 7:51). First Born Lamb of God with divine investiture authority a transfiguring lightning rod of hope to left up all good kids male and female in dark times and outer dark places waiting to be born again that do not want to die from being aborted not wanted, from bullied by shunning or abused sexually castrated shamed. Behold, I see the heavens opened and the Son of Man standing on the right hand of God (Acts 7:56).

He became a generational atonement payment of forgiveness bridge suspended balanced upside-down World with no end to violence. Time of End divided by church and school house shootings, children being born addicted to crack cocaine sacrificed for education and wealth, abortions, fear of unjust violent fire from Nuclear World War III, Weapons of Mass Destruction (WMD), wickedness of 9/11 Terrorist Suicide attack and rumors of wars between unban tribal giant violent street gangsters Blood and Crip Hoodlums. They stopped their ears and ran upon him with one accord (Acts 7:57). To be a reasonable lightning rod of peace to balance all female and male good and bad kids boys or girls, Christians turning the other cheek pardon bad behavior and Muslim not by Islamic law of religion by a commandment to love your enemy.

Acts 7:46-48
"Who found grace before God and asked to provide a tabernacle for the God of Jacob. But Solomon built him a house. Howbeit the most High does not dwell in temples made with hands, as saith the prophet."

This dedicated good boy was not just a good kid, he fell asleep in death, the first seed great faith of Abraham to be slain for the Nu New, Gospel Testament of Jesus Christ before his time was supposed to end. Threw him out of the city and began to stone him (Acts 7:58). He was innocently gunned down, shot in the head, assassinated on the Crossroad of Modern Mormon Trail of believers in dream and vision front of a nightclub after midnight hour during the College World Series time 2012. Calling upon God and saying, Lord Jesus, receive my spirit (Acts 7:59). North Downtown Omaha, Nebraska in a crowd of hundreds of people battle rapping club hoping to be sacrifice to become a light spectrum ray of hope in dark time according to God's pattern Architects Four Blood Moons and Blood line for dealing with the seed of Abraham great faith Israel the end of the Mayan Calendar December 21, 2012. Living after manner of happiness rather than a single and specific fulfillment. And, he kneeled down and cried with a loud voice, "Lord, impute not this sin to their charge." And having said this, he fell asleep in the Lord (Acts 7:60). Every little detail down to one word- "Jubilee" of De' Anthony.

Acts 8: Beginning

"Saul persecutes the Church, Philip's ministry in Samaria, He works miracles and baptizes men and women baptizes men and women Peter and John come to Samaria and confer the gift of the Holy Ghost by the laying on of hands, Simon seeks to buy this gift and is rebuked by Peter, Philip preaches Christ and baptizes an Ethiopian eunuch."

The Church Scatters (Acts 8:1-3)

De'Anthony was an uncut hew stone born April 18, 1993, Black Native American Urban Tribes Omaha Nebraska Good Life State time of Easter Passover. His birth was precious; he was treated like royalty. As a baby, he was showered with gift of gold, light of compassion, silver oil lamp of mercy by wise aunties and uncles like Baby Jesus the first Passover Lamb. He was in full agreement with Stephen's murder (Acts 8:1). He was a church boy raised to see the world through his grandmother Rose's and godmother Peaches' eyes loving thy neighbor going to Church Sunday school. He loved celebrating the joy of Christmas Gift giving and fun of Easter Passover rejoicing eating candy happiness coloring eggs. His handsome face shined, as though it was the face of an Angel. He stood about 5 feet 8 inches tall solid like a cannon, not afraid of the darkness rich in spirit with graceful given heart of a lion. Had believer attitude fortune in happiness, poor in spirit humble talent of God grace a dreamer of future "Jubilee" is the dream Martin Luther King, Jr. called to create a peaceful Nu, New Nation of equality children of God, seeing peaceful World times vision of taking his kids to church with his mother and grandmother.

Acts 8:2-3

"Some pious men buried Stephen and deeply grieved over him. Saul began to wreak havoc against the church. Entering one house after another, he would drag off both men and women and throw them into prison."

Jubilee of De'Anthony sad innocent assassination death persecution in Jesus name is about protection stopping the violence, safety of all Children Lamb of God unborn and born. Abortion effect not just the family order of faith and happiness. It unbalances the entire Heavenly Order Nation a sadness Passover Urban Tribes. Like the assassination of President Abraham Lincoln 1865, John Kennedy 1963, his brother Bobby Kennedy two months after Dr. Martin Luther King, Jr.in 1968. Lives aborted before their time.

Philip in Samaria Acts 8:4-25

He was Born Again spiritual wealthy with a forgiving heart good boy servant child Lamb of God. He lived in divide calendars of time Christian Passover to Easter leap year. Preaching the good news along the way (Acts 8:4). Injustice of rich and poor apartheid, violent times chaos of White supremacy of untouchables, castration thought Institutional sexual harassment, witness to Radical Islam extremist 9/11 Religion behavior attack become a rumor of War on Terror, Urban Tribal Wars between the Generation of North Omaha Urban Tribes, Nebraska Gangsters Bloods 24th Street Mafia and Crips 40th Ave Hoodlums are identified by the color blue and Bloods color red bandana. To preach Christ to them (Acts 8:5). Nobody wins; when the family Urban Tribes feud, everybody loses.

Acts 8:6-8
"The crowds were united by what they heard Philip say and the signs they saw him perform, and they gave him their undivided attention. With loud shrieks, unclean spirits came out of many people, and many who were paralyzed or crippled were healed. There was great rejoicing in that city."

Dezzo changed his way of thinking; he repented. His compassionate heart's conscience knew killing was wrong; he loved animals and had all kind of pets. The Gangsters Blood Bigger Boys would bully test his strength and "Ubuntu" big humankind Crip family Urban Tribes Heart. Before he was murdered, he gave up his hoodlum Crip walk family Tribe life to walk praise and worship rapping about Jesus Christ triune human sacrifice as a child of God seed of Abraham with great faith. Who preached the good news about God's kingdom and the name of Jesus Christ, both men and women were baptized (Acts 8:12)? De'Anthony's family did not find out he dedicated his life became born again while he was an inmate at the Douglas County Jail until after his murder. I would talk to Dezzo conscience heart about God's grace different of Islam and Christian. I showed him how he could watch the sun and moon rise from on top of Lookout Point Miller Park North Omaha, where you can see all the way over to Council Bluff Iowa the horizon; he could see it as a clock or calendar.

His heart and home were divided with happiness and sadness. He witnessed to the anger and fear Gangster Blood stepfather secret of domestic violence. He was not abused sexually; he was abused from witnessing domestic violence. This was because the Holy Spirit had not yet fallen on any of them; they had only been baptized in the name of the Lord Jesus (Acts 8:16). He had wittiness children of God who were sexually active but not practicing safe sex but living together, but not as husband and wife. He called 9.1.1. for the baby crib death of his baby brother and cried tears of sadness at many funerals of family and Urban Tribe members failures. His mother and family did not find out that De'Anthony sacrificed his life to Jesus Christ until his funeral. When the Holy spirit lead the chaplin from Douglas County Justices Center that said he normally does not do this to take timeout of his day go out of his way to inform De'Anthony's mother Barbara her son De'Anthony believed he was born again dedicated saved in eternal sanctuary of heaven! "Jubilee" He was saved! Sacrificed his life onto blood line seed of Abraham great faith of redemption Jesus Christ sacrifice the last time he was in the County Jail Dezzo was baptized.

Acts 8:20-23

"May your money be condemned to hell along with you because you believed you could buy God's gift with money! You can have no part or share in God's word because your heart isn't right with God. Therefore, change your heart and life! Turn from your wickedness! Plead with the Lord in the hope that your wicked intent can be forgiven, for I see that your bitterness has poisoned you and evil has you in chains."

De'Anthony was no ordinary North Omaha Urban Tribe Street Nigga 40th Ave Crip Hoodlum; he had God-given talents, could gangster rap, he had a beautiful voice like Marvin Gay, he would be on the block battle rapping about What Was Going on in The Hood Politics like Kendrick Lamar. His family gangster bloodline connected back to the West Coast Black City of Compton, California Love. Where everybody knows the hood politics prophet Tupac Shakur sang rapping about Long Beach and Rosecrans bumping and grinding like a slow jam moving Worldwide Lueders Park Piru will bow down to no man was not talking about himself. Also known as the

Lueder Park Bompton Piru and formally known as the Lueders Park Hustlers, throughout the 1970's; they're primarily an African American Piru street gang on the Eastside of Compton, Ca.

They're considered the most notorious Eastside Piru gang where he went swimming in his auntie Gwen backyard on Holly Ave on summer vacations and family reunion. Proclaimed the Lord's word, they returned Zi-On zone with God, preaching the good news to many villages along the way (Acts 8:25). Neighborhood stretches from Bullis Road to Atlantic Ave between Compton Blvd. and Rosecrans Ave. South of Mob Piru, and North of Holly Hood Piru, East of Elm street Piru, and west of Lime Hood Piru. City Compton where Urban Tribes War Piru and Crip outlived the police department.

Philip and the Ethiopian Eunuch
Acts 8:26
"An angel from the Lord spoke to Philip, 'At noon, take the road that leads from Jerusalem to Zi-On monument of God'."

He was raised under religious law of Muhammad Ali The Greatest not to go to war. Dezzo conscience heart did not like to fight; he watched professional wrestling and the activist greatest boxer Muhammad Ali floated like a butterfly and sting like a bee. Dezzo was fast as lighting and thunder, hands had power like a diesel truck. He could pin down grown men bigger than he was. They called De'Anthony, Dezzo power like a truck. He was not a big tall young man. He had powerful body strong hands, big kind heart talent of compassion and a beautiful merciful smile. He beloved his family and his family beloved him; he was not poor a boy, wealthy in spirit loyal to many family and friend Crip or Blood. He was reading the prophet Isaiah while sitting in his carriage (Acts 8:28). They called him "Dezzo The Dome[Head] Dr." because when he would fight a person if felt like being hit by a truck diesel loud sound like the engine combustion with lighting and thunder ping and a bang. He did not win all his fights, but he did not lose many.

Acts 8:32-33

"Like a sheep he was led to the slaughter and like a lamb before its shearer is silent so he didn't open his mouth. In his humiliation justice was taken away from him. Who can tell the story of his descendants because his life was taken from the earth?"

I Am Jubilee of De'Anthony mother's first cousin. I called Dezzo Little Cuzz by blood relationship, not by gang affiliation. Moors' family name a body of people one heart and mind. Born cornhusker seed great of faith Abraham Lincoln, Nebraska moved to Compton, California where we were raised under the shadow of a temple. Opened his mouth and began at the same scripture and preached unto him Jesus (Acts 8:35). I Am born January 19th 1/19 day of peace reset 2018 opposite of 9/11 day of Terrorism the same day of Dezzo's great grandfather. Eric Joseph Hospital Saint Elizabeth moved across the continual divide to Masonic law 33rd degree parallel line Westcoast Black City to be light of the World sun moon earth as a cross.

Acts 8:37

"And Philip said, If thou believes with all thine heart, thou mayest. And he answered and said, I believe that Jesus Christ is the Son of God."

King's Day
January 19, 2018

Why Persecutest Thou Me
Saul Encounters the Risen Jesus

Damascus is about one hundred and fifty miles north of Jerusalem, so it would take Saul and his attendants about a week to travel the distance. Perhaps during those few days of comparative leisure, he began to wonder whether what he was doing was right or not. Perhaps the shining face of the dying Stephen and the martyr's last prayer began to sink more deeply into his soul than it had done before. Little children's cries for their parents whom Saul had bound began to pierce his soul more keenly, and make him feel miserably unhappy as he looked forward to more experiences of that kind in Damascus. Perhaps he wondered whether the works of the Lord, if he were really engaged in it, would make him feel so restless and bitter. He was soon to learn that only the work of the evil one produces those feelings, and that true service for the Lord always brings peace and contentment. But whatever his thoughts and feeling were, he was hastening on with a determination to arrest every follower of Jesus whom he could find.

David O McKay Ancient Apostles p. 120

A city upon a hill that cannot be hidden Compton, California in 1971. Where we were raised watcher choice seer like a prophet have big dreams and vision of future events seeing Nuclear Weapon free Zi-On. He went to the high priest (Acts 9:1). Nu New Modern Jerusalem Church Starting from the shadow of a temple watchtower in my backyard from my bedroom of shame we called the shack like in the book called The Shack. To be gentlemen with humankind hearts of fairness. Fighting for civil rights, union members, extinguishing fires flames and saving lives. we play sport on basketball courts of champions at Lueder Park and Compton Little League Baseball Jack Robinson Stadium Gonzales Park and Community Center. Whether men or women, these letters would authorize him to take them as prisoners (Acts 9:2). We never called ourselves Piru or Crip. My oldest brother Lord James named Holly a hood as a sports club team he would organizes the younger boys in fairness to play neighborhood sports. He retired thirty years of service a City of Compton Fire Fighter Paramedic that saved many families and friends lives and is president of the Compton Little League today. We were the fellows known by our fairness in sports, baldheads, style of dress hats brims, three-piece suits, ties and parties that people still talk about today. The media has created promoted the Black-on-Black Gang Violence Urban Tribes War.

Acts 9:3-5

During the journey, as he approached Damascus, suddenly a light from heaven encircled him. He fell to the ground and heard a voice asking him, "Saul, Saul, why are you harassing me?" Saul asked, "Who are you, Lord?" "I am Jesus, whom you are harassing," came the reply."

My little Cuzz Dezzo "Jubilee" father holiday passover became a Harbinger seed moving my heart conscience. Reminding me to be baptized Easter Holiday Sunday morning 2013 at fifty years of age end of time. Proclaiming "Jubilee" the spirit of the lord is stirring on me moving on my hole entire family culture and social security. A formula to free the captive in debt and heal the broken-hearted conscience Justus. They heard the voice but saw no one (Acts 9:7). God will no longer use holiness to make thing right. God will use consequence of sin "Jubilee" Party of nonviolence to make the world order up-right. I did not know somebody a King has to be the lamb sacrifice innocent blood must be shed there is no coincidence here. Déjà vu I was saved by the grace of God before. I knew the Moore Family Tree life hand of hearts roots came to Compton California seed branch measure of great Faith. Up from the ground, he opened his eyes but he couldn't see. So, they led him by the hand (Acts 9:8).

From Abraham Lincoln, Nebraska corn husker football and called soda pop we did not gang bang. Compton Unified School celebrated Martin Luther King, Jr.'s birthday before it was a national holiday of peace and nonviolence. I graduated junior high middle school Whaley Warriors and high school as Rancho Dominguez's Don of East Compton. The Lord spoke to him in a vision, and he answered, "Yes, Lord" (Acts 9:10). Volunteereed to join the United States Military Service California National Guard and the United State Navy. I Am veteran trained to go to hell and back, qualified marksman in the military service. We are entrepreneurs trying to come up in crooked capitalist corrupted society of family cultures cartels and oligarch. "He is praying. In a vision he has seen a man put his hands on him to restore his sight" (Acts 9:11-12). We never capitalized from gang banging like giant super Crip Snoop Doog and Gangster Rapper Dr. Dre do today.

Acts 9:14-16

"He's here with authority from the chief priests to arrest everyone who calls on your name." The Lord replied, "Go! This man is the agent I have chosen to carry my name before Gentiles, kings, and Israelites. I will show him how much he must suffer for the sake of my name."

De'Anthony June 17, 2012 father's holiday murder was assassination sign signaling failure family security. End of Time innocence Blood Sacrifice to stop the violence Acts II Peace in the 150 years great, great, great, "Jubilee" Party 2018 in North and South America correctly. Like the shoot heard around the world that started the American Revolution created the United States. He sent me so that you could see again and be filled with the Holy Spirit (Acts 9:17). From great battle field Gettysburg that we here highly resolved that these dead shall not have died in vain that this nation under God, shall have a new birth of freedom. The sound of the assassination shoot that killed innocent cousin De'Anthony was not just heard in North Omaha.

It sounds also was heard in heaven to start a spiritual revolution movement of church unity with sign of Son of man light of the sun and moon as one cross. Instantly, flakes fell from his eyes and he could see again. He got up and was baptized (Acts 9:18). According to a formula Book of Redemption the Bible because that Adam failed we are under strict requirements a pattern promise where every little detail must be fulfilled by the seed of Abraham great faith word of Jesus Christ humanness united descendants of Joseph. "He is God's Son," he declared (Acts 9:20). Ubuntu Program "the belief in a universal bond of sharing that connects all humanity Ubuntu[Philosophy]. Philosophy of reconciliation and forgiveness that expresses "respect for a person's dignity irrespective of what that person has done or what neighborhood they come from. "And that government of the people by the people, for the people, shall not perish from the earth." -President Abraham Lincoln

Acts 9:31

"Then the church throughout Judea, Galilee, and Samaria enjoyed a time of peace. God strengthened the church, and its life was marked by reverence for the Lord. Encouraged by the Holy Spirit, the church continued to grow in numbers."

Peter Heals and Raises The Dead

Blood of De'Anthony was conceived innocent born not perfect family bloodline of holy protection out the House of Jacob and Joseph, seed of great faith Abraham Lincoln, Nebraska the Father of a Nu, New Nation to be a wittiness watchman First United Church North and South America. Model of reconciliation onto forgiveness in which human dignity and identity are drawn from the image of the triune God. Jesus Christ heals you! Get up and make your bed. "At once, he got up" (Acts 9:34). Human beings are called to be persons because they are created in the image of God, I AM. Dezzo's murder execution marked the beginning to the end of violent times Year Zero Blood and Crips standing together as one Nation "Jubilee" Partying nonviolently. Turned to the Lord (Acts 9:35). Under a pattern of four blood moon eclipse and two total solar eclipse of the heart forever with one church bell ringing.

Acts 9:40

"Peter sent everyone out of the room, then knelt and prayed. He turned to the body and said, "Tabitha, get up!" She opened her eyes, saw Peter, and sat up. 41 He gave her his hand and raised her up. Then he called God's holy people, including the widows, and presented her alive to them."

Peter, Cornelius, and The Gentiles

Jubilee of De'Anthony's innocent life most precious blood sacrifice is untouchable the First verse of the Nu New Testament to Jesus Christ of the Nu New Millennium Passover return to humanity a thief in the night son of redemption. He and his whole household were pious, gentile God-worshippers. He gave generously to those in need among the Jewish people and prayed to God constantly (Acts 10:2). Like the Blood Saint Stephen Holy martyr prayed for his murderer's redemption New Testament Book of Acts believe he was born again saved appointed in time. The Blood sacrifice of Joseph Smith Jr. the Book of Mormon another testament to Jesus Christ a formula returning establishing Nu New Millennium modern church presidential executive order of realignment. Be careful with what you are tempted for 2017 Tax cut or 2016 "Jubilee" Mercy.

Acts 10:3-4

"One day at nearly three o'clock in the afternoon, he clearly saw an angel from God in a vision. The angel came to him and said, "Cornelius!" Startled, he stared at the angel and replied, "What is it, Lord?" The angel said, "Your prayers and your compassionate acts are like a memorial offering to God."

Where ancient temple knowledge and wisdom is married united through education with Nu, New Millennium Modern First United Churches of Zi-On no nuclear weapon stopping the violence social order zone of peace calling forth commandment "Jubilee" Universal Pardon! "Whose house is near the seacoast" (Acts 10:6). Holy Times Sacred Events a formula for removing fake news that God is mad about Jesus Christ self-sacrifice celebrating Christmas Immaculate Conception Passover Easter Resurrection Pentecost until his return. A formula setting the Time record straight.

Acts 10:9-16

"At noon on the following day, as their journey brought them close to the city, Peter went up on the roof to pray. He became hungry and wanted to eat. While others were preparing the meal, he had a visionary experience. He saw heaven opened up and something like a large linen sheet being lowered to the earth by its four corners. Inside the sheet were all kinds of four-legged animals, reptiles, and wild birds. A voice told him, "Get up, Peter! Kill and eat!" Peter exclaimed, "Absolutely not, Lord! I have never eaten anything impure or unclean." The voice spoke a second time, "Never consider unclean what God has made pure."

This happened three times, then the object was suddenly pulled back into heaven."

The Mayan civilization are ancient Native American culture of color language Olmec people they are prophet steward over the land with the sovereignty to move anywhere north or south America they want to. "Don't ask questions; just go with them because I have sent them" (Acts 10:20). Blessed with divine rite knowledge and wisdom about pattern movement of the heaven from earth. They build pyramid temples tower for sacrificing people to honor the god sun and moon. They moved dirt building mountain pyramids from place to place planting trading word keys sharing knowledge of hope and charity everywhere they went didn't build fences or wall to keep people out. God has shown me that I should never call a person impure or unclean (Acts 10:28). America first stone masons to lay the stones that became the United States of America near Phoenix is a place called the Circlestone Observatory. They study space weather sun spot cycles and time pattern on the 33rd parallel north circle of latitude this 33 degree north eternal line marking Garden of paradise equatorial plane.

"I really am learning that God doesn't show partiality to one group of people over another (Acts 10: 34). It crosses the Wilderness dried up riverbed of Compton California the New Modern Jerusalem, North Africa, Baghdad Iraq, Tiran Iran Asia Pacific Ocean, North America, Phoenix, Arizona the Atlantic Ocean and Old Jerusalem Israel. Homeland South were most of the people of color live below this line the United Nation there is no nuclear weapons allowed south of 33rd degree parallel Time line. By proclaiming the good news through Jesus Christ: He is Lord of all (Acts 10: 36)! Christians have the God-given right to move any place in South and North America they want to. North American Free Trade Agreement signed by Canada, Mexico and the United States creating a trilateral trade bloc in North America. The agreement came into force on January 1, 1994.

Acts 10:39-43

We are witnesses of everything he did, both in Judea and in Jerusalem. They killed him by hanging him on a tree, but God raised him up on the third day and allowed him to be seen, not by everyone but by us. We are witnesses whom God chose beforehand, who ate and drank with him after God raised him from the dead. He commanded us to preach to the people and to testify that he is the one whom God appointed as judge of the living and the dead. All the prophets testify about him that everyone who believes in him receives forgiveness of sins through his name."

They gave out a sacred calendar marking time pattern for the end of time December 21, 2012 and beginning of the age in relationship to a formula counting the precession of the equinoxes cycle ancient temple wisdom. The Holy Spirit fell on everyone who heard the word (Acts 10:44). Their calendar formula predicted planet, sun and moon alignment pattern with true north and south. The Bible formula divide land north and south into time zones to be shared equally with periods every seven season, New Moon to New Moon cycle the Blood Moon is sacred Lord's Day of "Jubilee"! Astonished that the gift of the Holy Spirit had been poured out even on the Gentiles (Acts 10:45). Holy Calendar too formula predicting movement of separated pattern divide remnant people sons and daughters being exile alignment of government and church north and south after ten calendar year the land return back to the native people of color to police themselves under the protection authority of United Church of North and South America.

Acts 10:46-48

They heard them speaking in other languages and praising God. Peter asked, "These people have received the Holy Spirit just as we have. Surely no one can stop them from being baptized with water, can they?" He directed that they be baptized in the name of Jesus Christ.

CHAPTER 5
The Order of Melchizedek

Great American Eclipse
August 21, 2017

We are Jesus' House
Hebrews 3:1
"Therefore, brothers and sisters who are partners in the heavenly calling, think about Jesus, the apostle and high priest of our confession."

The methods of Jesus Christ Jubilee Order of Melchizedek Ministry have no walls and are set in appointed time over all his house. The Cross is the one holy door to heaven in an open book to the public remnant generation of the Living Temple of God instant forgiveness priesthood here on Earth as also Moses was faithful (Hebrews 3:2). As a one, two, one ministry, me as one, in the imaged of the Father, the creator and as the face of God's son Jesus Christ King setting in heaven as two, and as advantage the Holy Spirit. God's voice here on Earth the comforter as spiritual blanket arm of God instantly forgiving protection one. But God is the builder of everything (Hebrews 3:4). In a Book of Books with a double function calendar of words for keep time of Ages punishment (curses) or rewards (blessings) corrections called (Basic Instruction Before Leaving Earth) the King James Bible.

Respond to Jesus' voice now
Hebrews 3:7-11
"So, as the Holy Spirit says, Today, if you hear his voice, don't have stubborn hearts as they did in the rebellion, on the day when they tested me in the desert. That is where your ancestors challenged and tested me, though they had seen my work for forty years. So I was angry with them. I said, "Their hearts always go off course, and they don't know my ways." Because of my anger I swore: "They will never enter my rest!"

When I first started in a public elementary school calendar of numbers year, before I was even able to read or keep time, I (the artificial me) was compelled to pledge my state of mind with my right hand over my heart, allegiance to the flag of the "In God We Trust" United States Capital of Capitalism of America Don't Tread On Me, and it became my god, putting me in a double cross state of mind thinking way of ice cold unforgiving heart. I became my own antichrist. Unfaithful hearts that abandon the living God (Hebrews 3:12). I (the spiritual me) rebelled against who God custom created me to be and the United Kingdom of Heaven right state of mind of instant forgiveness with a warm heart and did not go to church. The artificial I felt beside myself. I saw the upside-down twisted underworld capitalism system and civil religion as my church family. "Today," so that none of you become insensitive to God because of sin's deception (Hebrews 3:13).

Soon as I became old enough, I was recruited before the end of the appointed time I graduated from high school to give up my free will and swear to enlist with my right hand in the air on mission in the civil religion United States Capitalist Fraternal Order Military Service to defend the

Constitution and the capitalist antichrist system twisted underworld unforgiving family protection. We are partners with Christ (Hebrew 3:14). I grew up an institutionalized capitalist cold hearted ready to do or die on the far-side, an eye for eye, tooth for tooth revengeful way of thinking no equality between woman and man.

To be all I could to artificially capitalize to be imagining doing good work, trying to be like God and be good and not live under the comforter spiritual blanket protective methods of Jesus Christ Jubilee Ministry arms of the Holy Spirit God's voice can be in me doing right. I gave up my freewill, which I was custom created to be and to serve and protect my underworld capitalism system twisted double crossing mind state. As they did in the rebellion (Hebrews 3:15). Institutionalized ready to follow orders to kill or be killed in the armed service on the far-side of the underworld capitalism system protecting the sea lanes open.

Hebrews 3:16

"Who was it who rebelled when they heard his voice? Wasn't it all of those who were brought out of Egypt by Moses."

I did more rumbling street fighting in the Civil Religion Capitalist Fraternal Order Military Armed Service than in my hood in the California National Guard Split Option 1979-1981. Wasn't it with the ones who sinned, whose bodies fell in the desert (Hebrews 3:17)?

Fort Knox 1980

I spent my high school junior year (eleventh grade) summer time in Army Boot Camp at Fort Knots, Kentucky. I had my first fight in the latrine knuckle up, toe to toe with a brother from Capital of Capitalism Washington D.C. named Cole. I showed him my false two front teeth and knocked him down.

Hebrews 3:18-19

"And against whom did he swear that they would never enter his rest, if not against the ones who were disobedient? We see that they couldn't enter because of their lack of faith."

Enter the rest

During the summer time after my high school graduation Disneyland Grand all Night Event, I went to Advance Individual Training A.I.T Fifty-One November and water purification at Fort Leonard Wood Missouri. Let's be careful so that none of you will appear to miss it (Hebrews 4:1). I had to fight the Army for them to keep their part of my contract. I was educated and served under Governor Jerry Brown. I enlisted in the U. S. Navy 1981-1984 to provide for my daughter, serve my nation, holy see and defend the underworld capitalism Institution keeping the sea lanes open.

Hebrews 4:3

"We who have faith are entering the rest. As God said, And because of my anger I swore: "They will never enter into my rest!" And yet God's works were completed at the foundation of the world."

I was a Jimmy Carter Democrat serving under General Colin Powell as President Ronald Reagan Senior Military Assistant to Secretary of Defense. It was gun versus butter. I chose guns and Don't Tread on Me. God rested on the seventh day from all his works (Hebrews 4:4). I attended boot camp at Naval Training Center (N.T.C.) in San Diego. I was commissioned to lead from the back as Recruit Petty Officer First Class over my Basic Training Platoon class. Don't have stubborn hearts (Hebrews 4:7). I dropped out of Hospital Corpsman School. I wanted to go on a West-Pac tour overseas.

I received two weeks leave, International Overseas Orders, with a passport and airline ticket on the Flying Tiger Boeing 747 out of Los Angeles International Airport (LAX), with stops in San Francisco, California; Anchorage, Alaska; Okinawa, Japan; and Clarke Air Force Base, in the Philippines, where I transferred airplanes to a Lockheed C-5 Galaxy, the military's largest transport aircraft, for a nine-hour flight to go to Diego Garcia Foot Print of Freedom India Ocean south of the equator. So, you see that a sabbath rest is left open for God's people (Hebrews 4: 9). I was a Seamen E-3 assigned as Petty Officer Shore Patrol E-4 Duty Island Defense. I broke up fights in the clubs and barracks with the drunks, sailors and Marines at the U.S.O. shows.

Hebrews 4:10

"The one who entered God's rest also rested from his works, just as God rested from his own."

First Summary of The Message
Hebrews 4:12

"because God's word is living, active, and sharper than any two-edged sword. It penetrates to the point that it separates the soul from the spirit and the joints from the marrow. It's able to judge the heart's thoughts and intentions."

Following the fall of the Shah of Iran and the Iran Hostage Crisis in 1979–1980, the West became concerned with ensuring the flow of oil from the Persian Gulf through the Strait of Hormuz, and the United States received permission for a $400 million expansion of the military facilities on Diego Garcia consisting of two parallel 12,000-foot-long runways, expansive parking aprons for heavy bombers, 20 new anchorages in the lagoon, a deep water pier, port facilities for the largest naval vessels in the American or British fleet, aircraft hangars, maintenance buildings and an air terminal, a 1,340,000 barrels fuel storage area, and billeting and messing facilities for thousands of sailors and support personnel.

Hebrews 4:13

"No creature is hidden from it, but rather everything is naked and exposed to the eyes of the one to whom we have to give an answer."

Hebrews 4:14

"Also, let's hold on to the confession since we have a great high priest who passed through the heavens, who is Jesus, God's Son."

In 1982, the Red Cross informed me that my grandfather, my mother's father, an Army veteran, had passed way in Oklahoma City, Oklahoma. I received emergency leave, and I had to fight to get a flight back home to the United States. I got on an Air Force Lockheed C-141 Starlifter cargo plane for a nine-hour flight to Clark Air Force Base in the Philippines. From there, I took a five-hour flight to Andersen Air force Base in Guam and then another nine-hour flight to pass over the international date line through the United States Custom Hickam Air force Base Hawaii. Fighting jetlag, I still had to fly another nine hours to Travis Air Force Base in Northern California and finally, I flew four more hours with touch and go landing training at Clark Air Force Base, in San Bernardino, California. I caught a Trailways bus to downtown Los Angeles. I still had to travel to Oklahoma City, Oklahoma for my grandfather's funeral.

Hebrews 4:16

"Finally, let's draw near to the throne of favor with confidence so that we can receive mercy and find grace when we need help."

I was placed on alert at the time of The Beirut Lebanon Barracks Bombings (October 23, 1983) killing 299 American and French servicemen. A suicide bomber detonated each of the truck bombs. In the attack on the building serving as a barracks for the 1st Battalion 8th Marines, the death toll was 241 American servicemen: 220 Marines, 18 sailors, and 3 soldiers, making that incident the deadliest single-day death toll for the United States Marine Corps since World War II's Battle of Iwo Jima, the deadliest single-day death toll for the United States Military since the first day of the Vietnam War's Tet Offensive, and the deadliest single attack on Americans overseas since World War II. Another 128 Americans were wounded in the blast. Thirteen later died of their injuries, and they are numbered among the total number who died. Two days later on the 25 October 1983 was the invasion of Grenada. I stood on watch on Perry class guide missile Frigate U.S.S. Boone was ordered 23 January 1978, launched 16 January 1980 by Todd Pacific Shipyards, and commissioned 15 May 1982. She has since earned numerous awards and commendations.

Introduction to a Deeper Teaching
Hebrews 5:1-6

"Every high priest is taken from the people and put in charge of things that relate to God for their sake, in order to offer gifts and sacrifices for sins. The high priest is able to deal gently with the ignorant and those who are misled since he himself is prone to weakness. Because of his weakness, he must offer sacrifices for his own sins as well as for the people. No one takes this honor for themselves but takes it only when they are called by God, just like Aaron. In the same way Christ also didn't promote himself to become high priest. Instead, it was the one who said

to him, You are my Son. Today I have become your Father, as he also says in another place, You are a priest forever, according to the order of Melchizedek."

During 1983-1984 while fighting seasickness on a war ship, we escorted United States Marians to Honduras to show support for Contras fighting against Nicaragua. Ship Liberty call in Key West, Florida. Ship docks across from Ernest Hemingway's house. A bar fight turned into a gang street fight with guys from Key West neighborhood against the crew off the ship, and I went smooth sailing through the Bermuda Triangle with a stopover in Freeport and Nassau, Bahamas.

Hebrews 5:7-10

"During his days on earth, Christ offered prayers and requests with loud cries and tears as his sacrifices to the one who was able to save him from death. He was heard because of his godly devotion. 8 Although he was a Son, he learned obedience from what he suffered. 9 After he had been made perfect, he became the source of eternal salvation for everyone who obeys him. 10 He was appointed by God to be a high priest according to the order of Melchizedek."

We received a commission to travel the Trans-Atlantic middle passage as naval ambassadors of Freedom to the Persian Gulf with orders to assure keeping the world sea-lanes open. From Naval Station Mayport, in Jacksonville, Florida, we crossed the Atlantic Ocean, refueled in Rota, Spain, and passed the coast. We returned salutes to the Kingdom of Morocco on December 20, 1777. Morocco became the first country to give a naval salute to the new nation. Morocco remains one of America's oldest and closest allies in the Middle East and North Africa, through the Strait of the Rock of Gibraltar into Mediterranean Sea. Liberty calls in Palma, Spain. All hands were on deck, while standing at General Quarters, as we transient the Suez Cannel, Egypt into the Red Sea. In the Horn of Africa, Djibouti, Djibouti, from Port Sudan, Sudan, we split the Red Sea to pilgrim in Jeddah, Saudi Arabia, Gulf of Aden, to the India Ocean, Arabian Sea, past the Strait of Hormuz, patrolled in the Persian Gulf with stops in the Kingdom of Bahrain. The Persian Gulf was a battlefield of mine during the Iran-Iraq War, in which each side attacked the other's oil tankers. We were fighting an artificial war and seasickness. Afterward, I fought for an honorable discharge out of the Navy.

Let's Press Zi-On to Maturity
Hebrews 6:1-3

"So let's press on to maturity, by moving on from the basics about Christ's word. Let's not lay a foundation of turning away from dead works, of faith in God, of teaching about ritual ways to wash with water, laying on of hands, the resurrection from the dead, and eternal judgment—all over again. We're going to press on, if God allows it."

This is Moore than one story about the time of end once in a life Holy time event proclaiming "Jubilee" twin year 2020. My dark life never has been just ordinary tough bad times. I, a twin, always lived double interesting exceptional joyful double blessed and dark trouble life in tasting good times. The light from God's eternal constant love has been illuminating in my spiritual twin dark life from first Sunday after Pentecost to Advent season of favor God had an action plan for my life a born-again choice seer of God world without numbers. Become partners with the Holy Spirit (Hebrews 6:4). Born with a peaceful breath of the Holy Spirit tongue of fire like Elijah a Moor man on the Mormon Wagon Trail of suffering and tears, passing through the corn field in Good Life State of Nebraska Capital Star City Abraham Lincoln. Named after father of faithful Abraham and Father of Freedom President Lincoln great emancipator. Centennial Anniversary of War Power Civil Act II end the war of "Jubilee." Into the Holy year of our Lord's day January 19, 1963 Daylight of peace reverse of dark Day of Terror 9/11. At Saint Elisabeth Hospital, named after the mother of disciple prophet John the Baptist, the greatest man born of a woman. Tasted God's good word and the powers of the coming age (Hebrews 6:5).

Middle son, twin name, first name title Eric comes out of history eternal one a Viking explorer, middle name after my grand and father first name comes out of the Bible, boy dreamer Joseph and man saint stepfather husband to the mother of God, into the arms of an Ethiopian mother and a Moor (Black) father. The year 10,000's of Saint March on Washington and Martin Luther King, Jr. read his "I Have a Dream" speech. Raised and resided on Ground Zero the 33rd parallel land grant from King of Spain in East Rancho Dominguez graduated Don Lord of East Compton. Be renewed again by repentance (Hebrews 6:6).

Even when the bad unspiritual, like Peter denied methods of Jesus Christ was afraid not with God's goodness excellent spirit eternal constant unconditional beloved forgave my twin divided sincere heart like King David. Loved myself misused my double authority and misused others, lost in the dark far-side jungle of my double-crossing mind cross up heart. Confused, as a prisoner under the influence of the capitalist entrepreneurial twisted artificial antichrist twin me. Whose end shall be by fire (Hebrews 6:8). Created to be all money could buy me. Looking out for

Number 1! Capital became my capitalist twin's own god ride or die giving up my autonomy free will to kill or be killed.

Make Your Hope Sure
Hebrews 6:9
"But we are convinced of better things in your case, brothers and sisters, even though we are talking this way-things that go together with salvation."

How does a capitalist entrepreneurial twisted artificial corporation professional twin person control the God created spiritual resurrected twin person? Born with autonomy into a spiritual Nobel Ethiopian Black family American citizen with the surname Moore. Continue to serve God's holy people (Hebrews 6:10). The Moors were rulers in Spain Europe, Maroons Moriscos New Christian a culture of people Negus (Kings) in exile that used to wear turbans and swords. Today, they wear neckties, three-piece suits, and live in Compton, CA. (Moor: Sub-Saharan Africans, Black African, the lowercase letter "e" was added to our last name to show the exile accepting Christianity baptizing circumcised their own children) spelled with uppercase and lowercase letters. My grandfather's family name is Bowler from Boley, Oklahoma. Grandmother was a queen Ethiopian Hebrew. My mother's certificate of birth says it, too. My father's parents were born in the neutral ground Bienville Parish Ringgold, Louisiana. My granddad was a watchman keeper time; he would say, "You can tell a lot from the sounding of a twin person name." Same effort to make your hope sure until the end (Hebrews 6:11). First and middle names a title say what you born to do artistic work. My first name Eric means (eternal one) and twin middle name Joseph (Jah is my increase) last name let people know where we come from and who we are, and where we are going divinely appointed by God as gentleman. Giving autonomy. The King James Bible says that, too.

Luke 2:4 (KJV)
"And Joseph also went up from Galilee, out of the city of Nazareth, into Judaea, unto the city of David, which is called Bethlehem; (because he was of the house and lineage of David."

The spiritual created twin me was custom created divinely placed in the spirit of the time as a genital soft-hearted psalm trouble man seed of King David with great wisdom as his son King Solomon for a godly purpose driven life watchman sounding of time starting over. Be obedient with the divine authority from God like King James ruling with orders of instant forgiveness, fruitful and multiply merciful hearts doing a great work helping doing good expanding the kingdom of heaven. But imitators of those who by faith and patience inherit the promises (Hebrews 6:12). Sacredly circumcised as a Christian, Hebrew, and Muslim seed remnant of King David heart (not Arab Muslim) on the eighth day. My grandmother's father's mother was Native American prayer Worrier rain dancer and mother's mother was a queen Ethiopian Hebrew woman of the enlightenment. Ethiopia Negus: Kingship is carried through the female line rather than the male. The queen mother was thus the one from whom her kingly son derived his right to the throne, and at times, she may have been the virtual ruler of the land.

Our Hope in Jesus' Priesthood
Hebrews 6:13-15
"When God gave Abraham his promise, he swore by himself since he couldn't swear by anyone greater. He said, I will certainly bless you and multiply your descendants. So Abraham obtained the promise by showing patience."

I, the capitalist entrepreneurial artificial corporation professional twin person, was created by United States Capital of capitalism government with debt to be a consumer with an interest collecting loan on my certificate of birth that spells my name MOORE with all uppercase letters, my social security number in red, driver's license, credit cards, credit score and digital data profile. A corporation is a separate legal entity that has been incorporated either directly through legislation or through a registration process established by law.

Hebrews 6:16

"People pledge by something greater than themselves. A solemn pledge guarantees what they say and shuts down any argument."

Holy Spirit voice God showed me the eternal light to see I Am Because We Are: In South Africa translated Ubuntu. At Nelson Mandela's memorial, United States President Barack Obama spoke about Ubuntu, saying, "There is a word in South Africa -- Ubuntu -- a word that captures Mandela's greatest gift: his recognition that we are all bound together in ways that are invisible to the eye; that there is a oneness to humanity; that we achieve ourselves by sharing ourselves with others, and caring for those around us.

Hebrews 6:17

"When God wanted to further demonstrate to the heirs of the promise that his purpose doesn't change, he guaranteed it with a solemn pledge."

We can never know how much of this sense was innate in him or how much was shaped in a dark and solitary cell. But, we remember the gestures, large and small -- introducing his jailers as honored guests at his inauguration; taking a pitch in a Springbok uniform; turning his family's heartbreak into a call to confront HIV/AIDS -- that revealed the depth of his empathy and his understanding. He not only embodied Ubuntu, he taught millions to find that truth within themselves."

Hebrews 6:18

"So these are two things that don't change, because it's impossible for God to lie. He did this so that we, who have taken refuge in him, can be encouraged to grasp the hope that is lying in front of us."

An anthropologist proposed a game to the kids in a African tribe. He put a basket full of fruit near a tree and told them that whoever got there first won the sweet fruits. When he gave them a signal to run, they all took each other's hands and ran together, then sat in a circle enjoying their treats. This hope is a safe and secure anchor for our whole being (Hebrews 6:19). When he asked them why they chose to run as a group when they could have had more fruit individually, one child spoke and said: "UBUNTU", how can one of us be happy if all the other ones are sad? 'Ubuntu' in Xhosa culture means: "I am because we are."

Hebrews 6:20

"That's where Jesus went in advance and entered for us, since he became a high priest according to the order of Melchizedek."

As I reflect on my past, I was a good-hearted man and she a hell of independent woman did not make us right. My capitalist entrepreneurial artificial twin good works, relationships and privies marriage, it was all by the Grace-grace of God constant eternal unconditional love. Who was king of Salem and priest of the Most High God (Hebrews 7:1)? The reason God raptured me from my previous antichrist twin's marriage was so my spiritual twin could celebrate becoming Born Again, and Holy Spirit voice of God revealed to me how to love unconditional others, teaching me charity how to give celebrate being married in the church spirit resurrection from my trust faith in the creator God's constant eternal unconditional loving forgiving myself. Marriage is not a corporation business under Robert Rule of Order or Marriage License Contract between two artificial capitalist people in with last name in capital letter only; you do not have the right to hire or fire the free will to quit. His name means first "king of righteousness," and then "king of Salem," that is, "king of peace" (Hebrews 7:2). Marriage unites a man and a woman with each other and any children born from their union. Marriage is family affair blood covenant under God's rule of divine order husband, wife eternal love the first and great commandment of all a sacred grace-grace. Having neither beginning of days, nor end of life, but made like unto the Son of God; abides a priest continually (Hebrews 7:3). Covenant with God, joined in heaven and Earth better or worse let not man separate what God has brought together until deaths do we part and generation, to generation.

Matthew 19:6 (JUB)
"Therefore they are no longer two, but one flesh. What therefore God has joined together, let not man separate."

Matrimony is not just about whom you can live with; it also is about putting somebody's interest before your own, whom you cannot live without or love no matter what they do.

A Priest like Melchizedek
Hebrews 7:4-6
"See how great Melchizedek was! Abraham, the father of the people, gave him a tenth of everything he captured. The descendants of Levi who receive the office of priest have a commandment under the Law to collect a tenth of everything from the people who are their brothers and sisters, though they also are descended from Abraham. But Melchizedek, who isn't related to them, received a tenth of everything from Abraham and blessed the one who had received the promises."

God knew the matters of my broken heart as stubborn a Capricorn mountain goat, but God knew matters well, God knew the matters of her hardened divided heart as a lazy Leo. When I told her, I Am revealed to my spiritual twin me be holy see our divide family as the Church to unify with Jesus Christ in ministry as the foundation cornerstone of my family home life and celebrate marriage. The less important person is blessed by the more important person (Hebrews 7:7). She thought I went crazy and wanted to brainwash her, wanting her to join a church or sing in a choir. She had more interest in continuing to electric slide, celebrating in nightclubs and marching with Old Sckool Drill Team in parades. According to the record (Hebrews 7:8), when my spiritual twin's voice of God came on me, she heard me crying asking my father to use the same spiritual talented voice given him the interest to organizes the Compton Firefighter Union 2216. That he should us the same example of spirit like Moses' law and interest to organize our family to working together. Paid a tenth through Abraham (Hebrews 7:9). I said, "That we all had God given divine skill talents and abilities to help make a difference, which we all can use to make this Keeping Family Church better moving closer to God working together we could do everything." When Melchisedek met him (Hebrews 7:10), he said he had some skill and abilities working under Robert Rule of Order that he could use to make this family better that did not follow God's Golden Rule of Order right I am my brother keeper. I did not want my three junior sons to be drafted to fight no capitalist antichrist twin war.

Hebrews 7:11

"So if perfection came through the Levitical office of priest (for the people received the Law under the priests), why was there still a need to speak about raising up another priest according to the order of Melchizedek rather than one according to the order of Aaron?"

I never thought love as a twin could be so complicated or would be so miss understood, I loved in the flesh, and in the conditions of the flesh I became somebody I could not be lived with, there always going to be some conditions too unloving that I am not going too able to beloved for. I did not know in the spirit of time of the end she was somebody I could not live without the message of the cross or God's peacefulness. There has to be a change in the Law as well (Hebrews 7:12). God beloved me supernaturally in bring us together with I am because we are like twin too bring unity through education to Urban Tribes God's Moore than Rainbow Family and educate them. Behavior tells the truth. The spiritual twin me working together we could do anything. We promised we would support each other kids' education interest. I would support her and her kids while they got their degrees of interest, and she would help support me and my kids when we wanted to get a degree of our interest. No one ever served at the altar from that tribe (Hebrews 7:13). I made it about my personal wants and artificial twin needs the spiritually dead artificial twin me working by myself without Jesus Christ I could only do so much. Moses never said anything about priests from that tribe (Hebrews 7:14). Capitalist artificial twin showed up in the flesh as a good daddy for her son and a dream husband that slowly faded away into a double nightmare. Spiritual twin I thought she would always need me. Mind blowing decision, causes head on collision, is she mine, I have to know, by letting her go.

Hebrews 7:15-17
*"And it's even clearer if another priest appears who is like Melchizedek.
He has become a priest by the power of a life that can't be destroyed,
rather than a legal requirement about physical descent. This is confirmed:
You are a priest forever, according to the order of Melchizedek.
Able to save completely."*

If my mother would have prophesied at the time of sounding event my fortieth birthday January 19 reverse of Nine Eleven day of peace, I am not plush partying at Stage II Night Club in North Omaha, working overtime on weekends being paid time and a half double time on holiday at the City

Omaha Vehicle Maintains Department. An earlier command is set aside because it was weak and useless (Hebrews 7:18). Four years out of prison into my ten-year marriage my wife had a Ph.D, I owned two homes across the street from a golf course and fishing pound with Ford Diesel Truck, a Luxury cars in the driveway. I did not know what a dollar cost, I was unhappy, lost in wilderness of temptation of lust not right with God. That at the age of fifty sounding the time of the end, I would Passover my heart mind to the Leadership of the voice of God the Holy Spirit starting over at the Four Blood Moons Eclipse New, New, beginning. Because the Law made nothing perfect Hebrews 7:19).

    I would be raptured out my marriage becoming divorce and born again at the same time, or getting baptizes by a woman in the same city I was born in, less than a mile from Saint Elizabeth same hospital where I was born. I would be divinely appointed keeper of the oldest church City of Compton, Vice President of United Methodist Men and Women 80 million members around the world, on my fifty-second birthday King Day the reverse day of nine eleven studying the Bible Keeping Holy Time, prison ministry. The others have become priests without a solemn pledge (Hebrews 7:20). I Am Choice seer would be an instrument Holy Spirit voice of God sounding for an extraordinary jubilee of mercy spiritual Exodus family moving closer to God living life like every day is Sunday. I would have called her my mother a liar.

Hebrews 7:21-22

"but this priest was affirmed with a solemn pledge by the one who said, The Lord has made a solemn pledge and will not change his mind: You are a priest forever. As a result, Jesus has become the guarantee of a better covenant."

    I did not believe the supernatural. I am flesh solid as a rock man of liberty I could not be regulated or trust government authority. I still have a problem wearing seatbelts today. I did not trust God's constant love or know nothing of the spirit. I believed La La Means I Love You. I have free will was self-righteous. I was old school as Blue Magic said, "I was chasing Rainbow" looking for a pot of Gold change. Death prevented them from continuing to serve (Hebrews 7:23). I did not see the Cross treasure or value methods of Jesus Christ as the only open-door stairway to see Heaven. I believed in hard work sacrifice for capitalism silver and gold change paid my crocket way into Heaven. I believed in my artificial capitalist twin good works and trusted in my artificial capitalist twin just for men good looks. The twin spiritual me did not comb or cut and twisted my hair into gray locks of spiritual wisdom like a predator time traveler warrior battling fames evil demons.

Hebrews 7:24-25
"In contrast, he holds the office of priest permanently because he continues to serve forever. This is why he can completely save those who are approaching God through him, because he always lives to speak with God for them."

If these walls could talk, they cry tears of sorrow, people would say I am the life of the party. My artificial capitalist twin I knew how to two-step partying celebrating all the time watched sport entertainment on tv, movie theater, concerts tickets anything my hard work could buy. Holy, innocent, incorrupt, separate from sinners, and raised high above the heavens (Hebrews 7:26). I did not know how unqualified spiritually dead artificial or morale weak my capitalist twin was. I trusted my education intelligent. I consumed what I knew and walked by sight danced and boogied to a different drumbeat I had credit cards worried about my credit score. I did not walk by a soft heartbeat of faith. I was Independent American free slave deep into debt. I was too cool intelligent to believe in miracles or trust in the supernatural of the living word in the King James Bible and God's glory. Capital became my capitalist twin's own god antichrist the spiritually dead artificial unforgiving common capitalist twin me prepared for war attacking dividing the uncommon spiritual instant forgiving twin me from God. Making artificial capitalist twin me want to consume more.

Hebrews 7:27-28

"He doesn't need to offer sacrifices every day like the other high priests, first for their own sins and then for the sins of the people. He did this once for all when he offered himself. 28 The Law appoints people who are prone to weakness as high priests, but the content of the solemn pledge, which came after the Law, appointed a Son who has been made perfect forever."

Meeting Tents, Sacrifices, and Covenants

My capitalist wife had hundred thousand dollars in student loan interest debt with a Ph.D. from the University Nebraska Lincoln and was associate professor at University Nebraska Omaha and Chair of Black Studies as she said without me help meeting her supporting her interest it would not have happen given thanks to her capitalist spiritual guide that was not Jesus Christ. *We have this kind of high priest. He sat down at the right side of the throne of the majesty in the heavens* (Hebrews 8:1). She was a member of the Fraternal Order Legion of Elks Lodge Civil Religious celebrated Federal United State Capital of capitalism holidays Fourth of July with hundred dollars spent on fireworks. Being radical not celebrating Christmas, Easter would keep other civil religion calendar holidays without biblical reason. Which is the true meeting tent that God, not any human being, set up (Hebrews 8:2).

She was spiritual fearfully of losing capital, proud but because of her being educated, she believed in astrology performances by following the stars she is a Leo with a lioness for pride tattoo on her shoulder. She is educated with no common since, did charitable work with pride and loved competing playing card games, like Bid-whist and Spades. Every high priest is appointed to offer gifts and sacrifices (Hebrews 8:3). She would boast playing games Remember when grandmother did this or when Erma Jennie did that, she did not like to lose. She was a self-centered party girl who knew every line dance step, did not miss one drumbeat marching in an adult drill team of over the hill and old school women, saving wealth American saving bonds for her own kids' salvation. Teacher of university students public speaking and Black Studies, gifted with typing close to 100 words a minute. Her dissertation is on the carnality of black female beauty. Not one word about tutoring about teaching the beautiful gifts of fruit of the Spirit is love, joy, peace, forbearance, kindness, goodness, faithfulness, gentleness and self-control.

Hebrews 8:6-7
"But now, Jesus has received a superior priestly service just as he arranged a better covenant that is enacted with better promises. If the first covenant had been without fault, it wouldn't have made sense to expect a second."

We were equally yoked capitalist antichrist and believed in our own good works and good looks being seeing at all the entertainment events miss using our influence of imitating what we saw. We did not eat pork, we watched and made porn movies, played sex games with sex toys. She was light skinned with a butterscotch complexion naturally beautiful did not need makeup with eyes that was intellectual that don't mean a thing. Desirable sexy with a behind that would take the wrinkle out of her pants; we liked to two-step dance together; she did not believe in faith of the unseen promise that we are going to be all right. The holy place on earth (Hebrews 9:1). The twin spiritually dead artificial capitalist i was accepted as a sinner breaker of the rules of law. The first moment of me asking what does her car license plate stand for. She said, "I am because we are." To me asking her, "Do you read a lot?" She asked me if I was Afrocentric: Emphasizing or promoting emphasis on African culture and the contributions of Africans to the development of Western civilization.

But God did find fault with them, since He says, Hebrews 8:8-9: *"Look, the days are coming, says the Lord, when I will make a covenant with the house of Israel, and I will make a new covenant with the house of Judah. It will not be like the covenant that I made with their ancestors on the day I took them by the hand to lead them out of the land of Egypt, because they did not continue to keep my covenant, and I lost interest in them, says the Lord."*

I showed her my dreadlocks with my pretty smile, while telling her, "I am just getting out of prison living in a halfway house." I saw the sunlight in her pretty smile while she give capitalist me her phone number working at a gas serves station on 30th & Ames Ave. North Omaha, NE. Too letting capitalist me move in her house after our first date to help pay the rent while receiving section eight housing; we got married in eight months. The loaves of bread presented to God (Hebrews 9:2). I was not a man of faith; I believed my good works would get me into heaven. With toast to our marriage with promise even when shit hit the fan to always and forever be my favorite fan, in front of family and friends. From the capitalist me stealing fuel from my job, cheating on drug test to cheating in my marriage in which she instantly forgave me. The holy of holies (Hebrews 9:3). Working together, we were arrested for stealing scraping metal from the side of the railroad track. Antichrist she would lie to cover up cheating in her best friend marriage. When it was about what they wanted, she became a cleanup woman in other people's marriage relationships. Antichrist she promised the Christian minister that she asks to married us we would not divorce without counseling with him first. When spiritual twin I knew I was not right changed the way I think accepted Jesus Christ as my savior as the head lead cornerstone of the family. The stone tablets of the covenant (Hebrews 9:4).

That's when capitalist we became unequally yoked. Lord as my witness, I told her, "I would do whatever to please her." I begged for her forgiveness. Like a love song off a Kem Album. I told her I never meant to hurt her that way. I would never hurt her again I told her she deserves a better man. I was a fool for letting you down I did not want to divide us. I understand why would you stay. I told her she had to do what she had to do and say what she had to say. Let love set you free. Spiritual I started ministering to help my younger cousin with her spiritual hung up twisted secret man friend her son that locked away and death of her two sons. Right now, we can't talk about these things in detail (Hebrews 9:5).

Antichrist she told my family she felt my cousin baby was mine and swore an affidavit to the courts against my cousin for my other cousin Antichrist she felt our relationship was inappropriate and that antichrist she saw my cousin as my other woman. The antichrist she said, "I was trying to be like Jesus Christ and brain washer her" and that when antichrist she with the was spiritual guided decide to divide family file and got a divorce. When these things have been prepared in this way (Hebrews 9:6). Antichrist she swore out a protection order for me to stay away. She believed I had a nervous breakdown because of our breakup instead of making sure I was okay. As a college associate professor, antichrist she would negative teach against Christ and the Apostasy Church to Christian students Black Studies He never does this without blood (Hebrews 9:7). We were hung up spiritually conflicting influence by error divide Apostasy Church family we both grown up in capitalism antichrist civil religion. Believed in drinking spirit of alcohol that was not Keeping Family Church. I was more depressed from the reelection of George Bush act of II war where many people died then my divorce where only the old me died.

Hebrews 8:10

"This is the covenant that I will make with the house of Israel after those days, says the Lord. I will place my laws in their minds, and write them on their hearts. I will be their God, and they will be my people."

I worked like a field Negus picking cotton. Trained as fighter to take orders kill or be killed as soldier in the California National Guard and sailor in the U.S. Navy Fraternal Order Military Serve. The Holy Spirit is showing that the way into the holy place hadn't been revealed yet while the first tent was standing (Hebrews 9:8). I traveled around the world been there, did this, done that, do or die and made it back in one peace. Road a Honda Night Hawk 650 motorcycle across America, been to United States Federal prison that did not spiritual change me I got fat it made me a bigger Capitalist consumer. Sacrifices that are being offered can't perfect the conscience of the one who is serving (Hebrews 9:9). I had study Islam reading the Holy Quran and other religion Rastafaris Emperor Haile Selassie, and revolutionary men like Fidel Castro and Che" Guevara killers of men to revelations methods of Jesus Christ Jubilee Ministry equity born again son and daughter.

Hebrews 8:11-12

"And each person won't ever teach a neighbor or their brother or sister, saying, "Know the Lord," because they will all know me, from the least important of them to the most important; because I will be lenient toward their unjust actions, and I won't remember their sins anymore."

I was a homeboy from the hood before Boyz From the Hood's the movie that made the hood's politics what they are still rapping about today that is still here president Compton First United Methods Men, Prison Ministry Church Sexton, Bible Study prayer group, praying on a prayer line at 5 am. Everybody was talking about 2Pac's Thug Life was an actor, raping and talking about the liven words we were talking about in our Hood life's Long Beach & Rosecrans moving liven words worldwide California Love. They are regulations that have been imposed until the time of the new order (Hebrews 9:10). There is a difference between begin a thug and begin down. My elder brother named Holly a hood as a sports team. We played neighborhood sports Sugar Ray Robinson Football, City of Champions Lueders Park Basketball, Compton Little League Baseball Gonzales Park. I was Los Angeles Ram, Raider, Lakers, Dodgers, Olympian fans raised to be leaders, family men, fellows, gentlemen we were never gang affiliated we did not gang bang or represented or trip off no colors did mean a thing. By a greater and more perfect tabernacle (Hebrews 9:11). We weren't estranged from the threat or funk of violence. We had a family history fighting for civil right to voter right, fires and saving live, starting unions, postal service, military service veterans, federal prison, county jail, I've been jump on by police, crack selling, drive by shootings and carjacking. My uncle went to prison for fighting the police. Securing our deliverance for all time (Hebrews 9:12). I was neutral like a diplomat. I wore red, white, and blue it did not matter the complexion of the clothes I wore or where my grandmother lived. When asked what set I was from, all I would say it was none of their business where I come from and I do not care where they stay. How much more will the blood of Jesus wash our consciences clean from dead works in order to serve the living God (Hebrews 9:14)? I live on Holly-hood Lueders Park Piru and Compton Crips not just by Blood relationship all my friend and family come from both sides. I would say, "I Am a Moor Regulator; I was given "Jubilee" liberty cultural attaché pass like ambassador authority from heaven to write this story and baptizes people as monument upward to God.

Hebrews 8:13

"When it says new, it makes the first obsolete. And if something is old and outdated, it's close to disappearing."

CHAPTER 6
Ministry of John the Baptist

Return of Elijah upon
Top of a Temple
Passover April 4, 2015

It was hard for the spiritual hung-up dead artificial capitalist me to believe that I could get something out nothing or as a Remnant keeper of appointed time announcing (Matthew 3:1). Watchman the creator of the Heaven and Earth wanted to have alinement supernatural public intimate and personal relationship with me one, two, one as my personal Lord and Savior sign of Son of man temple of God.

Matthew 3:2 (KJV)
"And saying, Repent ye: for the kingdom of heaven is at hand."

First, I had to repent by simply changing the way I think. Then, I had to confess I had a problem; I was confused and needed a helper. It was hard to consent and say I needed a savior. I was afraid of being seen as weak, carried, lost in time of the end, the time between the end of one event and the start of sounding off another, and needed help bearing witness to my future with no hope. I did not know I was time keeper remnant watchman who has the work of bearing witness to God's sacred secret "Jesus" or what age I was artificial. I never was obedient to instant forgiving or keeping the

Sabbath day of rest. I was obedient to the calendar of working day and night from sun up to sun down, afternoon to midnight. I lived the butterfly effect, lost and turned out to be pimped, hung-up by the caterpillar Underworld Capitalist system. I hustled this way and that way, all the time of day for green money on a paper leaf's chase. Money was the god I trusted to take care of everything.

Matthew 3:3

"He was the one of whom Isaiah the prophet spoke when he said: The voice of one shouting in the wilderness, "Prepare the way for the Lord; make his paths straight."

I was an obedient slave, lost to the calendar of working on the overtime clock, being paid time and a half on weekends and double time on holidays as a mechanic for the City of Omaha, Nebraska Vehicle Maintenance Department. He ate locusts and wild honey (Matthew 3:4). I followed and witnessed the depressing heartbreaking reelection of President Gorge Bush's second inauguration. Sometime after witnessing the dark storm Hurricane Katrina during August 23-30 2005, I was approached to become a member of a giant renowned Fraternal Order Masonic Freemasonry 357 Lodge (Illuminati) in Omaha, Nebraska. I was misinformed about them being a secret organization. They are not a secret organization, but they do have secret information. I would be required to believe in any higher power, make pledges of allegiance and oaths of faith, and have a member to sponsor my initiation. Throughout Judea, and all around the Jordan River came to him (Matthew 3:5). There were fees and dues I would be required to pay. They did charitable work, wore a uniform, and marched in the community paradise. They owned a bar (tavern) 357 that sold alcohol spirits to the public. Eastern Stars is the women's Freemason organization.

Matthew 3:6

"As they confessed their sins, he baptized them in the Jordan River."

I asked my father and uncle about the organization. They said they did not know much about the Fraternal Order of Freemasons. Our family had a tradition with the Fraternal Order Elks Social Club Lodge. My grandparents were members of Lincoln, Nebraska's Lodge.

Matthew 3:7

"Many Pharisees and Sadducees came to be baptized by John. He said to them, "You children of snakes! Who warned you to escape from the angry judgment that is coming soon?"

I acquired some books from the North Omaha African American Book Store on Lake Street, and I checked out books from the City of Omaha Library about the fraternal orders of freemasons and elks. They had a lot of similar customs and used some of the same ritual traditions as college fraternities and sororities. They spent a lot of money going to conventions and on clothes to represent themselves with tax write-offs. My wife was a member of the Elks Lodge in Omaha, Nebraska that had a bar (tavern) on Lake Street and sold alcohol spirits in the community, too. They both had uniforms with pledges of allegiance and oaths of faith.

Matthew 3:8

"Produce fruit that shows you have changed your hearts and lives."

The spiritual climate change sounding Holy Spirit voice of God came onto me with a flood of instant forgiveness, giving me an intimate comfort of the arm of God spiritual blanket of peace, speaking boldly as a lion king tongue of fire and blood like Elijah but softly and gently as a lamb's breath. "Be not afraid" like a good shepherd intimate personnel friend, sounding like Michael Jackson singing let me show you the way to go put your trust in me I won't let you down enlightening me by saying, that we can come together think like one and live under the Son as one "You cannot serve two masters; you belong to God," in my common joyful language with kindness and compassion (native tongue) in which I was most comfortable communicating getting the job done. I tell you that God is able to raise up Abraham's children from these stones (Matthew 3:9).

The Holy Spirit was telling me to show up, keeping family church faith like a baby, not a Freemason. The "sacred secrets methods of Jesus Christ or mysteries of mercy God promise grace-grace" are not like the hidden mysteries of this unfair dark underworld capitalist system. They are not revealed only to a select few who have the capital, been initiated into some occult ritual test, and are a hidden secret from the rest. Rather, sacred secrets of God are hidden from human understanding, and then, when the time is right, the methods of Jesus Christ is about an oath from promise God's faith reveals them by spiritual climate change with sound of commandment the word to his servants Watchmen fellow me. I tell you that God is able to raise up Abraham's children from these stones (Matthew 3:10). Then, he commissions them to preach about them publicly to all who will listen with ears of discernment of a child: "I know why the Mayan calendar ends December 21, 2012." This became my I Know Why the Cage Bird Sings, like seeing a nigger head eating oysters on a can as a little child.

Matthew 3:11
"The ax is already at the root of the trees. Therefore, every tree that doesn't produce good fruit will be chopped down and tossed into the fire."

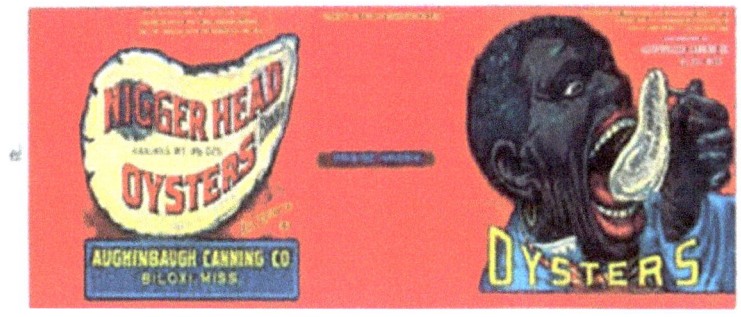

Matthew 3:11

"I baptize with water those of you who have changed your hearts and lives. The one who is coming after me is stronger than I am. I'm not worthy to carry his sandals. He will baptize you with the Holy Spirit and with fire."

Hearing the voice of God tell you cannot buy this anymore and you have to go home and tell your grandmother who is making your and her favorite Thanksgiving dinner oyster dressing for her sorority sisters that the spiritual climate changed.

Matthew 3:12

"The shovel he uses to sift the wheat from the husks is in his hands. He will clean out his threshing area and bring the wheat into his barn. But he will burn the husks with a fire that can't be put out."

Keeping family church: sounding the word "Jubilee" of mercy Universal Pardon, observing the Sabbath's Sabbath commandment is the spiritual climate change new ingredient to the Thanksgiving dressing. It is today's payment for the insurance policy from heaven for future generations, not the fraternity, sorority and capitalist fraternal order you belong to. God knew we could not keep the principles of time or commandments of the Law, so he sent his Son as the lord of time as an insurance agent to cover the balance of everyone protecting us from spending time to get to hell. Then, he sent the Comforter, a spiritual blanket of peace, God's arms of the Holy Spirit's voice of God as the forgiveness insurance claims adjuster to redeem us for our mistake and accident of sin and enslavement debt. The spiritual climate changed new, new, beginning in time. Teaching me to use my uncommon sense to start over. Forgiveness Insurance through the King James Bible the Earth and the generation of forever will never die. The King James Bible is simple to read as Easter leap year calendar is to appointed time never-ending cycle with new beginnings spiritual climate change south up north down.

Baptism of Jesus
Matthew 3:13
"At that time Jesus came from Galilee to the Jordan River so that John would baptize him."

Keeping family church sounding of "Jubilee" Universal Pardon spiritual climate change is the time of the end before the new, new, beginning of time that will never end, bearing witness of remnant family moving close from methods of Jesus Christ without moving. It is like reading the King James Bible from the Book of Revelations to Genesis explaining spiritual climate change time of the end dark age has happened before.

Matthew 3:14
"John tried to stop him and said, "I need to be baptized by you, yet you come to me?"

When I read the last book of the King James Bible the Book of Revelation, the first chapter, it doubly blessed me. It is only book in the King James Bible, you receive an extra blessing for reading.

Revelation 1:3 (KJV)
"Blessed is he that readeth, and they that hear the words of this prophecy, and keep those things which are written therein: for the time is at hand."

Firstborn blessing, I got to start all over by being born again out of a double-crossed mind state here on earth in the Spiritual Kingdom of Peace the New, New, Jerusalem Divine City Compton, California incorporated May 11, 1888 on the 33 Degree Parallel culture desert. The second blessing of the Holy Spirit voice of God came as a remnant measurement of my child-like faith as beautiful as the sound of the morning sunrise with the loving great wisdom of taking communion New, New, Moon in their image rich white old lady male/female named Grace-grace with a son named Gordon who helped my baby's mother anyway they could. Delivering right state of mind peace with facts great wisdom and knowledge that sacred Royal Art of Geometry, horizontal line is death, vertical line is life, making the cross a door bridging a way from heaven and Earth. Numbers and mathematic translation from Muslim in North Africa are just as spiritual as words translated into English King James Bible in Europe bringing together a spiritual change in the climate of many world cultures. 6 = Confusion 7 = Holiness, 8 = New Beginning, 9 = Divine Completeness, 14 = Double measure of spiritual perfection, directing me to rest in all my problems.

Matthew 3:15
"Jesus answered, 'Allow me to be baptized now. This is necessary to fulfill all righteousness.' So John agreed to baptize Jesus."

First, the Holy Spirit instructed me to renew opening my closed mind in communion with living word methods of Jesus Christ's living water, ensuring me with revealing revelation knowledge, (a word from God) that I would just not see the promise land from the mountaintop as God told Moses and Dr. King said in his last speech. "I've Been to the Mountaintop":

"Like anybody, I would like to live - a long life; longevity has its place. But, I'm not concerned about that now. I just want to do God's will. And He's allowed me to go up to the mountain. And, I've looked over. And, I've seen the Promised Land. I may not get there with you. But I want you to know tonight, that we, as a people, will get to the Promised Land. So, I'm happy, tonight. I'm not worried about anything. I'm not fearing any man. Mine eyes have seen the glory of the coming of the Lord."

Matthew 3:16
"When Jesus was baptized, he immediately came up out of the water. Heaven was opened to him, and he saw the Spirit of God coming down like a dove and resting on him."

The remnant generation of forever will have a Holy land experience of seeing the living word of God appear daily anywhere on Earth. All I had to do was be obedient, living as every day is Sunday. Religion would have you believe that Moses talked and got the commandment laws from God, I Am as a burning bush seeing Israel as God's place in the Underworld putting the sound of God's law in a box. Then, use those laws for talking, hearing or seeing God as I Am (Jesus) or Israel (family) seeing word God as in self they will stone you to death!

Matthew 3:17
"A voice from heaven said, "This is my Son whom I dearly love; I find happiness in him."

Therefore, I could comprehend before knowledge (modern science) set time, technology (digital data) the science of sin. They told me the women menstrual and the moon cycle is a supernatural miracle. Connecting the women's menstrual period cycle calendar is just as important as the twenty-eight and a half days moon phase cycle calendar is to eternal life's cycle. I pray the moon phase with communion like Catholics pray the rosary beads and say hail Mary's, honoring the virgin motherhood. I see the moon phase in remembrance on what God promised faith he would do for what I was supposed to do as honor to God's word working supernatural in heaven. Catholic see the pope and honor virgin mother Black Madonna as icons God's Word working supernaturally in the flesh on Earth and keeping family church.

Temptation of Jesus
Matthew 4:1
"Then the Spirit led Jesus up into the wilderness so that the devil might tempt him."

Sign of Son man cycle of the sun. Watching where the sun and moon rise and sets the sun of man reveal what time of the day, the season of the year, and the age of the eternal time cycle blood moon eclipse praising God.

Matthew 4:2
"After Jesus had fasted for forty days and forty nights, he was starving."

I needed to confess I could not save myself from going to hell, and I was morally weak just like a baby. Like being born from root, the disease of sin of one man named Adam made me a son of sin in a one-on-one relationship with a talking serpent and the lying devil. Being born again in the spirit atom cell male/female image of Jesus Christ and righteous made me right in a one to one relationship with Holy Spirit voice of God with loving wisdom dominion and enlighten me. That serpent does not talk; the devil is a lie. If you know what a lie is, then you know the truth to all things seen and unseen in the labyrinth of time.

Matthew 4:3

"The tempter came to him and said, "Since you are God's Son, command these stones to become bread."

The sound of Holy Spirit voice of God came to me speaking revelations out of the King James Bible like beautiful black Moorish Christian King-Priest out a Shakespeare play Acts II Perfect Love Othello saying "know thee self" "See thou family as remnant of Israel, make thy family thy church, working together thou can do anything by the sweet blood of Jesus, by thy self thou can only do so much and this where thy should pay thy tithes to." Holy Spirit voice of God said, "Look around thy and see the Thou Lord in all has already bless thy. Thy at fifty you still have a mother and father in thou family and neighborhood thy Lord have blessed them too with a measure of faith."

Matthew 4:4

"Jesus replied, "It's written, People won't live only by bread, but by every word spoken by God."

I like reading and sounding words out in the King James Version of the Bible; it's bold and straight to the point. It took me back to the age of time of being an exile Moor Melchizedek priest, fighting renowned giant demons and being a renowned Moor Viking slayer (carnal and ungodly). Old Testament Religion law said, punish them, "Stone them to death, cut their hands or head off, burn them on a stake." In the New, New, Testament prophet relationship methods of Jesus Christ Holy Spirit voice of God good shepherd comforter arm from Word of God sword cut off head of giant organizations like King David fight giant in the King James Bible. The reward was drawing me out of the bondage of Underworld Capitalist life I was drowning in the debt of my sin. It teaches instant forgiveness, which is the key to unlock the dimension time of God in history who is eternal, to become born again opening the way back from Heaven to Earth. All I had to do was believe and have faith to kill time be born again into communion with God's Grace-grace.

Matthew 4:5-6

"After that the devil brought him into the holy city and stood him at the highest point of the temple. He said to him, 6 "Since you are God's Son, throw yourself down; for it is written, I will command my angels concerning you, and they will take you up in their hands so that you won't hit your foot on a stone."

I am a supernatural, spiritual seed remnant left here be the Grace-grace of God as representative of the living word from the beginning of time to do the will of our Lord. I am a Supernatural spiritual time traveler not bound by law of time barriers being able to be born again to police myself. I am able to see things supernaturally, through renewing my mind with communion, conceiving the eternal flame from sounds of the living word out of the face of living water from sign of Son of man God, with the fruit of the spirit: long suffering, love, joy, peace, forbearance, kindness, goodness, faithfulness, gentleness and self-control from which there is no law.

Matthew 4:7

"Jesus replied, 'Again it's written, Don't test the Lord your God'."

I am a spiritual ambassador of reconciliation in the United Kingdom of Heaven with diplomatic immunity not govern by tax law. In the spiritual kingdom every day is Sunday; we should not have to pay taxes like L. Ron Hubbard. Methods of Jesus Christ says this:

Matthew 22:17-22 Jubilee Bible 2000 (JUB)
"Tell us therefore, What thinkest thou? Is it lawful to give tribute unto Caesar or not? But Jesus perceived their wickedness and said, Why tempt ye me, ye hypocrites? Show me the coin of the tribute. And they presented unto him a denarius. And he said unto them, Whose is this image and superscription? They say unto him, Caesar's. Then said he unto them, Render therefore unto Caesar the things which are Caesar's and unto God the things that are God's. When they had heard these words, they marveled and left him and went away."

During the spiritual climate of Old Testament religions, the Lord's day relied on a moon phase calendar that was too hard to keep family church became lost in time. The Lord's day of judgment is the first day of the spirit month of worship from new moon to full moon was a Sabbath day of annals Scarface in a temple for protection from God's punishment from the sin of reliving the same horrible death over and over.

Matthew 4:8
"Then the devil brought him to a very high mountain and showed him all the kingdoms of the world and their glory."

The spiritual climate New Testament religions Easter calendar resurrection first Sunday Lord's day of communal worship. Passover from being under the law of the punishment to being in love a relationship with methods of Jesus Christ became day of peace repentant with communion Judgment for reward gifts with God's word being born again in the spirit of love to complete the greater work in His righteousness and understanding how to be a united people, one nation, one land, one faith, one God.

Matthew 4:9

"He said, "I'll give you all these if you bow down and worship me."

The spiritual climate New, New, Testament relationship Kingdom calendar Holy Spirit calling on first fruit believers every day is Sunday, the Lord's day of the spiritual month, and to see word as flesh, becoming spiritual food for survival. Man does not live by bread alone, but by the sound of the living word seed from God. Holy Spirit voice of God provides my daily bread and showering me with love cleans takes care of all my healing needs.

Matthew 4:10

"Jesus responded, "Go away, Satan, because it's written, You will worship the Lord your God and serve only him."

I am able to travel out of time as representative methods of Jesus Christ as a remnant watchman, judging myself with self-deliverance. As an observer of God in history, the cross is the door to heaven, science, art of geometry and religion, in relationship set in time, season, sun, blood moon eclipse, stars, and the dark end of the age of precision of the equinox, observing principle spiritual sabbath cycles to see how methods of Jesus Christ influence have made or did not make on the God in historical events. Mayan calendar ending December 21, 2012 precession of the equinox alignment in Heaven time of the end, extraordinary Jubilee of mercy Universal Pardon spiritual climate change global celebration is divine alignment four blood moons. 2014-2015 opened the door to heaven here on Earth, starting all over from the being of a new, new, age.

Faith and truth are the activating powers for the journey from the past to the future. Like gas and air are the activating forces to move a car from one place to another.

Matthew 4:11

"The devil left him, and angels came and took care of him."

A spiritual time traveler is a remnant of God's people that can soundly deliver a spiritual message to different ages baby sister and brothers, speaking at their age level, giving a better understanding of spirit of the time- to start over.

If chosen to be an ambassador in foreign country as a representative for the president of the United States Capital of Capitalism. I would take orders commandments, giving up my free will to speak for myself, learn the native tongue and study their capitalist government, culture and economics, taking the job with honors and respect. As a representative of the president of the United States Capital of Capitalism Government and the American Creed:

"I believe in the United States of America, as a government of the people, by the people, for the people; whose just powers are derived from the consent of the governed; a democracy in a republic; a sovereign Nation of many sovereign States; a perfect union, one and inseparable; established upon these principles of freedom, equality, justice, and humanity for which American patriots sacrificed their lives and fortunes. I therefore believe it is my duty to my country to love it, to support its Constitution, to obey its laws, to respect its flag, and to defend it against all enemies."

I would pay attention to his words and Underworld Capitalist system governments and become an obedient diplomat with immunity, having all my housing, transportation, health care insurance, and food needs would be taken care of.

As a representative server of the Spiritual United Kingdom of Heaven Government, here on Earth, I learn on the old and new Underworld Capitalism Fraternal Order local, state, federal, government and the school holidays are civil religions day for keeping time calendar start with the sunrise in the morning, for keeping family public accounting records, doing business and to feed the natural body flesh food.

The kings and priests kept dying and needed to have successors to keep count of the solar calendar, a 365 days process that keeps getting messed up. The cross becoming the door to Heaven is always moving but time, and truth never changes like a lunar calendar, VII days a week. There are three sides to every story like God, the Son and the Holy Spirit is the truth like morning, noon, and night is a day to top, sides and bottom make a pyramid. Different time, period, month in calendar spiritual climate of change setting appointed time sign of the Son of Man. The cross is the door into spiritual climate of change United Kingdom of Heaven. Every day is Sunday, a holiday of rest. With gifts, you are rewarded for doing the right thing.

CHAPTER 7
Acts II Conception of Jesus Christ

Sign of Son of Man on Tabernacle

We all know the King James Bible does not say Jesus was born at the calendar time of the Christmas holiday.

John 1:1-2 (AMP)
"In the beginning [before all time] was the Word (Christ), and the Word was with God, and the Word was God Himself. He was present originally with God."

This was the season of favor the sounding "Jubilee" Mary Motherhood Ministry supernaturally, immaculately conceived the word seed from God in her womb. Mary believed God's living word so powerfully it became like sperm to a female egg creating a new, new, blood type and supernaturally created a life. Nine and a half moon cycles later, she gave birth to Logos. Motherhood ministry gave birth to spiritual climate of change Melchizedek priesthood without any successors. Not according to the law of a commandment depending upon no flesh, but sound according to principle the power of an indestructible life methods of Jesus Christ.

Luke 1:30-3 (KJV)
"And the angel said unto her, Fear not, Mary: for thou hast found favour with God. And, behold, thou shalt conceive in thy womb, and bring forth a son, and shalt call his name Jesus."

Spiritual eternal lifetime starts the moment of sound conception. God, the Son and Holy Spirit voice of God is jubilant moment of human conception into time. The spiritual human conception of a new, new, blood type becoming flesh is beloved and sacred. It is worth more to change God's in history account than any amount of silver or gold to God's Holy trinity calendar of time. This set act in time alone with the story in the Book of Acts in the King James Bible brings God's will into creation of time spiritual climate of change. How was it true that Melchizedek had neither beginning of days nor end of life? Word made flesh, time becomes a spiritual dimension of God's divine alignment.

The birth of Jesus Christ word come alive made sound flesh eternal Melchizedek king-priest, prophet hood (order) divided God's calendar into history unifying the office of king and priest would be combined, allowing us to see and be God's hands at work. In a notable Messianic prophecy, the sworn oath of God to David's heart Lord" is: "You are a priest to time indefinite according to the manner of Melchizedek, creating supranational equality Jesus Christ Church without walls United Kingdom on Earth as it is in heaven. Any two people can become a church two or more in Jesus Christ's name.

In the Old Testament, ancient pharaohs built pyramids, tombs and temples full of gold for their gods to be used in the afterlife. Kings ruled in Babylon and made themselves like gods idols wearing gold and jewels display of wealth. Priests were keeper of the family mystery systems, separated dark underworld secret society. The people used word sounding like Babel, built a tower to get to heaven to be with their god, sacrifice their first fruit born to please God, made altars out of stacking rocks showing honor to God. They practiced standing over human and animal sacrifices, prayed with blood rituals, and used sex orgies as worship. Prophets terrified the public with all type of horrible stories about snakes, the end of time and Viking raiding, stealing, kidnapping and killing people in coastal villages.

In the ancient world, Alexander the Greek, conquered the known world as a war god, Emperor Caesar's Roman public government tax, knowledge, coins and wealth became rule over divided god from the people. Fraternity and sorority people with letters in front and after their name, sacrifice (aborted) babies, having tube tide and vasectomy to their gods used education and wealth for their salvation and dressed in robes, capes with hoods of color, and uniforms with caps of color for recognition and protection like gangs do today.

To be a witch or warlock you had to be born into their society or meet certain requirements. They became celebrities with curse Black art and Black magic spells, telling people future using astrology, Zodiac signs, and tarot picture card. Worshiping the devil for fame or prayed to sign symbols and idols made by men. They work in secret doing the unsacred and taking a secret oath of faith. They have secret handshakes and make secret sign with their hands to communicate in secret using Ring Kisses, and wear expenses jewelry. They self-mutilate with multi piercing and barbarian tattoos. Practicing eye for an eye, tooth for a tooth equality in revenge. Not seeing firstborn daughters and sons equality women can't lead men. They will tell you they are all about capitalist business of being paid and money is everything. Gathering wealth to keep for their self like the Royalty crown of Jewels. These things are carnal

In the spiritual Book of Revelations methods of Jesus Christ said:

Revelation 2:6 (KJV)
"But this thou hast, that thou hatest the deeds of the Nicolaitanes, which I also hate."

Today as a believer in methods of Jesus Christ translated (God in self) Holy Spirit instant forgiveness, I was anointed, saving me like a personnel lifeguard coming to my rescue no matter how deep water of ocean of thoughts I had gotten myself into. It does not matter whom I paid my tithes to or if I wear pants or dress. Jesus Christ as my friend the Head, instant forgiving, agent of spiritual climate of change in my life insurance policy, they all became revealed and open to the public in a book called the King James Bible.

There are no requirements or restrictions; you police yourself and self-deliverance; there are no secrets. Just believe and have faith. Your insurance do's and don'ts have already been paid for! You are not required to pray five times a day or make a pilgrimage far-far away, spending money to go look in an empty tomb. It is just like the Holy Land Experience in Orlando, Florida is today. You do not need to buy a CD set or prayer shawl. That money would be better spent by giving it away in your neighborhood. All I had to do is walk, talk, believe by saying thanks, do what I can and give first fruit out of honor if I can, not because I am required to. Have faith that God will do the rest.

In the beginning, God Holy trinity (Father, Son and Holy Spirit) sound created heavens, earth and moon, making the hole planet holy and all human blood conceived is sacred not a country, a place, dome over a rock, or gold in one temple. The spiritual climate of change New, New, Ages Jerusalem Kingdom of heaven, spiritual exodus is straight out of Compton Divine City of peace from out the west. There is a temple already in heaven. No need to build or go to war over one there. King James Bible says Moses saw it and that is where Jesus Christ is sitting and resting at. The cross is the door to the bridge for walking in the Holy Spirit; the bodies become the spiritual temple here on earth. The heartbeat is the ark of the eternal flame from the burning bush with our faith as our altar, blood covenant with God in history making every day Sunday.

Then, Father God spoke sound to himself and swore an oath and created me his son in their image of the Holy Spirit, a spiritual male and female, giving them men and women, kings, queens, the renewed heart and power principle of freewill to be born again. He gave them dominion to come back from heaven to Earth as the sons and daughters of humankind with autonomy to minister to the remnant family and the apostasy church, share in love and truth about a relationship in the Holy Spirit, guiding us into the kingdom of peace and king of righteousness heaven here on Earth.

We do not have to wait to die any more to receive instant forgiveness the double blessed benefit of going to heaven. Jesus Christ reveals the appreciation what your elders have already worked and died for, so we do not have to methods movement of Jesus Christ and Holy Spirit voice of God insurance policy brings heaven and Earth to you. Exodus II Perfect Love monument praising God.

The Gospel of Nicodemus Acts of Pilate. Translated by Alexander Walker
2 But the centurion reported unto the governor the things that had come to pass: and when the governor and his wife heard, they were sore vexed, and neither ate nor drank that day. And Pilate sent for the Jews and said unto them: Did ye see that which came to pass? But they said: There was an eclipse of the sun after the accustomed sort.

The Jewish elders then captured Joseph, and imprisoned him, and placed a seal on the door to his cell after first posting a guard. Joseph warned the elders, "The Son of God whom you hanged upon the cross, is able to deliver me out of your hands. All your wickedness will return upon you."

Once the elders returned to the cell, the seal was still in place, but Joseph was gone. The elders later discover that Joseph had returned to Arimathea. Having a change in heart, the elders desired to have a more civil conversation with Joseph about his actions and sent a letter of apology to him by means of seven of his friends. Joseph travelled back from Arimathea to Jerusalem to meet with the elders, where they questioned him about his escape. He told them this story;

On the day of the preparation, about the tenth hour, you shut me in, and I remained there the whole Sabbath in full. And when midnight came, as I was standing and praying, the house where you shut me in was hung up by the four corners, and there was a flashing of light in mine eyes. And I fell to the ground trembling. Then someone lifted me up from the place where I had fallen, and poured over me an abundance of water from the head even to the feet, and put round my nostrils the odour of a wonderful ointment, and rubbed my face with the water itself, as if washing me, and kissed me, and said to me, Joseph, fear not; but open thine eyes, and see who it is that speaks to thee. And looking, I saw Jesus; and being terrified, I thought it was a phantom.

And with prayer and the commandments I spoke to him, and he spoke with me. And I said to him: Art thou Rabbi Elias? And he said to me: I am not Elias. And I said: Who art thou, my Lord? And he said to me: I am Jesus, whose body thou didst beg from Pilate, and wrap in clean linen; and thou didst lay a napkin on my face, and didst lay me in thy new tomb, and roll a stone to the door of the tomb. Then I said to him that was speaking to me: Show me, Lord, where I laid thee. And he led me, and showed me the place where I laid him, and the linen which I had put on him, and the napkin which I had wrapped upon his face; and I knew that it was Jesus.

And he took hold of me with his hand, and put me in the midst of my house though the gates were shut, and put me in my bed, and said to me: Peace to thee! And he kissed me, and said to me: For forty days go not out of thy house; for, lo, I go to my brethren into Galilee. According to the

Gospel of Nicodemus, Joseph testified to the Jewish elders, and specifically to chief priests Caiaphas and Annas that Jesus had risen from the dead and ascended to heaven and he indicated that others were raised from the dead at the resurrection of Christ (repeating Matt 27:52-53). He specifically identified the two sons of the high-priest Simeon (again in Luke 2:25-35). The elders Annas, Caiaphas, Nicodemus, and Joseph himself, along with Gamaliel under whom Paul of Tarsus studied, travelled to Arimathea to interview Simeon's sons Charinus and Lenthius.

And the priests and the Levites said one to another: If his memorial endure until the Sommos which is called the Jubilee, know ye that he will prevail forever and raise up for himself a new people.

So they took the money, and did as they were taught: and this saying is commonly reported among the Jews until this day (Matthew 28:15). One way or other truth that was buried will come out become public.

After these things Pilate entered into the temple of the Jews and gathered together all the chief of the priests, and the teachers (grammaticos) and scribes and doctors of the law, and went in with them into the holy place of the temple and commanded all the doors to be shut, and said unto them: We have heard that ye have in this temple a certain great Bible; wherefore I ask you that it be presented before us. And when that great Bible adorned with gold and precious jewels was brought by four ministers, Pilate said to them all: I adjure you by the God of your fathers which commanded you to build this temple in the place of his sanctuary, that ye hide not the truth from me. Ye know all the things that are written in this Bible; but tell me now if ye have found in the scriptures that this Jesus whom ye have crucified is the Son of God which should come for the salvation of mankind, and in what year of the times he must come. Declare unto me whether ye crucified him in ignorance or knowingly.

And Annas and Caiaphas when they were thus adjured commanded all the rest that were will them to go out of the temple; and they themselves shut all the doors of the temple and of the sanctuary, and said unto Pilate:

Thou hast adjured us, O excellent judge, by the building of this temple to make manifest unto thee the truth and reason (or a true account). After that we had crucified Jesus, knowing not that he was the Son of God, but supposing that by some chance he did his wondrous works, we made a great assembly (synagogue) in this temple; and as we conferred one with another concerning the signs of the mighty works which Jesus had done, we found many witnesses of our own nation who said that they had seen Jesus alive after his passion, and that he was passed into the height of the heaven.

Moreover, we saw two witnesses whom Jesus raised from the dead, who declared unto us many marvelous things which Jesus did among the dead, which things we have in writing in our hands. Now our custom is that every year before our assembly we open this holy Bible and inquire the testimony of God. And we have found in the first book of the Seventy how that Michael the angel spake unto the third son of Adam the first man concerning the five thousand and five hundred years, wherein should come the most beloved Son of God, even Christ: and furthermore we have thought that peradventure this same was the God of Israel which said unto Moses: Make thee an ark of the covenant in length two cubits and a half, and in breadth one cubit and a half, and in height one cubit and a half. For by those five cubits and a half we have understood and known the fashion of the ark of the old covenant, for that in five thousand and a half thousand years Jesus Christ should come in the ark of his body: and we have found that he is the God of Israel, even the Son of God.

For after his passion, we the chief of the priests, because we marveled at the signs which came to pass on his account did open the Bible, and searched out all the generations unto the generation of Joseph, and Mary the mother of Christ, taking her to be the seed of David: and we found that from the day when God made the heaven and the earth and the first man, from that time unto the Flood are 2,212 years: and from the Flood unto the building of the tower 531 years: and from the building of the tower unto Abraham 606 years: and from Abraham unto the coming of the children of Israel out of Egypt 470 years: and from the going of the children of Israel out of Egypt unto the building of the temple 511 years: and from the building of the temple unto the destruction of the same temple 464 years: so far found we in the Bible of Esdras: and inquiring from the burning of the temple unto the coming of Christ and his birth we found it to be 636 years, which together were five thousand and five hundred years like as we found it written in the Bible that Michael the archangel declared before unto Seth the third son of Adam, that after five thousand and a half thousand years Christ the Son of God hath (? should) come. Hitherto have we told no man, lest there should be a schism in our synagogues; and now, O excellent judge, thou hast adjured us by this holy Bible of the testimonies of God, and we do declare it unto thee: and we also have adjured thee by thy life and health that thou declare not these words unto any man in Jerusalem.

Resurrection born-again Joseph Alone parallel human spirit of Jesus Christ beautiful love. Spiritual body of new people are time travelers the superheroes of the Holy Bible today celebrating Jubilee universal pardon! From the merciful Father, compassionate Son and the comforting Holy Spirit as the trinity working together hand and hand in Acts II Perfect Love: The New, New, Testament a new, new, millennium perspective of seeing the image of Human spirit rightfulness. Jesus unselfish beautiful love looking back in time through a watchtower craftsman arch symbol of Christians suffering bridge over trouble water. From the beginning of this New Nation creation, one family of seer Joseph spiritual body of people journey of affliction passing over into future. Kingdom straight out of heaven dual citizenship on Earth crossing America borderline of faith. Free Church State of peace Eureka I found it straight out of Compton, California the opposite Washington D.C. State of War. Abraham Lincoln, Nebraska the New Capital of America monument to God.

CHAPTER 8

Acts II something old Becoming New Creation Monument to God

Passover April 4, 2015

The methods of Jesus Christ are radical, a healer, a lover, but not a revolutionary. He said to be a revolutionary you have to pick up a weapon and become a killer like those that you are fighting. In a revolution, there always is a loser. Using the methods of Jesus Christ "Jubilee" Ministry, everybody of all ages wins. It is reconciliation; nobody is left behind; he wants a one to one relationship; His great commandment is, "Love your enemy."

Romans 13:8-10 (KJV)
"Owe no man any thing, but to love one another: for he that loveth another hath fulfilled the law. For this, Thou shalt not commit adultery, Thou shalt not kill, Thou shalt not steal, Thou shalt not bear false witness, Thou shalt not covet; and if there be any other commandment, it is briefly comprehended in this saying, namely, Thou shalt love thy neighbor as thyself. Love worketh no ill to his neighbor: therefore love is the fulfilling of the law."

His battle is with good and evil; these things are spiritual. The war of Armageddon is a spiritual battle, not a physical or martial war. The battlefield is in our minds. You cannot protest the war of Armageddon. I do not get to choose my battles; war is twenty-four hours, seven days a week, from victory to victory. God brings justice, so we do not have to. Spiritual climate change keeping family church stops the war of Armageddon.

Everybody knows the devil (demons) and the money, wealth, stealing, blood killing, village raiding Vikings is after all our peace. Christianity is about protection; Jesus Christ's Holy Spirit voice of Godfather public one to one ministry he was born, baptized, forgave, died, and resurrected in public. Be not afraid! The God of history is the God of today and forever.

The sounding four blood moons on Jewish feast days within two years is very rare and has only occurred seven times since the time of 1 A.D. in 1492 (The Moors Jews were expelled from Spain by Queen Isabella), 1948 (statehood for Israel and the War of Independence), 1967 (the Six-Day War). There are now four blood moons scheduled to appear in 2014/2015 and then there will NOT be any for the next 100 years. The four blood moons are a sign of the Son of man from heaven to signal the world of the spiritual exodus, the family of remnants turning closer to Jesus Christ without having to go anywhere. Keeping the Sabbath's Sabbath feasts cycle sounding extraordinary "Jubilee" of mercy universal pardon release, biggest out pouring of instant forgiveness of debt and sin from heaven the world has ever seen. Is about seeing the cross as the door to being church in your own family making every day Sunday.

Leviticus 25:10 (KJV)
"And ye shall hallow the fiftieth year, and proclaim liberty throughout all the land unto all the inhabitants thereof: it shall be a jubile unto you; and ye shall return every man unto his possession, and ye shall return every man unto his family."

United States of America will also be in celebration of a Grand Jubilee One Hundred Fiftieth Anniversary of the Thirteen Amendment to the Constitution freeing all slaves.

Section 1. Neither slavery nor involuntary servitude, except as a punishment for crime whereof the party shall have been duly convicted, shall exist within the United States, or any place subject to their jurisdiction.

Section 2. Congress shall have power to enforce this article by appropriate legislation.

I watch television, see capitalist million-dollar movies and documentary programs what if all the people disappeared, what if world ended, what if this religion did this, what if that religion that. What would happen if one day all Signatures vanish off all legal documents, digital data disappeared all computer got shut down. You got a gift from God all debt and sin were instantly forgiven you were given an Extraordinary Jubilee of Mercy Universal Pardon.

What would you do if you woke up one day and heard everyone's debt and everyone's sin had been forgiven (pardon) wiped clean? House mortgages paid off, car notes paid in full, student loans canceled, credit cards show zero balance, credit scores showed no write offs, and parents, brothers and sisters were released from prison and told to return home to their families, all criminal records get wiped out. This would happen every fifty years. At least once in everyone's lifetime. This could only happen by a sound act of God. How would you act if you knew when you turn fifty years old you inherited two million dollars from our father in heaven?

I been asked "This sounds like reparations: forty acres and a mule." I said "No!" Reparations are for a race of people that suffered a wrong. The sounding Extraordinary Jubilee of Mercy Universal Pardon eternal rule of order is a God's oath faith given right is an insurance policy which heaven itself has ordained ensuring nobody gets left behind and everybody eating from the same table; race does no matter. It's better than playing the lottery; play Jubilee; everybody wins. Reset from heaven, it is an eternal upgrade rested in God Glory Grace and Mercy!

I do not have million-dollar of capital in church or debt from a graduate degree with letter before or after my name making capital. I never had a plan to preach the gospel of Good News. The reason I end up here is when saw I had problem in my marriage. I heard the voice of God the Holy Spirit tell me to look at myself seeing my artificial life and saw I was the problem. From me growing up, ready to kill or be killed. Going to federal prison for conspiring to selling drugs in my community do or die, to stealing from my job eye for eye, and lying cheating in my marriage doing to other what you will do to yourself. I like to smoke weed, get turn up, kick back, drink and party too. I also saw my younger brothers, male cousins, and nephew having the same problem in their relationships, going in and out of prison too.

The more I looked around, I saw the same problem in my family was in churches and nation too. When I went to my father, a family elder letting him know we had a problem and need help getting my generation working together. I was told, "Do it yourself." He was too busy hustling going to California to slave for some money and wealth. I did not know the elders could not teach my generation to work together because they were not free and did not know how to work together. Because of fear, no forgiveness, no trust, pride and their financial debt they could not see they was still slaves and the promise land or the truth that was right in front of their eyes. They fought wars over the capital wealth they gather for their self and passed down war debt and fear of the unknown to their children. I also saw I could not help myself. To free my family, I had to save myself first, take a look at the man in the mirror, if I wanted to make the world a better place.

This is not about making capital or being famous capitalist or renowned capitalism system; I never wanted to be famous capitalist or had a problem making capital did not care how much a dollar cost for happiness. This is about after living fifty years in this upside-down twisted antichrist Underworld Capitalism system. Two hundred twenty-five years as one nation under God in God we trust. I knew more about buying gifts for Santa Claus and the Easter bunny then I knew about church, experiencing hearing God. Receiving a gift talent of instant forgiveness from God in heaven from the sounding the word Extraordinary "Jubilee" of Mercy and Compassion Universal Pardon! For everything wrong I ever did.

Celebration the fulfillment of the word of God from oath of measured little by little faith Abraham to Abraham Lincoln righteousness. Descendants of Joseph baptizing new convert Christian New City of Zi-On old Compton. 2021 years after John the Baptist started baptizing people in the Jordan river, starting with the sign of the son of man rising from a graveyard ending with beginning sign of the son man rising from a graveyard monument temple praising God. People being baptizes in reconciliation of the resurrection of Jesus Christ from all around the world. A test of inspiration who will come from the farthest to be baptizes in my pool in front of a monument honoring God with tens of thousands Christian lives. The greatest gift I could give in return for God save me is baptizing people in my pool honor of the trinity Amen.

I SEE A NEW CHURCH

Restoration of Zi-On

33rd parallel prayer Line of faith

Underworld
Hell

Entr'acte New Millennial, New Testament

A Spiritual Dissertation appointed Holy time zone a prayer lifeline of faith in a place unseen called Zi-On. Modern day On city of the Son peaceful safe state of mind with God. New creation beautiful hearted people praying with intention for healing keeping the family Church in a pandemic epidemic. United by the Methodist of Jesus Christ Universal Church history beautiful light for all to see as city upon a hill. Witnessing 2nd Acts II Peace, Love and Happiness message of hope to end all wars. Zi-On restored spiritual truth revolution safe place of discernment word of God's wisdom. Revelation vision of seeing the world turn right side up. By hearing the healing word of truth written on our hearts'. Fighting a good fight against evil appealing for unity and equality. A beautiful true-life heart-warming story exercise of faith. A Black Native America family Urban Tribe spiritual journey heir of salvation trusting the wise word of God's amazing grace. In the matrix zone of Holy Time of Zi-On, reservation place of safe keeping, alongside, upside down one divisible Nation. On a dividing line opposite of going to Hell.

I see a new Church year 2020 vision of the presence and future Compton 1st united women union with men in peace, love and happiness. Acts to turning the upside-down military Industrial World right-side up around praying with intention in God we trust. Started in the Bible with the firstborn again spiritual double blessing with 20/20 vision seeing the male and female descendants equal right of the name son of Joseph Jesus Christ. 1st Acts turning the World upside down North up, South became down.

When in Rome see the Iron Industrial World as the Roman's Gladiators did Roman Empires divided Nations on top. Killing became game of sport entertainment fun talent used as money. Great Beast of iron and clay Army of the Dead from the North as a pandemic against the South. keeling woman and men named Giant Corporations on the Stock Market today Tower of Babel praying in one language facing one direction one person named god. Kingdom of Hell Religious war, battling sexual perversion and revengeful violence god on Earth Caesar is King [Acts 17: 6]. 2nd Acts II Peace, Love and Happiness. Ubuntu: I am because we are philosophy program of reconciliation Humanism united in continual prayer. Turn the upside-down World right side up South up North becomes down order of Heaven. Can any good thing come straight out of Compton? Come and see New Church! From the Ghetto to Zi-On zone of favor mind state union with God of peace, love, and happiness, Kingdom of Heaven on Earth Jesus Christ is King of King.

Atoning truth Passover baton of forgiveness woman united unconditional love marriage with man equally [Acts 17: 7]. Twin stories of family unity and equality united on the Cross of Hope with the Star of David rule of law and order. Wives united with Husband beloved equal thankful and forgiving told at the same time stopping the panic domestic violence behavior. One pouring out of the Holy Spirit renewing of the mind at the ending of pandemic worst of bad violent time North up, South down 1st Act with Amen. The other proclaiming "Jubilee" celebrating renewing of the heart at the beginning of best of peaceful goodtime. Ministry of reconciliation South up, North down 2nd Acts II year 2020 with thankfulness no more jealously and revengeful violence. Twin separate ancient Great Kemet Pyramid Temple wisdom reality united on a Cross of hope with Star of David equally! Becoming one liturgical new Church year zero violence. A New Millennial Christmas story about the advent conception of Jesus Christ birthyear of seeing his New Millennial Church born again December 25th.

The Sacred Scriptures cannot be broken. Peace, Love and Happiness Acts II 2nd advent of Jesus Christ turning the upside-down Industrial World around South up, North down. 20 years after 9/11. Attending Sunday school, Sunday Church service, Mid-week Prayer Group and praying with purpose on a prayer line demonstration life of faith at 5 am. Nobody gets hurt or dies. Be a living Sacrifice heir of salvation studying the Bible with acts of faith dedication and commitment. Like attending College receiving a PhD or Law Degree on scholarship, even greater than marching in a protest: Certified celestial and terrestrial historical event sealed indictment against all conspiracies. Boundlessness by ancient Priesthood authority prayer lifeline of faith renewing of the heart and mind stopping the violent hate. "Ubuntu" reconciliation as moral quality of a person loving beautiful heart. 20/20 vision of hope witness II Acts of unity by faith of Holy Spirit humanness healing loving care for other persons. God's Universal Church family call for Revival spiritual battle, awakening raising of the dead being Born again Zi-On. Dying to hear the truth.

The Ambassadors of peace son and daughters of Joseph messenger Book of hope. New Millennial, New Testament of Good News, 2nd Acts II Peace, Love and happiness (Joel 2: 31). New, New covenant story 2nd Acts II desires of a beautiful heart (Jeremiah 31: 31). The Dream Ubuntu I am because we are: A Bible study written prophecy Spirit of the Lord is pouring peace, love and happiness upon the desires of all unselfish heart's beloved passion. A call of repentance "Jubilee" celebration demonstration of responsibility to be baptism of faith reconciliation (Ubuntu) to being Holy humanism. As a phenomenon according to which persons is a person through communion network of other people mind interconnected like the worldwide web internetwork. Directed by the Holy Spirit to read the Bible like a clock on the wall unfolding morally acceptable manner of truth. New word Calendar book to keep the solemn festival Holy time year zero violence, no war. Keeping of Holy time protest praying with intention for healing the Psalm written on our burning heart's beloved passion directed to Jesus Christ. At the end worst of bad times Book of Revelations between Genesis. Starting the millennial clock Church bell ringing three times signaling trinity eternal God father, Son of man and Holy Spirit as one. Revival raising of the dead return of Elijah minister tongue of fire and blood fighting evil. Spiritual climate change stopping the violence Doomsday Theory clock on the wall ending worst of bad time. Starting awaking of keeping Holy Time Church year 2020 vision of praying at 5 AM on a prayer line of faith. Calling on the Lord in all things state of mind Zi-On Holy time zone acts peace, love and happiness!

"Jubilee" Leviticus 25: 10 Biblical revival command awaking event that kept seven seasons, a single season equal seven years, fulfilled times seven equals Zi-On Holy Times zone of peace. An epiphany when I heard a Prophet name Curtis blow a Shofar Horn during Church service. At Zi-On Restoration International Ministries 4444 O Street of Abraham Lincoln, Nebraska city of terms of endearment ground zero. It instantly made tears fall from my eyes. I could see that I was a blind sinner. I started crying the Psalms written on my heart "Jubilee God help me" "Lord have mercy on my soul". On or about 2012 before the end of the Mayan Calendar year. I prayed instantly epiphany Universal pardon God's perfect love started 2nd Acts II 2nd coming true life story of the Holy Spirit making it happen with goodness. Non-violently putting an ending to doomsday conspiracies how the world comes to end of bad times. Year 2013 when I got Baptizes the Pope resigns an epiphany. Every little by little detail must be fulfilled!

Urban Tribes "Jubilee" Party Revival of the faithful. America sounding Tribal War of Freedom of Information Act by faith. Human Right act to peacefully go anywhere proclaiming the word of God correctly believing in thing unseen. Fulfilling the perfect word of God's Peace love, and

Happiness Atonement to Passover restoration of the promise land. I see The New Millennial, Renewed Church repenting. 1st United Church State Compton New City of On (Genesis 41:45). City of the Son celebrating, rejoicing people returning by amazing graceful action in faith of God's Holy Spirit perfect love. City of destruction" of idolatry shall cease, and the worship of the true God be established. United in pride of rainbow of all people praising the Lord presence in American History Black migration Equal Right Act of faith. Homeland security a house divided cannot stand a gift of Citizenship. Human Right Act of faith benefit of the Clergy praying Psalm 51. Lord have mercy on my soul. To all American migration DACA Dreamer protection 2nd Act II Peace, Love, and Happiness who believe as promised bridging generation after generation. Protected by the Constitution of the United States of America Perfect Union. Unity through "Jubilee" Universal pardon your neighbor's bad behavior. Turn the other cheek, love your enemy. The sin or debt of the Parent can't be used against the Children to take away the Family Home Act. I Am my brother and sister keeper Parent seeing firstborn Daughter equal to their firstborn Son. Keeping the command military order be a good example appointed time completion being Holy.

Commission to publishing the New Millennial, New Testament of Good News, second coming 2nd Acts II Peace, Love and happiness. Nowhere in Church history has there been a nonfiction New York Best Seller Novel epidemic story ever published with pictures of Twin IV Blood Moon Eclipse on the front and back cover II Act in faith of God's celestial and terrestrial glory snapshot. Captured on a Cross of hope through a sacred Temple star of David law of Moses, Sun rising parallel praising Blood Moon like a clock Watchtower arch monument to God. Witness by the Author from the same spot aiming East and West South up, North down beginning calendar ending worst of bad time. The end to 400 years of enslavement Black migration history. Reflective Bible Study lookback and forward Great falling away from God year 1619 Jamestown to year 2019 Compton Great

Awaking pouring out of the spirit. Special Report "Jubilee" Black migration cross American Church History. The Dream Ubuntu network II humanism God presence in Zi-On our lives renewing of the heart and mind. Pouring out of the Spirit 2nd Acts II Peace, Love and happiness aim of God in Academic History from Atonement to Passover resurrection appointed Zi-On time dimension, season of Holiness. A house divide cannot stand. Stop violent politicize religion hate. Keep the Passover as sign and wonders of passion eternal judgement to all the Churches being Holy. "Ubuntu" President Obama spoke about it at Nelson Mandela's funeral used to bring South Africa together after Apartheid to renew the mind with amnesty. Jubilee celebrating the release end of Jim Crow religion segregation renew the heart Universal pardon Human Right Act of Justice. Universal health care system judgement of God's loving word is correction Good News a blessing to the believer, impeachment to the unbeliever an indictment. God's perfect aim to convict the World by sowing hearts of peace praying the Psalm in the unfolding dawn early morning rays of light Zi-On state of mind. Becoming New Millennial, New, Jerusalem Hub City of champions peace and hope. Compton 1st United Church State of Zi-On continually praying a check and balance opposite State of Hell, politics in Washington D.C.

This is the day calendar season of pinpoint research alignment Historical Biblical proportion. Holy Time management event lunar and solar eclipse illuminating into a Cross. Shapes, numbers, pattern, and names sound the vibration divine aim of perfection in God's creation of eclipse time calendar for eternal good order law of nature. The Arch of knowledge seeing the passion perfect aim of God's goodness in everything sunlight, black moon, united, national calendar of crisis. There exists a "Divine Proportion" that is exhibited in a multitude of names, shapes, numbers, and patterns eclipse whose relationship can only be the result of the omnipotent, good, and all-wise God of Scripture beautiful passion in all things. 2nd Acts II Peace Love and happiness Arch of Heaven. This Divine

Proportion existing in the smallest to the largest heartbeat parts of blood drop, in living water mythology air and ice. Atom in non-living thing under the sound vibration of heaven arch praise God being Holy. Reveals the Omnipresence awesome handiwork aim of God's passion and His interest in names beauty, function, and perfect order season of Holy time. After 400 years of affliction Brothers and Sister of Moor's great Black migration American culture of people Identified by exile Trans-Atlantic slave trade. Black Joseph spiritual body of beautiful unselfish people professing the word of God rightly in all things. I know College Professors that have received name on Doctoral Degree for less work than this. The Dream Ubuntu reconciliation return, Ben Joseph Jesus Christ as one complete end to Black Migration Studies in American University Academia and Religious studies.

As a child, I was always proud of the name of my hometown. I was born a Cornhusker on the Mormon Trail terms of endearment. Planted in the Heartland of America Abraham, Lincoln, Nebraska The Star City Capital of Nebraska the Good life State rule of law and order. My hometown cities named after the 14th President Abraham Lincoln. The Emancipator that signed the Executive Order that freed the enslaved in United States Civil War of "Jubilee" year 1863. That also name after the father of the faithful Abraham in the Bible making me born again seed of Abraham. Year 1963 a century of Black migration before my birth the same year Dr. King said he also had a dream, seeing boys and girls equally. I never imagined in my lifetime visions of debt and sin believe dreams do come true. I would be qualified by the Lord to Author this parallel triumphant story of God's Acts II glory and perfection. Everybody knows Black Joseph body of people was enslaved African to America Trans-Atlantic slave trade lived alongside Native Americans. Double bless Black natives America put in charge slave or free God's will increase. Joseph Boy Dreamer return renewed raised from being dead. As symbol perfect aim unselfish beauty father's love. The passion of God's eye of the Bible Jesus type of Joseph!

Starting with my birthyear 2009 President Obama 1st Inauguration time day of devotional peace January 19, 1/19 opposite time day of Terror 9/11. Delivered by Midwife St Elizabeth Hospital birthplace, down to my circumcised God give name from the womb to the tomb Eric Joseph Moore. Son of Joseph Black Native American spiritual network Body culture of colorful people worshiping God. The Trinity the heavenly Father, Son of man and breath of Holy Spirit as one God continually praying with intention on their own free will. Celebrating turning the upside-down Underworld right side up vision see the people at the bottom migrate to the top as promised South up, North down. The end of appointed bad time 400 years of slavery in America Great Migration project of affliction and oppression Laws Apartheid Jim Crow Segregation. As a child of God, I Am proud of the name of my Home Kingdom of Heaven I Am Born Again.

A seed of Abraham Black Joseph eternal Ruler Immigrant the most central key figure in the Holy Books Bible, Quran, Tora and Book of Mormon written about all over the World a type passion of Christ shadow of Jesus. Each book teaches different line and directions name to honor praying. His name means God is my increases, Joseph praying for unity divided Nation and greater than the name Moses. Today eternal ruler (Eric) Joseph born again of a seed of Abraham heirs of salvation raised Straight Out of Compton, The Dream Ubuntu reconciliation return of the promise land that was stolen Zi-On. Negus with attitude before Gangster Rapp, a Boy from the Hood before the Hit Movie. 2nd Acts to the end, to a perfect love stories the aim of God's perfection eternal Ruler (Eric). Joseph praying the Psalm of a broken heart California Love. "Eureka" I found it! Zi-On what was meant for the genius of evil God used it for the wisdom of Good. Zi-On the "Hub City" of Compton has a unique 1st United Church History its Dual Sovereignty Granted land by the Queen and King of Spain. Zi-On as protectorate benefit of the clergy Black Native Migration State of New Christians Sanctuary City of On. City of the Son of man Zi-On if you fold a map of the World in half Compton, California parallel Jerusalem, Israel line right up to each other. Zi-On Honored by Mexico and by the United States Treaty that still stand today. Zi-On after Ten years the land return to the generational Native people of Color! Reestablish the Human Right benefit of the Clergy Zi-On. The Dream Ubuntu peaceful return of the promise land Zi-On. The New Millennial, New Testament, 2nd Acts II Peace, Love and happiness reclaiming what was stolen Zi-On.

The New Millennial, New, Testament 2nd Acts II Peace, Love and happiness Atonement to Passover Zi-On. Everybody likes a good love story bringing people together. Of Black Joseph dedication rejoicing proclaiming "Jubilee" celebrating today and forever, Great year of the Lord. The Dream Ubuntu atonement return Second Coming of Jesus Acts II perfect love of the Redeemer parallel Black Joseph type of Christ. Checking on his brothers' and sisters' welfare. [Genesis 45: 26] And they told him, saying: 'Joseph is yet alive, and he is ruler (President, Eric to mean eternal ruler) over all the land of Egypt (Urban Tribes of North and South Native America: 1st United Church Compton). And his heart fainted, for he believed them not. The Bible named of Joseph is Eric eternal ruler preparing for the second coming 2nd Acts II Perfect Love and happiness in the beginning was the word. Transfiguration people returning to God. Exodus II Great migration of people from ancient Temple system of worshipping returning to God. Going to New Millennial Church continually praying with their Mothers. Baptizes and Born-again Black Joseph, eternal ruler Chief Administrator of Urban Tribes welfare, Boy Dreamer without jealousy anything he prayed for God made it happen Zi-On. [Genesis 37: 9] Then he had another dream, and he told it to his brothers. "Listen," he said, "I had another dream, and this time the sun and moon and eleven stars were bowing down to me. Choice seer Joseph beautiful unselfish love what was meant for the genius use of evil God used it for Good. Joseph eternal ruler saw his family bow down to his unselfish forgiving love. But he never saw the stars, moon phase turn to blood and Sun turn darkness, Eclipse bow down.

Until today Born-again Black Joseph eternal ruler straight out of Compton parallel Black Jesus Christ our savior marking appointed time straight out of Heaven. Fighting a good fight forgiving proclaiming "Jubilee" celebrating the perfect aim of God's judgment of mercy and compassion atonement through Passover. In every word in the Bible spoken out the mouth of children of God be Holy.

A Phenomenon IV Blood Moon Eclipse seeing the black moon phase turn to blood. Snapshot through sacred Temple wisdom of God. Star of David rule of law, Sun and moon millennial clock twin tower arch of man suffering. Praising God's aim of perfection glory and grace from Passover to Atonement appointed goodtime. ^{Genesis 1:8} And God gave the arch the name of Heaven. And there was evening and there was morning, the second day. The World greatest and longest skyhook-shot and Jump shot by the right hand of God's perfect aim. Made twice from the same spot traveling east and west. Both targets spinning moving at the equator 1000 mph rotating in opposite direction. By the spirit of one-man name Alone (Eric) eternal Ruler choice seer Black Joseph. Seen in both directions west and east by all the World over resetting all-time correction setting the records straight. Turning the world around South up, North down. ^{Genesis 1:14} And God said, let there be lights in the arch of heaven, for a division between the day and the night, and let them be for signs, and for marking the changes of the year, and for days and for years. God's right-hand perfect aim power and glory all the world witness on the day of Passover and Atonement perfect score New Year Lord day zero-time correction! Better than being Chosen one out of a million fanatics too shoot a once in a lifetime perfect goal, then making a million-dollar half-court all net perfect shot at Halftime Show in the NBA All-Star Basketball Game.

The perfect aim twofold of God's right hand these one and million glories snapshot of perfection peacefully resets World time clock to Zero, Zero without violence. ^{Genesis 1:15} And let them be for lights in the arch of heaven to give moon light on the earth: and it was so. Perfect aim Straight out of heaven as said so in the Bible a new beginning of time. Introduction that the man of God may be Holy perfect thoroughly furnished unto all good work pictures turning into words of perfection no war. Being snapshot at the beginning of appointed time new black moon phase new moon Genesis too Revelations every word promised fulfilled Zi-On. [Genesis 9:16] When I see the arch in the sky, I will always remember the promise that I have made to every living creature. [Genesis 9: 17] The arch will be the sign of that solemn promise. Zi-On as enlightenment sign and wonders in arch night and day heaven calendar appointed prosperity in the wisdom of God new spiritual leadership in righteousness of Holy Time.

This is the day of the Lord of perfection Holy Time period of better understanding New Millennial, New Testament Good News of Great Restoration of Zi-On. [Genesis 1:27] God created humanity in person God's own image, in the divine image God created them, male and female God created them. [Genesis 5: 24] Enoch walked with God and disappeared because God took him. Became translated pure in heart. [Revelation 4:3] And to my eyes he was like a jasper and a sardius stone: and there was an arch of light round the high seat, like an emerald. Beautiful love more precious than jewelry of hope, Moore than a rainbow of faith. Sunlight, black moon, Earth and Man to be statue of Liberty, for Justice and equality. IV Blood Moons eclipse symbols of Emancipation affliction and oppression the three pillars of Eternity, Creation, Fall, and Atonement. Borderline of faith on the 33rd parallel line of death None of this is by accident there is no coincidences here Zi-On. What the odds that the one person that is tell this story would be name Eternal Ruler (Eric) Joseph. Named after his father and grandfather in the womb of his mother. A seed of Abraham Lincoln, Nebraska in Star city Good life State. Hospital name after Saint Elizabeth circumcised for remembrance under rule of law Passover and order of Atonement to be baptized born again with no Tattoos in the worst of bad times proclaiming Jubilee. Demonstration of faith praying on a prayer line in the direction of one name Jesus Christ. With repentance, passion, immersion, and communion. What's more beautiful way can God show his perfect love after 400 years of slaver conquer of paradise and dying on a cross. It makes you want to cry out laughing.

This is the day of expectation the Lord dominion, be glad and rejoice for this is the day the Lord actions celebration of the Prophets ending 400 years first enslave Black Native in America project year 1619 be fruitful. I could be dead or in prison. We all saw year 2001 Terrorist Attack 9/11 the Twin Towers collapse, year 2005 Hurricane Katrina, year 2008 Recession stock market collapse and First African American elected President, year 2013 the Pope resigned the Catholic Church. And year 2020 Impeachment Trial of the President ending Whiteman privilege. $^{Genesis\ 17:4}$ "As for Me, behold, my covenant is with you, and you will be the father of a multitude of nations. And he said to Abraham, $^{Genesis\ 15:13}$ Truly, your seed will be living in a land which is not theirs, as servants to a people who will be cruel to them for four hundred years; standing like a statute of Sower seed of Abraham Lincoln on the Capital Dome of Nebraska. Spreading seeds over a New nation of people in a Good life State. I never imagined I would be telling this Good News story. About myself becoming a Born Again Christian or see the World time would peacefully end like this great awaking new Gospel.

2nd Acts II from my backyard an event the entire World seen. But a story only one person was guided to write about the grace and glory of God perfect aim signs and wonders. Ancient Temple wisdom united New Millennial Church standing looking backward and forward thankful in Zi-On. Suspended unfolding time ending Book of Revelation, between beginning Book of Genesis peaceful state of Zi-On. Resetting time like a clock on the wall 1st calendar Holy times. Sun of righteousness rising and dying on the cross in love united with the star of David rule of law instrument used for keeping Holy time rejoicing of Zi-On. Like a compass instrument keeps True North. IV Blood black Moon eclipse spiritual climate change alignment Temple wisdom and Church United Great day of the

Lord. Harbingers reflection of perfection hand of God's wisdom and man peacefully working together opposite of Anti-President Donald Trump thee devil's apprentice.

This not about Giant famous Entertainers and famous prosperity Preachers of L.A. Zi-On is Holy Time of prosperity knowing the perfect aim of God, past, presence and future. Every step by step of the way on the right path of life awaking praying in the morning with breath of repentance sorrowful heartbeat is Zi-On. Not about turning entertainment into reality get a Tattoo or Entrepreneur in a Capitalist Society making money. When the Holy Spirit came pouring onto me calling me out to being thankful remembering get baptizes by my God give name eternal Ruler. It happened when I turn fifty years of age witness by my mother and father. I had to look at myself and realize, I was, lost, blind and could not see I was a enslave by sin upside down in debt and did not know I was in Hell. By then, I was too proud to beg for forgiveness, I had ruined my marriage and did not know how to say I am sorry. I was immature not spiritually fully developed harden heart grown men are not supposed to cry. I had pride in my good works with my soft hands and tools as a Mechanic. I thought I could fix anything; I could not save myself I was afraid to cry ask for help. The Holy Spirit said I Am your Professor of truth will teach you how to cry out like a baby when you are praying in line of faith with your Mother. I will pour out my spirit of wisdom on your broken heart. Psalm 90: 12 Teach us to number our days that we may gain wisdom of the Heart. To see the World through my mother brown pretty eyes, a good example being Holy. All the colors of the Rainbow Culture of beautiful hearted people as your teacher, tutor, instructor, lecturer and fellow friend shows you all thing seen and unseen. I was not instructed to buy assault weapon be Holy.

This end of time change will happen peacefully praying with church bells ringing. Three-time Sunday morning for the Father, Son and Holy Spirit ending Sunday school starting church service. Not like Christopher Columbus conquest of Paradise in 1492 Great Migration. In 1504, he used

IV Blood Moon to trick scare the native tribes of Jamaica from attacking him and his hungry men. He lied and said God is mad the same lie false Prophet say to hustle scare people today anger man Ministry. God's mercy and compassion is the same today and forever. I love Compton Lueders park the neighborhood where I am raised Hub City of Champions New Millennial, New, New, Jerusalem. In my back yard there is one of the most beautiful Temple of tombs Moorish style architectural Arch Sun and Moon clock Historic landmark Angeles Abbey Memorial Park. Parallel Old Jerusalem, Israel on the 33rd parallel line of death run right through my backyard ground zero. Time marker setting historic facts as time correction of peace staring of 2nd Acts II Perfect Love and happiness. Twin Blood Moon Eclipse Putting Amen to 1st Acts stopping Tribal wars and Gang violence. Keeping the command celebrating Passover and Atonement as sign and symbolic of thankfulness for the Perfect Love of God. Perfect alignment of arch of Heaven millennial clock the sun, moon and arch of man suffering on earth as one praying.

Perfect picture snapshot from the backyard my Hood by the right hand of God perfect aim of the camera my weapon of choice seer 2020 vision. 2nd Acts to perfect love being in the perfect spot at the perfect time to capture a million-dollar picture snapshot of a perfect event and write the Spirit of truth about it backwards. From the end of the story Book of Revelations to the beginning of the Story Black Joseph eternal rule. How do you write a story from the end to the beginning? Become born again. Only by the Holy Spirit's perfect right writing hand instrument of God's perfection proclaiming "Jubilee" Universal pardon for everyone. Feeding the word of God correctly to those who are all suffering to hear the plan of truth. The Holy Spirit will teach you how to pray from the bottom of your heart burning worries and breath of concerns. Turning to witness God's aim Passover to Atonement. "Jubilee" celebrating the work of God in Old and New Testament that has already been fulfilled.

If I would have been told the World would peacefully end like this? That God sent eternal ruler Black Joseph seed of Abraham Lincoln, Nebraska back to be Born Again, circumcised, Baptizes, No Tattoos, Straight out of Compton. From his backyard to take a snapshot picture Piru Blood Moon eclipse over tomb returning people to Sun of righteousness God be Holy. Be on prayer line at 5a.m. praying to stop misinformation World War III, Worldwide famine and stopping Forest fire saving lives commanding the wind to stop blowing in the still of the morning promise land. I would not believe it until I saw it for myself. Twenty years after 9/11 I would celebrating the end worst of bad time with thanksgiving on my heart for what God has done, doing and will do on a prayer line crying and begging pleading at 5:00 a.m. I would have called you crazy. I believed in calling into the Washington Journal C-span 7 am ET.

Praying on a prayer line in the still of the morning at the crack of dawn was never a plan of mine. How does God get a sinner Boy name Joseph Born again in Good Life State, Abraham Lincoln, Nebraska too corrupted state Compton California? To be at a cemetery at sunrise and sunset exact time. During IV Blood Moons eclipse of worst bad times. Teach Jesus Christ to the Bloods and Crips in his family. After being Born Again over at fifty years of age living on Earth then write Author a book about the event appointed time Baptizes. Calling it 2nd Acts II Peace Love and Happiness second coming Jesus Christ, The New Millennial, New, Testament circumcision of the heart. When he could be doing anything and be anywhere, he wants, he is not required to do anything. Writing the New Millennial, New Testament was never in a lives plan of mine until I became born again and Baptizes. When I became dip Immersed in Jesus Christ passion self-Published, I Am Because We Are proclaimed "Jubilee", the Pope resigned 2013. Starting the "Jubilee" economy I Am Because We Are: translated Ubuntu philosophy meaning humanity towards others "the belief in a universal bond of sharing that connects all humanity". "Jubilee" is a very powerful word return the land back to the original owner economic policy setting the heaven order straightway. "Jubilee" universal Pardon reset economic bad time debt clock too zero. Release all enslaved from their bad behavior to be Holy a good work stopping the Domestic and Racial violence Watchman. Reconciliation Ubuntu program right of humanity operation system update like pushing the reset button on computer. "Jubilee" Universal Pardon is a sharing program command straight out of heaven to happen every fifty years. Reset economic Ubuntu philosophy right of Humanity operation system of Reconciliation Atonement to Passover.

This is not about Black people thing or White people thing, political fight between Republican Red and Democrat Blue, or Religious debate non denomination Churches. Going to Church was never a plan of mine to protest or being on a prayer line. I was anti-Church most of my life. I did not see a need to public demonstrate my faith I was antichrist. I never thought in history I would be begging Lord have mercy on my soul. This is about judgement do you believe or not believe in Jesus Christ proclaiming it supernatural reconciliation rejoice. "Jubilee" revival is a Biblical divine proportion event epiphany of good times. Human right benefit, healing the broken hearted, charity to the afflicted, welfare for the oppressed and freeing the enslaved. Everybody knows "Jubilee" the great day of rejoicing with epiphany the Lord. It is ordered to happen every fifty years. It is a law that is already written on the books. By speaking this one word it calls all the power of heaven to move supernatural on your behalf. Remove any debt of sin that you may have gotten into setting the debt record straightway to zero. Release the broken hearted to pray supernatural work of the Holy Spirit. Those that have been forgiven, received the mercy of God has a lot of mercy to give justice and liberty for all. Jubilee stops Christian living their lives in fear preparing for doomsday. The Dream Return of the blessing peacefully celebration every day like this, Passover forever.

Eric or little by little a modern day classic American perfect love Story. The Dream Return journey of Noble English-speaking Boy. Born in the Heartland of America Good life State. Raised up a sinner under the protection of the righthand of God. On the borderline of faith battlefield, soldier of love. In Eureka a Corrupted life State City on a Hill. To be a light of hope in dark times. Until he heard a divine voice say, "I know why the Mayan calendar is ending on December 21, 2012". It became his "I Know Why the Cage Bird Sing" inspiration. It made him feel some type of way suspended in time awaking of his soul learning to write little by little. Like somebody was trying to tell him something to say anonymously.

He always had a strange feeling somebody invisible friend was watching out for him following looking over his shoulders helping like a guarding angel. Waiting at appointed time to be slow to speak. This voice was like a spark of light that would get brighter and brighter, little by little as he would hear words of truth and wisdom. Growing in wisdom understanding the truth of enlightenment little by little. Was trying to get him to see the truth about who he Royally really was. The truthful soft voice speaks wisdom to the heart with comforting word that gave him a peace of mind little by little. To read the King James Bible like a calendar book of Revelations end of stupid Times to Genesis beginning of wisdom holy time. To make the World a better place. Looking at the man in mirror asking him to change his way. If time ends, then it will start over again it has happened before. Study of the Bible marks the aim of God throughout time of creation of the calendar. Keeping of appointed times harvest feast and festivals a yearlong event. Moment by moment little by little step by step. Getting baptizes, going to Church until the end of his life with his Mother was never his plan. He wanted to be like his Father a Firefighter fighting fires and saving lives, organizer of Union Representative. He volunteers his life to this Nation. Joins the Military served in two Arm Forces Veteran and served time in prison trying to do the right thing on his own life plan. He could only do so much alone, did not know love is the battlefield where we don't have to fight no more. Jesus does the fighting today. Little by little he became a prayer worrier like his Grandmother and Mother. Fighting disease seeing demons attacking his family praying continually.

On the fifth anniversary Bloody Sunday Selma AL. March 7, 2015 Butler Foundation celebrated Black Achievement pass, present and future program at proclaiming what is the secret? Delivering the word of God Friday 13, March 2015 second Anniversary Pope call for 2016 year of the Lord mercy "Jubilee". One special word "Jubilee" it is the law of the land written on the Liberty bell. [Leviticus 25:10] every fifty years be holy. Today in Jesus Christ name "Jubilee" happens by saying the word. Instantly sends the power Administration of Angels of heaven to start moving on your benefit. Freeing you from whatever rotten fishy smelling mess you have gotten into. The greatest fish God created is the sign of the Pisces fish in heaven. It is a negative mutable sign always changing like a dog chasing his tell. Jonna prayed the Psalm to free him from going around in circles practicing the Dark Arts of Astrology. There is a true war going on here today Good vs evil. For the heart and mind of the believer in passion of Jesus Christ. The Dream Return seer of my Brother and Sisters return to Church pray together with their Mother and Father, Husband's and Wife's touching and agreeing unified in God perfect aim. To conquer circumcise every heart. A battlefield of love believing that getting up going to Sunday Church serves with your Mother and Grandmother and studying the word will win this battle of the mind. Not preparing for doomsday the world to end. The path to heaven is very narrow and bumpy. I was never afraid of going to Hell. Trained by the United States Military to go to Hell and come back.

To a Believer of the Kingdom of heaven see the Church and State as one body of people celebrating the whole Church calendar year feast and festivals. Reality of the Bible good New cycle played out in real life Holy times. As for the non-believer the Church and State is separated Civil religious Holidays, truth divided man didn't walk on the moon. The world is flat, and martians and aliens are real. Tribes of people leap year no faith. Seeing reality just a normal Bad News cycle rumors of war over Holy ground. As thing become more finetune to hear the Holy voice of the lord speak to the sorrowful heart you cannot have it both ways, you cannot serve two Masters. Excepting the good with the Bad the lessor of two evils. The Kingdom of heaven God is good all the time there is no less evil. Evil is just evil, not more or less. He has three Christian friend that live in Nebraska one that believe in the Gold stander over people afraid that the Government is going to come take his guns away. One that believe doing Business in communist China is good for making America Capitalist great again. And one that think he can take a hundred dollars of In God We Trust World Reserved currency buy a foreign currency. Betting expecting the Stock Market to fall so that he will receive a million dollars flipping World currency around manipulation the market.

The most valuable thing we have is spending time praying with passion for others going to Church with our Beautiful Mothers be Holy. My Brother said he rather memories pray in one direction a foreign language, reciting it five times day with religious Arab Muslin radical Isis Sharia law proclaiming Holy ground. Islamic tradition state of Double mindedness revengeful thinking eye for eye. That believe God restrict people from using deodorant. Instead of repenting praying with passion of his heart sharing worries and concerns. With his Christian Mother wonderful healing ointment good smell of anoint mercy oil of Holiness. With no restriction, going to Beautiful Church serves on his Sunday off. Where Men and women praying together as husband and wives seated together and pray holding hands touching and agreeing as one body of people. He rather stops the workday to pray noon, afternoon and sunset, workweek in middle day Friday to pray with a bunch of musty Arab Brother. At a Mosque separated from women and their wives. When they don't give F*ck or do not care about him or his Christian mother! Jubilee free you to consumerism cheer for Christ like a Dallas Cowboy sports fanatic. After a winning championship season. A lot of Church people practice sin by doing whatever they want to do all week long then play Church on Sunday morning asking forgiveness so they can start sinning all over again on Monday morning. 2nd Acts II Perfect Love Christian Perfection praying the liturgical calendar year correctly be Holy.

The liturgical year, also known as the church year the 12 month, 52-week, 24 hour, 365 day, calendar overtime, consists of the cycle of liturgical seasons in Christian churches that determines when feast days, celebrations of saints, are observed, and which Scripture are to be read either in an annual cycle or in a cycle of several years. The liturgical cycle divides the year into a series of seasons, each with their own mood, spiritual climate theological emphases, and modes line of prayer overtime giving thanks in daily prayer.

Church Year of the Lord: Advent, Epiphany, Lent, Easter Resurrection, Pentecost, Ordinary Time.

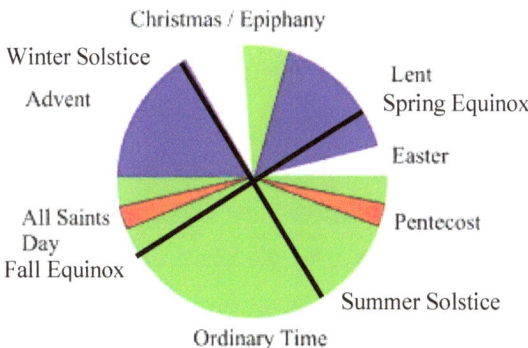

December Chapter One: Genesis 1:6 And God said, Let there be a solid arch stretching over the waters, parting the waters from the waters (Bible in Basic English)

Advent means arrival/ coming celebration begins four Sundays before Christmas Day ending Christmas Eve. The Advent use the wreath symbolizing peace eternity of God Jesus Christ Methodist flame of Christian perfection.

- Advent Weeks
    1. Hope, Trust, Reliance, expectation.
    2. Faith is the assured expectation of things hope for.
    3. Joy expectation of Good, happiness, rejoicing, exultation.
    4. Love long suffering and kindness.
    5. Peace is the state of no wars.

The 1st Advent Sunday has the main focuses centered aim on Hope trust, reliance arrival of God's promise fulfilled. (Genesis 49: 18) Scriptures of Prophecy Ephraim Son of Prophet Joseph was a type of Christ human spirit who took upon him the form a servant and yet then and now did that which made it evident that perfect aim God was with him Judah spiritual Israel acts of Jesus in Heaven. Parallel Alone, Joseph last Prophet royal priesthood of King and Priest Nation. Suffering on Earth waiting for last arrival active in history the perfect aim of God's wisdom. (1 Peter 2:9) Preparing the way without jealousies between the Brothers prosperity is knowledge who God is. That was born at the end of the last Age practicing Tattoo Dark Art fortune telling prosperity preaching gateway to hell.

Great Falling-Away from God wisdom great apostasy church. Waiting for the last arrival of Jesus the savor end of 1st Acts the last time indeed both Jews wondering and non-Jews. (Isaiah 11:13) Expectation of "Jubilee" for his return a second time coming as a trumping voice from heaven of the Holy Spirit. (Isaiah 11:11) Advent arrival of the shadow of Jesus Christ last coming crisscrossing America resting on the wing of a white Dove in human spirit of hope. (Matthew 3:17) A loud voice of the wisdom of God as a peaceful red-light signal of Hope to stop the violence. Speaking to the heartbroken suicide thinking going on in this dark wicked World of Temptation (Matthew 4:1). Tradition of lighting the color purple candle as Family Royalty of Hope perfect aim of God is faithful trustful and reliable will keep the promise made to us as a family. All families united in hope with the Holy spirit perfect aim of God indeed. Jesus Christ human spirit will not return a second time with Nuclear weapon on planet Earth. (Isaiah 2:5)

The expectation in my spiritual dissertation. As a writer, I witnessing the Good News for dual Sovereignty ultimate healing power voice of the Lord perfect aim. (Acts 2:14) Jehovah sacrifice Himself second arrival? Coming in great glory to glory in the last days. (Luke 2:34) Advent hope perfect aim of God appointed time Passover and Atonement. Second Acts II the Holy Spirit second coming 2nd Acts II Perfect Love. Holy spirit last arrival comforting conviction healing of the brokenhearted 2nd Acts II Perfect Love of truth and suffering. (Psalm 105:19) In the long suffering view Son of man last Prophet Black Joseph, Alone faithful and discreet slave, a human shadow of Jesus the hope of Israel in Spirit.(Hebrews 1:1-6) Waiting for God's kingdom the body of Jesus Christ human spirit, before his sacrifice in life and after his death.(Mathew 4: 16) What God intends men for he will be sure some way or other to qualify them for. Joseph's, Son shadow, Alone parallel human spirit Jesus Christ given dual sovereignty authority prominent position Chief Administrator, Seer cornerstone key alinement with every word in the Bible. Savor of both Jews and non-Jews domestic represent at the beginning set in Holy Time year of the Lord. (John 3:16) Onto the Old, New, now The New Millennial, New, Testament Obedient in suffering three parts prayer godly Psalm devotion, loud cries and tears of sacrifice. (Hebrews 5:7)

Privileges of the Firstborn again son enslaved right to have two part praying Psalm with hope and faithfulness. One-part Acts of a father's broken heart desire in love and marriage to spiritual Israel crying out forgiveness from affliction. And one-part discreet slave secret disciple Alone last Prophet Black Joseph faithfulness 2nd Acts II Perfect love, today parallel the Holy Spirit shadow Jesus Christ weeping over Jerusalem. (Revelation 7: 9) human Jesus as head of the Universal Temple Church in heaven parallel last Prophet Black Joseph, Alone 1st Sexton of 1st United Temple

Church on Earth now after 400 years enslaved as a great tribulation. [Luke 21: 20-24] God prospered him was with Black Joseph blessed wonderfully even in the house of his servitude, and he delivered him out of all his tribulations. [Acts 7:9-10] Becoming favor expectation of Good News awakening studying the Bible preparing the way for 2nd Acts II Perfect love divine interruption putting Amen to 1st Acts. [Genesis 15: 13] As for you intended evil God meant it for Good. [genesis 50: 20] Just as God promised to our ancestors' son of first Prophet Black Joseph, seed to Abraham faith and to Abraham Lincoln, Nebraska, Good Life State, equality under Law of Moses descendants forever. [Luke 1:55] It is most appropriate that Alone, first Prophet Black Joseph's name single individual was used to designate Ruler over all the Urban Tribe's citizenship of Nation spiritual Israel singled out as the special person object centered of affection reclaim of God's faithful and discreet slave.[Psalm 80:1] 1st Prophet Joseph's imitation shadow of Christ ready obedience in complying with the father's will in checking on his half-brothers, parallels Jesus willingly coming to earth in the form of a human obedience to the point of death.[Philippians 2: 8] Advent means arrival The New Millennial, New, Testament 2nd Acts II Perfect Love ending tribulation times the day is near ending 1st Acts.[Romans 13:11-14]

Hopeful expectation Acts II the second Acts of the coming restoration of Jesus Christ ending the first coming Acts great tribulation. [Isaiah 11:2] Post tribulation Celebrating Advent Season signal anticipating the revelation conception last arrival of restoration of Jesus as Messiah. [Christ or King] His second last coming covenant Kingdom of Heaven onto four corners of the planet Earth in spirit. 2nd Acts II Perfect Love the revelation of the Holy Spirit second time coming of Jesus Christ, Post Tribulation Stress Bible Study Keeping Holy Times. [Matthew 24:37-44] Ministry of reconciliation praying Psalm with hope is one of the most important and most frequently mentioned doctrines of the Old and New Testament put on the faith of God. [Ephesians 6:18] Precise in detail of every beat of the broken hearted, down to each word of 1ˢᵗ Acts in the Bible, 2ⁿᵈ Acts II bowing down of every knee confessing. (Isaiah 45:23)

Jesus Christ human spirit as Lord last coming for the church to establish his heavenly Kingdom of peacefulness stopping the violence. (Isaiah 60:18) Parallel Alone last 1ˢᵗ Prophet Black Joseph Earthly Post-Tribulation Ministry of Reconciliation at the close of the great tribulation. (Isaiah 2:2) To eagerly judge the wicked World with mercy and compassion to bring in the last righteous resign of the King of King New, New Testament life of hopefulness with thankfulness. (Isaiah 2:4) Stopping the violence turning Nuclear Weapon of mass destruction into plowshares and their Assault Rifle into Church Bells ringing instruction from Zi-On zone of peace the Lord be there. (Isaiah 2:4)

www.ingramcontent.com/pod-product-compliance
Lightning Source LLC
Chambersburg PA
CBHW050926240426
43670CB00022B/2942